EMPRESS AND HANDMAID

EMPRESS AND HANDMAID

ON NATURE AND GENDER IN THE CULT OF THE VIRGIN MARY

Sarah Jane Boss

CASSELL
London and New York

Cassell

Wellington House, 125 Strand, London WC2R 0BB

370 Lexington Avenue, New York, NY 10017-6550

First published 2000

British Library Cataloguing-in-Publication Data
A catalogue record for this book is available from the British Library.

ISBN 0-304-33926-1

Typeset by BookEns Ltd, Royston, Herts.
Printed and bound in Great Britain by
Bookcraft (Bath) Ltd, Midsomer Norton

രുന്നുന്നുന്ന

Contents

For
Tina Beattie
and
Philip Endean SJ

Plates

ട്ടേ0ട്ടേ0ട്ടേ0

Acknowledgements

This book is based on a doctoral thesis submitted to the University of Bristol in 1993. The acknowledgements at the beginning of that work include the following: the St Matthias Trust, Bristol; Elizabeth Boss, Jeffrey Boss, Steve Collins, Chris Finlay, Peter Gee and Mark Haeffner. I am sad that my supervisor, Ian Hamnett, has not lived to see the publication of *Empress and Handmaid*. Denys Turner and John Milbank were the examiners of my thesis, and they encouraged me to turn it into a book.

Over the past eight years, John Harding has given me tireless support, both materially and morally. I owe him a great debt of gratitude.

I do not know whether I could have written this without the encouragement and stimulation of members of the Marian Study Group, and of people associated with the Marian Study Centre. Among these are Kevin Alban O. Carm, Mary Grey, Peter Seed and Eamon Duffy. Particular thanks are due to Simon Coleman, Cathy Oakes, Chris Maunder, Tina Beattie and Philip Endean SJ. Tina and Philip have been consistently encouraging (and sometimes argumentative). With deep affection I dedicate this book to them, because they understand why it matters.

Preface

Empress and Handmaid tries to locate the ever-changing place which Marian devotion has occupied in the history of Western civilization, and particularly in the history of technological change and of related ideas about nature and gender. The study is necessarily inconclusive, not least because the method I employ is deliberately open-ended. Also, many corrections will need to be made by future scholarship, since the subject is vast and this is the first work to address it as a whole. But this is a start.

Since the concept of *domination* is central to the work, there is an Appendix giving a brief account of the social theory from which the concept is drawn.

Abbreviations

AAS   *Acta Apostolicae Sedis* [*Acta Sanctae Sedis*] Rome, 1865–

DEC   *Decrees of the Ecumenical Councils* (ed. Norman P. Tanner) two vols; London: Sheed and Ward, 1990

PG   *Patrologia Graeca* (ed. J.-P. Migne) Paris, 1857–1866

PL   *Patrologia Latina* (ed. J.-P. Migne) Paris, 1844–1862 cɔɛ⁄ɔɛ⁄ɔɛ⁄ɔ

Introduction

In 1964, the Second Vatican Council published its decree on the Church, *De Ecclesia*. This includes a chapter on the Blessed Virgin Mary, in which it is written that 'the immaculate Virgin ... was ... exalted by the Lord as queen of all things so that she might be more fully conformed to her Son, the Lord of lords and victor over sin and death'.[1] This sentence expresses the classical Catholic understanding of the honour which God bestows upon Mary as a consequence of her contribution to the divine work of salvation; yet the Mariology of the past thirty years has hardly been influenced by it at all. Indeed, to find the most powerful expressions of Mary's regal status, and the universal authority which this status entails, it is necessary to look as far back as the Catholic culture of the eleventh and early twelfth centuries, when she was the undisputed 'mistress of the world and empress of the universe'.[2]

One of the notable features of the art of this high medieval period is the type of Romanesque statue known as the Virgin in Majesty, of which the most remarkable examples come from the Auvergne region of central France (Plate 1).[3] These statues show the Virgin enthroned, with Christ as a small but mature-looking figure seated on her lap. Both mother and child have a bearing of majesty; but many observers comment that they are especially striking for the way in which they seem to look at the viewer. As you gaze on the image, the Virgin in particular might give the impression of looking into you and through you, so that explicit tokens of lordship, such as the throne, are undergirded by the impression of some power which is greater than the political, but less easily defined. As the viewer of such an image, you

1

might feel yourself to be the object of the statue's gaze, and to be in some way subject to its uncanny authority. In the words of the anthropologist Sophie Cassagnes-Brouquet: 'The image fixes its black eyes upon us and, with the aura of mystery which surrounds it, takes command of us with its tantalising stare.'[4]

Statues of this type were no longer made after the end of the thirteenth century. But several hundred years elapsed before European culture produced a genre of imagery which was to be the true antithesis of the Romanesque Virgin in Majesty. For, as I shall go on to argue, the antithesis is found in the visual media of pornography; and if the Virgin in Majesty is characteristic of the Middle Ages, then pornography is typical of modernity. Where the twelfth-century wooden Virgin seems to look at and have command over the viewer, the user of pornography, by contrast, is frequently reassured that it is he who looks at and has command over the characters in the images which he views. Many commentators on pornography note that it renders the human being an object of manipulation – a machine rather than a living person. Moreover, in pornography, it is men who are the observers, and it is commonly (though not invariably) representations of women which are observed. So the male observer hopes to have mastery over the female object of observation. Thus, in the Marquis de Sade's *Juliette*, Saint-Fonds, the royal minister, tortures a girl; and when she starts to cry he says, 'That's how I like women ... if only I could reduce them all to such a state with a single word!'[5] As the literary critic Susanne Kappeler notes, 'the usual consumer of pornography' expects 'the woman in the piece [to be] reduced to object, means to a certain end, vehicle for his pleasure'.[6] Similarly, the title of Susan Griffin's book *Pornography and Silence* refers to the way in which the pornographic victim is rendered voiceless and powerless by techniques which include being gagged, bound and, eventually, killed.[7] Whereas the worshipper before the Virgin in Majesty is the servant of the Lord and Lady whose presence the statue conveys, the actors in the pornographic film or photograph are servants of the pornographer and viewer who summon and pay for their presence.

Furthermore, where the Virgin in Majesty is intended to instil in the devotee a sense of the sacred, the pornographic image is concerned with its denial. From the earliest days of pornographic representation, clergy and religious have frequently been the focus of its attention. And at times and places when the Church was a politically powerful institution, pornographic attacks on its representatives could be used in the interests of political criticism.[8] Yet the undermining of institutional power was not the sole intention of such texts. One pornographic 'classic' of the eighteenth century was the *Histoire de Dom Bougre, Portier des Chartreux* (*The Story of Father Bugger, the Carthusian Porter*). Since Carthusians have never wielded great institutional power, and have always been noted for their austerity and strict observance of monastic rules, they are not an obvious choice for political satire. It therefore seems likely that a text describing promiscuous sexual activity in a Charterhouse is attacking Catholic ideals of holiness in themselves. The writings of De Sade make explicit attacks on those very things. The cultural critics Theodor Adorno and Max Horkheimer observe that De Sade's heroine Juliette 'demonizes Catholicism ... The energies which were devoted to the blessed sacrament, are applied to sacrilege instead.'[9] Early pornographic texts thus go beyond the satirical; they also set out to profane sacred objects, places and rituals, such as crucifixes, churches and the Mass.

In the twentieth century, even though pornography is no longer a vehicle for political criticism, the motif of the violation of sanctity has remained present in pornographic writing and imagery. Susan Griffin argues that the desecration of the holy is in fact at the foundation of the pornographic enterprise. The human person, she asserts, is a unity of body and soul, and as such, is known to be sacred. Pornography, however, declares the human being whom it represents to be 'only flesh' – flesh without spirit, body without soul, merely an object for control by the pornographer. According to Griffin, pornography is the product of a culture which cannot tolerate nature, and in its domination of the pornographic victim, culture tries to punish and suppress that which is 'natural', such as bodily feelings and emotions. So pornography silences the idea that 'culture might mediate nature's power for us, and might make of our own minds and bodies the sacred vessels which transform experience into meaning'.[10] Yet the union of spirit and flesh in a sacred vessel is the mystery which the Virgin in Majesty is intended precisely to reveal. The child on her lap is the eternal Word of God made flesh, and she is the human woman who conceived and bore him in her womb and is therefore the Mother of God.

The child looks like a small adult. He raises his right hand in a gesture of authority, and in his left hand holds a book which signifies that he is the eternal Word of the Father. These things indicate the boy's divine status. Yet at the same time, he is a barefooted child on his mother's knees, and as such is a mortal, carnal human being. He is God incarnate – God enfleshed; and when the eternal and infinite God took upon himself the fleshly bounds of the human condition, it was his mother who gave him his humanity. So in an elegant movement of reflection and reciprocity, the human woman who gives her body to divinity becomes the Mother of God, and is thereby exalted to a position which is higher even than that of the all-spiritual angels, for she is enthroned as Queen of Heaven. The willingness of the spirit to be united with matter, the potential of matter to receive the spirit, and the bonding of divinity with the physical creation: these are the truths which the Virgin and Child embody and which pornography denies. The pornographer tries to punish and subdue his own sensibilities by punishing and subduing the subjects of his pornography. But he is also punishing and subduing real human beings.

Susanne Kappeler has argued that the pornographic image must be understood as a communication from the pornographer to the viewer, in which the one who sends the message is making a statement about his power over the people in the picture.[11] The fact that a man is able to photograph a woman in a state of humiliation and subjection, and then to publish it for other men's pleasure and his own profit, is itself an exercise of power over her, and that power is then advertised to all those who see the photograph. Here again, the Virgin in Majesty provides the starkest contrast to the pornographic image. Many of the Majesty statues have legends concerning their origins – legends which guarantee that sacred power resides with the image itself, and which defy human pretensions to wield control over it. A claim which is commonly made for statues of this kind is that the image was found by an animal, or sometimes by a herdsman, in a natural setting such as a bush or a spring. Typically, it is claimed that the local people took the statue into the village and put it in a place of honour in the church, but the next morning, the statue had returned to the spot in which it was discovered. Every time the people move it back, the statue miraculously returns to its original place. After several days, the people realize that Christ and the Virgin intend their image to remain in the place in which it was found, and so the devotees build a shrine for it there. A legend of this type implies that the statue does not have an ordinary human origin, and that it is in certain respects more powerful than those who try to take charge of it. Unlike the subject of a pornographic image, who is in the power of the pornographer, in the case of the Romanesque statue, power is believed to reside in the subjects themselves, who are the Virgin and Child.

Another common myth concerning the origins of Virgin in Majesty statues is the claim that the statue was carved from life by St Luke. In this case, a human artist is identified, but he is of such sanctity – as is the circumstance that the carving was made from the Virgin herself – that knowledge of the human artist enhances, rather than diminishes, the image's sacred power. Statues which are said to have sacred or miraculous origins are almost always accorded the power to work miracles.

One of the most famous statues of the Virgin in Majesty is Our Lady of Montserrat, patroness of Catalonia. The many legends surrounding her include both the motif of carving by St Luke and that of the extraordinary discovery in a wild setting. The statue is said to have been carved by St Luke and brought to Barcelona by an apostle. At a time of Moorish invasion it was hidden from the infidel, on the Sierra de Montserrat, and its whereabouts subsequently forgotten.[12] Then, in the eighth century, a group of shepherds were led to it by an angelic choir. When the statue was discovered, the Bishop of Vic decided to have it removed to the nearby town of Manresa; but when they tried to move the statue it grew heavier and heavier, so that in the end it had to be left in the place in which it was found. The great monastery of Montserrat subsequently grew up around the sacred site.

The association of special powers with particular images and particular places is another feature which distinguishes the Virgin in Majesty very sharply from pornography. One aspect of the porno-grapher's human-as-machine is the absence of individuality in the figures of pornographic literature and imagery. In pornography, one human being is interchangeable with any other of the same general type. The functions which the actor performs are unrelated to any personal qualities. Adorno and Horkheimer observe that there are a number of ironies in contemporary culture's promotion of 'the individual', and several of these are connected with the visual representation of men and women.[13] For example, photographs in magazines depict real people, in the sense that actual human beings are the models in them. Yet in fashion magazines, or pornographic magazines, the real human models – mostly women – are very carefully selected for their physical characteristics, and these characteristics are broadly similar within any one genre of photography. In addition to this, the models are elaborately made up and they pose for the camera so that only certain postures and angles of view are represented. What the magazine shows to the world, then, is a highly contrived and selected impression of what human beings, and in particular, women, look like. The physical characteristics of models in magazines are exceptional; they are not ones which the majority of people either can or ought to possess. Yet because the people in the pictures are obviously real people, and because the same few types of representation are ubiquitous in contemporary culture, the types become imprinted on the mind, and one is easily cajoled into believing that one can and ought to find precisely these types of beauty in the everyday world.

As a counter-example to this, take the iconography of Eastern Orthodox Christianity. The icon always represents a human being, but in a manner which deviates from naturalism – for example, by using perspective which does not imitate normal three-dimensional vision. The viewer of the icon is thus able to contemplate a beauty which does not impose expectations as to what physical attributes one should find beautiful in another person. The viewer can turn away from an icon to perceive the varied beauty of other men and women, without the intrusion of the magazine photographer's dictatorial lens. In this way, the medium which seems to represent 'individuals' – the photography of fashion and pornography – in fact imposes stereotypes for replication in social reality. Yet the icon, which makes no pretence at physical literalism, allows the viewer the freedom to find the individual beauty of particular human beings.

In this respect, the Romanesque Virgin in Majesty is like the Orthodox icon. Each statue has key elements in common with every other, and none raises the expectation of physical imitation by living women and men. Moreover, each statue is treasured for its particular legends and miracles, and – perhaps most of all – for the unique sacred site in which it dwells. The Marian devotee will say that the image of Our Lady of Montserrat and her sacred dwelling-place have a character which is all their own, as does any other statue and site in which the Virgin has chosen to make her special home. Adorno and Horkheimer argue that the stamp of sameness which is imposed upon the subjects of pornographic abuse ('them all', says Saint-Fonds of women) is typical of modernity, and seems to be an imitation of mass-production in the factory system. The rationalization of ever-larger areas of social and economic life – for example, in expanding bureaucracies, and the production of objects for mass consumption – mean that particularity and variety are gradually destroyed. Furthermore, whether I buy a pre-packed, quality-controlled meal in the supermarket, or conduct my business by means of a global computer network, I participate increasingly in systems of action which render me the object, rather than the subject, of that action. Pornography provides vivid images of the moral underpinning and consequences of such a mode of life. For social processes of rationalization are fundamentally concerned with world-mastery, rationalization being a mode of action in which human beings come to dominate humanity, together with animals and the rest of the natural world.[14] And here again, the Romanesque Virgin in Majesty stands in opposition to such an ideology. As has already been noted, many of the shrines which house Virgin in Majesty figures are away from human habitation, in places which are wild, or semi-wild. It is as though the meeting of God and humanity occurs most powerfully in separation from civilization – that God is met most surely amongst plants, animals, rocks and springs, rather than buildings. As if to underline the meaning of the Incarnation, the natural is experienced as the locus of the spiritual.

In the light of what has gone above, then, it is perhaps not surprising to find that in pornography, the meaning of animals, plants and wild places is the very opposite of this. If a pornographer represents a woman with an animal, or in a field, then he is telling the viewer that she is merely flesh. Like the supposedly soulless animal which lives by instinct alone, she is a body which craves bodily satisfaction; she is purely 'natural' and without a soul. Whereas a Marian shrine, by its story, its statue and its place, will proclaim that a sacred presence is inherent in the material creation, the pornographic image declares matter to be devoid of all spirit, and ultimately, of all meaning.

According to Griffin's analysis, the pornographer is unable to accept his own bodiliness. His weak flesh and his mortality are things he finds humiliating. He therefore projects them onto the pornographic subject: so it is now she (or he) who is identified with the flesh. But the pornographer's feelings are his own, and they return to demand attention. The pornographer despises them, and finds them humiliating, and so he despises and humiliates the pornographic subject who symbolizes them. Eventually, she (or he) must be bound, tortured and even killed – events which are all more or less common in the various pornographic media. Yet the pornographer's own emotions still will not leave him. He is on a hopeless quest to deny or destroy his own integrity, that is, the unity of body and soul, spirit and matter, which is a human person. But matter without spirit would be devoid of meaning, and to deny the truth or to attempt to destroy the reality which is the nature of one's own species will likewise lead only to emptiness and despair. The pornographer may imagine himself to be elevated over another person, but in attempting to deny and humiliate his own physical condition, he only debases himself. Indeed, the sadist and the masochist are two halves of the same mind.

Here again, pornography stands in opposition to the Romanesque statue of Christ and his mother. The pornographic image is degrading to its maker and user; but the Virgin in Majesty ennobles her devotee. You may prostrate yourself before her and proclaim yourself her servant, or pour out your sins to her; but in return she will fill you with that dignity and sense of worth by which she first commanded your attention. The pornographer perpetrates the lie that the human condition and the physical world are naturally vile and degraded; but the Mother of God and her Son say truthfully that the whole of creation is destined for the highest honour.

What, then, has become of the image of the Virgin Mary since the Middle Ages? If great Majesty statues are no longer made, then how is Mary portrayed in the art of the age of pornography? Certainly not as a commanding monarch. On the contrary, she is typically shown with the posture and gestures of humility, rather than authority (see Plate 2, Our Lady of Lourdes). The marked difference between Romanesque and modern representations of the Virgin was noted by the Anglican theologian B. F. Westcott when he visited the shrine of La Salette, near Grenoble, in 1865. This shrine had its origin in 1846, when the Virgin appeared to a young boy and girl who were herding cattle. It became a site of miraculous healing, and was a popular place of pilgrimage when Westcott and his companions made their journey there twenty years later. Westcott was favourably impressed by the devotion which he found at La Salette, and of the statues which had been erected there he wrote:

> There is nothing like the black image of Le Puy, or Dijon, or Notre Dame de Bon Secours at Rouen, which creates an involuntary sense of repulsion or even of disgust as if we were in the presence of some fetish-

worship. The figures of the Virgin which are the object or symbols of
devotion are perfect in taste and beauty. They claim to represent simply
an historic fact. The very purity in which the popular faith is presented
makes its novelty more conspicuously evident.[15]

The black Virgin of Dijon is a Majesty statue of the twelfth century, and
that at Le Puy is a copy of a similar Romanesque figure which was
destroyed at the French Revolution. The principal statue at La Salette,
by contrast, shows the Virgin in a simple form corresponding to the
description given by the two cowherds. The impression of sacred
power which surrounds the Virgin in Majesty is experienced by
Westcott as repulsive, and is contrasted unfavourably with the less
commanding image which has a more narrative character. Westcott's
reaction is articulated as a Christian response to something pagan –
'fetish-worship'; but his feelings are probably typical of many Europeans
of the nineteenth and twentieth centuries, for whom Mary is only ever
meek and unassuming.

If the Virgin in Majesty truly does convey to the viewer a sense of
divinity in the physical world, then it is worth considering that modern
reaction against such an image may in part be a reaction against this
central meaning.[16] If pornography distinctly opposes the unity of spirit
and matter, modern Marian iconography merely avoids any allusion to
it. But that avoidance, like pornography's opposition, may be born of
modernity's fear of 'nature's' power.

Furthermore, the Virgin's subordination is not only depicted in
modern iconography, but is found also in the written texts of
twentieth-century devotion. Mary Daly, a feminist opponent of
Catholicism, writes of the Annunciation:

> the angel Gabriel appears to the terrified young girl, announcing that she
> has been chosen to become the mother of god. Her response to this
> sudden proposal from the godfather is totalled nonresistance: 'Let it be
> done unto me according to thy word.' Physical rape is not necessary
> when the mind / will / spirit has already been invaded.[17]

And elsewhere she says: 'The male-angel Gabriel brings poor Mary the
news that she is to be impregnated by and with god. Like all rape
victims in male myth she submits joyously to this unspeakable
degradation.'[18]

Daly's rendering of the Annunciation would not stand up to scrutiny
if treated as a commentary upon, say, the homily of St Bernard (c.1090–

1153) in which he describes the whole of creation waiting anxiously upon Mary's word of assent, so that the accomplishment of the world's salvation depends upon her decision.[19] But as a description of much modern Marian writing, Daly's account is disturbingly close to the truth. Susan Griffin comments:

> The image of woman as a void is a dominant theme of pornographic culture. A woman is less. She is less strong, less intelligent, less creative, less spiritual. She does not exist for herself. Rather, she is a shadow whose existence depends on the real existence of men. She exists for men and is not, in Freud's words, 'an end in herself'.[20]

The motif of 'woman as a void' is found also in writing about Mary. Such writing is certainly more beautiful than its pornographic counterpart, but to a Christian believer, the points of correspondence between the two must be disturbing. Caryll Houselander's book *The Reed of God*, which is a meditation on Mary, begins with these words:

> That virginal quality which, for want of a better word, I call emptiness is the beginning of this contemplation.
>
> It is not a formless emptiness, a void without meaning; on the contrary it has a shape, a form given to it by the purpose for which it is intended.
>
> It is emptiness like the hollow in the reed, the narrow riftless emptiness which can have only one destiny: to receive the piper's breath and to utter the song that is in his heart ...
>
> [Our Lady] was a reed through which the Eternal Love was to be piped as a shepherd's song.[21]

Several virtues other than that of usefulness to a musician might be attributed to a reed with its hollow; but Houselander significantly ignores this, so that Mary here stands in a relationship to God similar to that of the pornographic victim to the man who uses her.

Yet pornography is concerned not with the mere assertion of a woman's emptiness, but with the denial and obliteration of her humanity. Susanne Kappeler analyses a section of D. M. Thomas's novel *The White Hotel*, in which the fictitious character Lisa Erdman allows herself to be subjected to sexual violence by men. Erdman says of them: 'I didn't mind which one of them was in ... it was good to feel part of me was someone else, no one was selfish in the white hotel.'[22] Kappeler comments:

> Selflessness: the definition of perfect femininity, the goal of virtue for wife and mother, for womanhood ...

No one was selfish in the white hotel. This one is woman, rapidly becoming a no one herself. Everyone else, in the white hotel, is very selfish: they all want to fuck her, have her. They assert their subjectivity by means of her object-body and her evacuated humanity.[23]

Kappeler observes that the 'female' character in pornography may be shown as resisting her own violation, or – as in *The White Hotel* – she may be 'voluntarily and infinitely available to his impositions'; but either way, 'The options are strictly defined within the one imperative that it *will* happen to her; "she" can choose an attitude.'[24]

Modern Catholic writing on Mary lays great emphasis on the totality of her assent to God's will, so that she gives herself to him as freely and completely as Lisa Erdman gives herself to the men in the white hotel. Adrienne von Speyr – a woman of influence in modern Catholic theology – writes of Mary:

From the moment in which she pronounced [her assent], she forms it continuously, submitting herself perfectly to God in everything, and thus lets the assent shape her whole existence. This formation of the assent means . . . that she renounces once and for all any self-shaping of her own life.[25]

In assenting, she renounces herself, makes herself nothing, in order to let God alone become active in her.[26]

Against this Catholic understanding, the modern Protestant theologian Karl Barth denies that Mary's free assent plays any important part in the Christian story of salvation, asserting that Mary is merely the instrument of God's will.[27] But how important is the theological distinction between these interpretations when, as Kappeler observes, 'the one imperative' is that 'it *will* happen to her'?

Now, a theological argument could be made to oppose the case which I have outlined above. It might be objected that there is an important difference between assertions of Mary's assent to and dependence upon God, and the subordination of woman to man in pornography: namely, that whereas the world really does depend upon God, and whereas people of both sexes should assent to God's will, no human being should lay claim to such a relationship of absolute power over, or dependence upon, a fellow human being, and it is therefore immoral, and even idolatrous, to try to order relations between men and women in this way. Thus, there is nothing wrong with the Marian devotion of Houselander and Von Speyr, but there is everything wrong with the literature of pornography.

The difficulty with this objection is that Christians have not always viewed Mary in the way in which Houselander and Von Speyr do. Comparisons with the Marian devotion of earlier centuries indicate that the presentations of these authors are part and parcel of the wider culture in which they wrote. There are striking historical correlations between the varying character of Marian devotion and other cultural changes, including the growth of pornography. For while it may be true, theologically speaking, to say that humanity is totally dependent upon God, and is called to serve and obey him, the historical fact is that, over the centuries, Christians have interpreted Mary's relationship to God in a variety of different ways, and have done so within the bounds of orthodoxy. The placing of a huge emphasis upon Mary's personal submission and selflessness is a fairly recent development, which, like pornography, is characteristic of modernity.

Furthermore, although the monotheistic faith which Christians profess holds that God is before and beyond gender (which is an aspect of God's creation), a certain trend within modern Catholic theology nevertheless tries to attribute a kind of maleness to God. At the same time, this theology claims that at the Annunciation, a particular importance is attached to Mary's femininity, so that the relationship of God to Mary is in some sense that of male to female. John Saward, giving an account of the theology of Hans Urs von Balthasar, writes:

> God in his transcendence, as the primary actor and initiator, is analogically male with regard to the creature; the creature in its dependence on God is open and receptive, *capax Dei*, and therefore, in a certain sense, feminine ...
>
> Woman is the classic creature. It is supremely fitting, therefore, that a woman on her own ... should have represented creation in consenting to the Incarnation.[28]

This explicitly gendered presentation of the relationship between God and Mary underlines the similarity between the structure of some modern Marian writing and that of pornography. It may or may not be possible to defend this phenomenon in terms of theological orthodoxy; but the modern emphasis on Mary's 'openness' and self-denial represents a broader cultural trend which, according to the values both of Christianity and of many secular philosophies, is morally unacceptable.

Nevertheless, a central argument of the present work is that throughout Christian tradition, Mary is indeed, as Saward suggests, a representative figure for the creation in relation to the Creator. Over time, Christians have conceptualized this relationship in different ways – sometimes seeing Mary as the wielder of Christ's imperial authority, at other times as the maidservant of Nazareth. The principal question which I am addressing is what social and economic developments have contributed to this sort of change in the cult of the Virgin? And I also ask whether this process occurs in reverse: in particular, whether contemporary Marian devotion has the potential to inspire economic and political transformation in society at large.

In Christian theology and devotion, Mary stands for creation in relation to the Creator. More particularly, she stands for creation in what is supposed to be its right relationship with the Creator. So, for example, Catholic theology holds that, by the grace of God, men and women can and should co-operate with God's will, and in this way assist in God's work of salvation. Accordingly, Catholic theologians typically present Mary as the finest example of one who co-operated with God. She agreed to be the mother of Christ who is God incarnate, or God made flesh. Since Jesus had no human father, it was from Mary alone that he took his human flesh, and since the Incarnation is the beginning of the world's redemption, Mary, in giving him his flesh, made the fullest contribution that any human being could have made to that redemption.

In stark contrast to this, Calvinist theology (such as that of Barth, referred to above) holds that since nothing good ever happens except by the grace of God, any talk of human 'co-operation' in redemption is misplaced: it attributes too active a role to one of God's creatures, and does so at the expense of a proper recognition of the Creator, who is the only source of salvation. Mary, therefore, is not to be regarded as playing any kind of decisive part in the Incarnation. She merely receives the miracle which God bestows, and thus typifies the relationship of the world to its Maker.

Again, in Catholic teaching, the material world can be the bearer of divine presence or grace. The real presence of Christ in the bread and wine of the Eucharist, or the power which is invested in saints' relics, are instances of this. But the material object which is the supreme example of such God-bearing, is of course the body of the Virgin who carried the incarnate Lord. It is she who is accorded the greatest devotion after Christ himself.

13

In opposition to this, Calvinist teaching tends to regard any veneration of the material world as being too close to idolatry, that is, the worship of a creature rather than its Creator. The created order exists by the grace of God, but nothing should suggest that the two might be in any way confused. So the religious cult of a material object is considered unacceptable. Consequently, whatever honour God bestowed upon Mary in making her the mother of Christ, her child-bearing does not provide grounds on which other human beings should do her homage.

These and many other examples show the persistence with which the attitudes of Western Christians towards Mary reveal distinct understandings of the theology of grace and creation as a whole. More particularly, they show that she is seen to be representative of the created world in its right relationship with the Creator.

Christian understanding of the relationship between Creator and creation has been subject to a number of changes over the centuries. Some of the technical formulations of Catholic theologians have remained fairly constant, but other manifestations of Christian devotion make clear the transformations that have occurred. For instance, a famous French manuscript illustration of the thirteenth century shows God 'setting a compass on the face of the deep' in the work of creation (Proverbs 8:27). The Lord holds a craftsman's dividers over the primal waters of creation, as though his work is analogous to that of a thirteenth-century builder or stonemason. The thirteenth century was a period of extraordinarily rapid technological development in Western Europe, and God had never previously been represented in this way. In earlier depictions, made by monks and nuns who devoted themselves to prayer and scholarship, God's creative work was a purely intellectual activity, involving only the head, and not the hands. But as humanity's relationship with the natural world was transformed in the application of new technology – originally undertaken by Benedictine monasteries – so humanity's conception of the relationship between God and creation changed in parallel movement. For Christians generally imagine that God's creative activity conforms to the dominant mode of human creativity within their own culture.

Now, if the relationship between God and creation is comprehended on the model of humanity's relationship with its natural environment, and if Mary is a representative figure for creation in relation to the Creator, then changes of technology and economy – changes in humanity's relationship with the natural world – should be accompanied by corresponding changes in the cult of the Virgin. I argue that this is indeed the case, so that the development of Marian devotion in Western Europe provides an index of humanity's increasing mastery over the natural and social orders, and its aspiration to ever greater domination. The high medieval perception of Mary as the powerful Queen of Heaven was produced by a society in which people experienced themselves as dependent upon their physical environment, and in which that environment was the bearer of sacred power, as Mary herself was the bearer of God incarnate. The modern image of the Madonna as a humble young girl at prayer signifies on the one hand a Christian culture in which the created order is seen as very distant from its Maker, and on the other hand a wider society in which 'nature' is supposed to be ever more subordinate to control by human invention.

Authors of the so-called 'Frankfurt School' of Critical Theory, especially Adorno, Horkheimer and Herbert Marcuse, argued that humanity's domination of nature underlay and corresponded to domination of other kinds, including that of women by men. Using a revised form of Marxism, and Freudian psychoanalytical theory, they built up an understanding of modern society which posited close connections between different modes of domination, including social processes of rationalization and psychological repression. Feminist scholarship has pursued some of the same themes, and I draw on both classical Frankfurt theory and more recent research on gender to construct a framework in which to interpret evidence concerning Marian doctrine and devotion.

The cult of the Virgin Mary is intimately bound to social relations of domination. There are correspondences between domination of different kinds (those of class and of gender, for example), and consequently, the history of Marian devotion can be associated with domination in any one of a number of spheres of social action. However, my analysis gives priority to humanity's domination of 'nature' (a category whose meaning has itself changed during the course of European history). This prioritization makes possible a reasonably coherent account of relations between the different modes of domination, and also provides a plausible explanation as to why important changes in Marian devotion occurred at the times and in the manner in which they did. The theoretical perspective of the Frankfurt School assumes the priority of technology and economy over other aspects of culture, and this assumption is supported by more recent research, for example, by Peggy Reeves Sanday's cross-cultural study of male dominance.[29] Nevertheless, there are other aspects of human culture, including the religious, which have a determining influence on the development of a whole society, and the question arises as to whether Marian doctrine and devotion has itself the capacity to effect change in social action.

Technology and economy are concerned with the use and management of the natural environment, and in most human societies these processes have necessitated a measure of self-denial on the part of those who practise them: the postponement of immediate pleasure in the interest of longer-term well-being. A man cannot satisfy every craving for food, sleep and sex, and at the same time put his energy into the planning and execution of, for example, a major engineering project. Desires are therefore denied and repressed. So the domination of nature finds a counterpart in psychic repression, which in turn might be characterized as the domination of the human person's own nature. But the desires do not go away; and from their hidden position, they come to be the unacknowledged dictators of human action. The unrecognized desires find their own, now distorted, channels of expression, and by their very existence it appears as though the objects of domination are themselves presenting a threat to the oppressor.

The domination of nature, both external and internal, easily gives rise to the domination of other men and women – and in the first instance, to the domination of women by men. A variety of environmental circumstances can favour male dominance in economic and social life; but in addition to this, the denial of immediate sexual satisfaction necessitates a man's controlling or distancing himself from women who remind him of his desire and threaten its denial. Woman thus becomes associated with desires which must be repressed, and which in turn are associated with the natural environment that is the object of human control. Through these sorts of processes male identity comes to be constructed as a self which is separate from, and must gain mastery over, an 'other' which includes women, nature, and the man's own physical needs.

The different relationships of domination share a common, dyadic structure, in which the superior party, or 'master', in the relationship perceives himself to be 'other' than, and in opposition to, the subordinate. At the same time, he treats all members of the subordinate

16

group as though they were, in all significant respects, the same as one another, and thus fails to recognize their individual differences. This is the kind of relationship which feminist theorists have referred to as 'dualistic'. Dualism is maintained by members of both sexes, but sociological and psychological considerations make it seem likely that men at present have a greater propensity than women to construct the world in this manner.

If, as has been suggested above, Christians understand God's relationship with the creation in terms which are analogous to those on which humanity constructs its relationship with the natural world, and also in terms of the relationship between male and female, then at least some of the characteristics which Christians attribute to the relationship between God and creation might best be understood as a psychological projection, and perhaps a social legitimation, of the state of human activities of the economic and social order at a given time and place. Correspondingly, then, the relationship which is envisaged to exist between God and the Virgin Mary, who is representative of the created order, will be indicative of social relations of domination.

However, the relationship between male and female, humanity and nature, and even between races and social classes, is rarely one in which one group exercises uncompromised control over the other. On the contrary, domination is frequently concerned with managing or subduing the other's power. The infant would have no life at all were it not for the care of its mother or her substitute, and the process of growing up involves separating oneself from the overwhelming power of the mother. Depending on circumstances, the separation from the mother may entail a rigid defining of the self in opposition to the maternal other, and a sense of need to suppress everything which in any way evokes her powerful presence, since the mother's presence signifies comfort and the satisfaction of basic needs, and these are things which the adult must control and postpone. So for the male, the mother comes to stand for things which are desired but forbidden; and other women, because they are like the mother – the 'original' woman – can come to stand for the same things.

In like manner, the natural world of which humanity forms a part and which entirely sustains it appears initially to be the bearer, or rather, the multiple bearers, of sacred power; and the development of modern technology has been an attempt at progressive separation from this sacred universe, and of increasing control over natural powers – which is to say, it has been a process of de-sacralization. Like a child who cannot believe that he is separate from his mother, and cannot accept his dependence on physical nature, the civilization of Western Europe has fought ever more against 'Mother Nature', from the time of the Carolingian empire until the present day. And Western Christians' perception of Mother Nature finds constant reverberations in representations of Mother Mary, from the glorious queen of Romanesque art to the dutiful servant of contemporary devotional texts.

The Blessed Virgin Mary is Mother of God, and as such, she guarantees the capacity of material things to be infused with divinity. But in a society whose fundamental economic life depends upon the denial of that capacity, either Mary must be ignored, or attention distracted away from her divine motherhood, so that her own sacred power is denied. As both Mother of God and Mother of Christians, she is the focus of a great web of desires and fears which are aroused by maternal associations at different times and places, and in modernity, these associations have become to an extraordinary degree ones which arouse fear and hatred.

Yet Marian devotion in the twentieth century is shot through with contradictions. It is easy to find instances of Mary being allied to political forces of domination: indeed, Nicholas Perry and Loreto Echeverría have contended that Mary has always been associated with political repression.[30] When it occurs, Mary's alliance with forces of domination is due in part to her role as 'perfect creature', where this is defined in terms of a relationship of mastery and subservience, but it is due also to her position as a mother. She recalls in devotees the memory of infant closeness to their own mothers, and in this she seems to offer them a safe haven from the turbulent waters of social change. This enables her cult to act as a refuge from the challenge of social liberation. Perry and Echeverría are, however, mistaken in giving the impression that Mary has been invariably associated with right-wing or reactionary social movements, and in recent decades, this has been seen clearly in the base communities and liberation theology of Latin America. Here, Mary is presented as a sign of hope to the poor and oppressed: her virginity signifies freedom from all kinds of violation, whilst her immaculate conception is a promise that humanity will be restored to paradise.[31]

Ironically, the psychology of Mary's association with liberation is in one respect very similar to her alignment with conservatism. For in both cases it is the devotees' remembrance of childhood closeness to their mothers which inspires their ideals and actions. The most fundamental human knowledge of joy and contentment is that which the infant experiences – or even just suspects might be possible – in its relationship with its mother. The memory of this experience is therefore the ultimate source of hope for a 'second Eden', which will be the state of freedom from all domination; and this hope is the necessary inspiration for any struggle towards liberation. It is not that liberation will consist in a return to an infantile, unsocialized condition. On the contrary, regression to such a state would be the substitution of one kind of domination for another. Rather, liberation might somehow be a state in which those achievements of civilization which can be used in such a manner will be put to the service of a state of well-being whose existence we can believe is possible because we have already known the joy of an earlier fulfilment.

The Critical Theorist Ernst Bloch believed that the value of religious ideals – especially those of Judaism and Christianity – lay in the hope which they offered for a world transformed beyond our present imagining. The God of Moses and of Jesus takes people outside the oppressive structures of conservative religion and promises a future of liberation, but a future which is essentially unknown.[32]

The Hebrew Scriptures make it abundantly clear that God himself cannot be represented in any image created by human hand, and indeed, that the Deity is ultimately beyond all human imagining. Theodor Adorno and Max Horkheimer would sometimes appeal to this notion of God when explaining their refusal to present any definite picture of the ideal towards which they were striving.[33] Their task was one of criticizing the present age in the light of a possible future which as yet could not be envisaged; this was a future of liberation which could not be adequately pictured while human vision was still distorted by relations of domination. Hence, perpetual criticism of the present time was the only possible activity – but also the absolutely necessary one – in the intellectual contribution to the struggle against domination of all kinds.

The God whom Horkheimer and Adorno referred to was a god of history: a god who acts not only in the cycles of physical nature but also in the ever-changing arena of human politics; a god whose demands upon his people include not only prescriptions for the correct performance of ritual, but also the social requirement of justice. The religious emphasis upon ethical behaviour forms a counterpart to the belief that the Creator God has endowed men and women with the potential to create and remake many aspects of the world which they inhabit. For it is precisely this potential which gives rise to the responsibility for wise judgement. Even the belief that the first vine was planted by Noah, a human man, and not by a supernatural being, reveals a strong awareness of humanity's power to affect its environment; and this sense of human power is matched by a corresponding belief that the Creator's creation is not itself divine. Therefore, in their dealings with the different aspects of the physical world, men and women can come to believe that they need not be greatly restrained by taboos or by fears of committing sacrilege. Eventually, however, the creation will come to lack not only divinity, but even sanctity.

The path has been a varied one which has led from the world of the magician to the universe of the scientist. The 'scientific' belief that the universe is rationally ordered was both a cause and a consequence of the conviction that the workings of all things might be exposed and then manipulated by human agency. Over time, these projects of exposure and manipulation have become essentially atheistic, but both intellectually and practically, the process of large-scale rationalization has emerged predominantly out of Western Christianity; and so, likewise, did the Enlightenment. By this route, modern society owes much of its character to the monotheistic belief in a single and final Creator, who is also the Lord of history before whom each and every person stands judged. It is the belief in this sort of god and his creation which has made possible many aspects of modernity: concepts of individual liberty, for example, fall into this category, as does the perpetual pursuit of an ever-widening scope for human intervention in the natural and social environment, and, most strikingly, the possibility of accomplishing these aims through the technical procedures of science and politics. Adorno and Horkheimer acknowledged the debt which their own concern with liberation owed to its religious forebears.

However, the God of the Bible is, as he himself reports, a jealous god. He offers freedom and justice at the cost of abandoning the worship of all other deities or idols. It is ironic, therefore, that the ideal of technical achievement, which monotheistic religion helped to make a practical reality, has itself become an idol which, as such, is no longer subordinated even to human well-being, let alone to any higher virtue.

The belief that nature is not divine is a precondition for its exploitation. But the technology of exploitation has itself come to be seen as an ultimate end, a final good in itself, and in that sense is divinized. The irrational demands of competition in the economy and technology are now given preference over any appeal to reason, although on reflection, it can be seen that the very fear of idolatry has itself been partly responsible for the establishment of these idols of modernity.

Throughout the Christian Scriptures there is uncompromising opposition to the gods of the nations. Many of these deities are intimately associated with aspects of the physical world: they are venerated through sacred objects, such as wooden poles and statues; or they require elaborate ritual performances which reflect and guarantee the continuing cycle of the agricultural year. The baals, the asherahs and their European counterparts are especially associated with rites of fertility, and it is this in particular which reveals to the Jew or the Christian that these gods are no gods at all. For the true God is alone the author of all life, and he transcends the world in such a way that he is not party to the incompleteness of creaturely generation. The gods of the nations are the gods of stasis and repetition, who seduce people into worshipping the creation rather than the Creator. The God of Israel and of Jesus, by contrast, is a god who turns his worshippers' hearts away from an unworthy dependence upon creatures who have no business to command human needs; he is the God who leads people onward through the vicissitudes of history to a world which will be transformed – a world which will be quite unlike the one which we now inhabit.

Yet what is to be the basis for this faith in the unseen God and his unknown future? The gods of the crops and the seasons provide nourishment and pleasure to their devotees. They seem to promise that, given the right conditions, plants, animals and humans will flourish within the boundaries of a physical and moral universe which is substantially familiar to its current residents. These entirely pagan gods fill their world with sacred meaning, so that every detail of human experience bears religious import. Yet the God of Christianity (far more than the God of Judaism and even of Jesus) fails in all these respects. He offers few guarantees for the here-and-now, and the bearers of his 'good news' turn the present age into little more than a waiting room for the age to come. Put like this, it is hard to see what is the attraction of Christian monotheism. But then, for much of Christian history, Christian faith has been put rather differently from this.

21

From a psychological point of view, the possibility of following an invisible God to an unknown destination depends upon worshippers having within themselves a deep sense that they are being upheld and cared for, and that they have hope for the future. Without this support, the challenge of the Christian God is too frightening or depressing to be bearable. According to psychoanalytical theory, this fundamental awareness of support and encouragement derives from the infant's primitive experience of closeness to its mother. It is this most primitive source of joy and contentment which is able to sustain the adult who is faced with obstacles and uncertainties, as it is the memory of this experience which provides the emotional grounds for the hope that conflict and division will not prove to be a necessary condition of society but can eventually be supplanted by relationships which are peaceful and fulfilling. It therefore seems reasonable to anticipate that a religious culture which encourages such a sense of fundamental safety will be one in which the institution of motherhood is held in high esteem, or in which maternal symbols occupy a dominant position.

Within Christianity, these maternal functions have, on occasions, been performed by God the Father, by Christ and by the Holy Spirit. But with greater frequency than any of these, it is Mary, the mother of Christ and, in more recent devotion, of Christians, who has been associated with that sense of continuing comfort and nourishment which recalls the devotees' infant desires. It was Mary who rescued Theophilus' soul from the Devil,[34] and she is the only saint whose intercession can never be refused by Christ the Judge. Gerard Manley Hopkins addressed Mary as 'world-mothering air', comparing her to the all-embracing and life-giving air which we breathe.[35] With such an abundance of confidence, it is possible to venture a great deal in the hope of attaining something still greater.

Yet Christians have frequently been sceptical of such apparently easy reassurance, and have suspected it of idolatry. The Calvinism of Weber's *Protestant Ethic* has no place for such maternal imagery.[36] But the loss of the maternal image erodes the most fundamental ground of hope for the future; and hence, the instrumental reason which might possibly have been converted to the service of the noblest aspirations has become a meaningless end in itself. Domination through and by instrumental rationality insinuates itself ever more widely, as the image and hope of freedom is progressively forgotten; and while religious people guard against the idolization of Mary and nature, new idols of human invention are established without Christian opposition. Mary nevertheless remains a vital presence for millions of Christians throughout the world, where she is a potential inspiration for subversive criticism, and where she can provide something else, whose importance Bloch denies. For he believed that the hope which was promised in Judaism and Christianity could and should continue without belief in the God who was originally considered to be the source of that hope. Yet without belief in God, the hope is ultimately unsustainable, and Mary as the Godbearer brings her devotees not only hope for a world transformed, but also the God who is the source and dwelling-place of that hope. Against a culture which is set against nature, and in which all flesh is meaningless, the Mother of God is still able to proclaim God's presence within the blood and the milk, the cells and the atoms, of the material creation, and in this too she constitutes a potential point of subversion of the present social order.

Notes

1. *DEC* pp. 894–5.
2. This phrase is used several times by Eadmer of Canterbury (1060/64 – 1141), in *Tractatus de Conceptione Sanctae Mariae*, ed. H. Thurston and P. T. Slater (1904).
3. The most extensive single study of these is Ilene Forsyth, *Throne of Wisdom: Wood Sculptures of the Madonna in Romanesque France* (1972).
4. Sophie Cassagnes-Brouquet, *Vierges Noires: Regard et Fascination* (1990), p. 9.
5. Quoted in Theodor Adorno and Max Horkheimer, *Dialectic of Enlightenment*, trans. John Cumming (1979), p. 111.
6. Susanne Kappeler, *The Pornography of Representation* (1986), p. 95.
7. Susan Griffin, *Pornography and Silence*, (1981).
8. See, for example, Lynn Hunt, 'Pornography and the French Revolution' in Lynn Hunt (ed.), *The Invention of Pornography: Obscenity and the Origins of Modernity, 1500–1800* (1996), pp. 301–39, and other essays in the same volume.
9. Adorno and Horkheimer, *Dialectic of Enlightenment*, p. 94.
10. Griffin, *Pornography and Silence*, p. 71.
11. Kappeler, *The Pornography of Representation*, pp. 5–10 and *passim*.
12. This legend may express an abiding antipathy to Islam. See Chapter 5 for a discussion of the connections which Marian devotion has had with anti-Jewish sentiment.

13. Adorno and Horkheimer, 'The culture industry: enlightenment as mass deception' in *The Dialectic of Enlightenment*, pp. 120–67.
14. Wolfgang Schluchter, *Rationalism, Religion and Domination: A Weberian Perspective*, trans. Neil Solomon (1989), p. 360.
15. Quoted in A. M. Allchin, *The Joy of All Creation: An Anglican Meditation on the Place of Mary*, (1993), pp. 164–5.
16. A genuine anxiety about idolatry may have underlain the Anglicans' discomfiture, but that raises the question as to why certain images are more prone than others to arouse such a concern. Issues of this kind are discussed in David Freedberg, *The Power of Images: Studies in the History and Theory of Response* (1989), especially Chapter 14, pp. 378–428.
17. Mary Daly, *Gyn/Ecology: The Metaethics of Radical Feminism* (1978), p. 85.
18. Mary Daly, *Pure Lust: Elemental Feminist Philosophy* (1984), p. 74.
19. Bernard of Clairvaux and Amadeus of Lausanne, *Magnificat: Homilies in Praise of the Blessed Virgin Mary*, trans. M.-B. Saïd and Grace Perigo (1979), pp. 45–58, especially pp. 53–4. See below, Chapter 1, p. 32.
20. Griffin, *Pornography and Silence*, pp. 217–18.
21. Caryll Houselander, *The Reed of God* (1944), p. 1.
22. Kappeler, *The Pornography of Representation*, p. 89.
23. Kappeler, *The Pornography of Representation*, pp. 89–90.
24. Kappeler, *The Pornography of Representation*, p. 90.
25. Adrienne von Speyr, *Handmaid of the Lord*, trans. E.A. Nelson (1985), p. 10.
26. Von Speyr, *Handmaid of the Lord*, p. 9.
27. Karl Barth, *Church Dogmatics* vol. I: *The Doctrine of the Word of God*, part 2, trans. G.T. Thomson and Harold Knight (1956), p. 140.
28. John Saward, *The Mysteries of March: Hans Urs von Balthasar on the Incarnation and Easter* (1990), 1990, p. 67.
29. Peggy Reeves Sanday, *Female Power and Male Dominance: On the Origins of Sexual Inequality* (1981).
30. Nicholas Perry and Loreto Echeverría, *Under the Heel of Mary* (1988).
31. See, for example, Ivone Gebara and Maria Clara Bingemer, *Mary, Mother of God, Mother of the Poor*, trans. Phillip Berryman (1989).
32. Ernst Bloch, *Das Prinzip Hoffnung* (Frankfurt am Main: Suhrkamp, 1959) vol. I, pp. 191–298; cited in Tom Moylan: 'Bloch against Bloch: the theological reception of *Das Prinzip Hoffnung* and the liberation of the utopian function' in J. O. Daniel and T. Moylan (eds), *Not Yet: Reconsidering Ernst Bloch* (1997), pp. 97–100.
33. Rudolf J. Siebert, *The Critical Theory of Religion: The Frankfurt School* (1985), p. 347; Zoltán Tar, *The Frankfurt School: The Critical Theories of Max Horkheimer and Theodor W. Adorno* (1985), p. 185; Martin Jay, *Adorno* (1984), p. 20.
34. An account of the legend of Theophilus is given in Chapter 2. It is one of

24

the oldest of the miracles of the Virgin, and it appears in all the major collections of such miracles (see, for example, Paule Bétérous, *Les Collections de Miracles de la Vierge en Gallo et Ibéro-Roman au XIIIe Siècle*, 1983–4). The story is the forerunner of Faust, who in Marlowe's version is left with no one to save him (Christopher Marlowe, *Doctor Faustus* in *The Complete Plays*, ed. J.B. Stearne (1969), pp. 259–339).

35. Gerard Manley Hopkins, *Poems and Prose*, ed. W. H. Gardner (1953), pp. 54–8.

36. Max Weber, *The Protestant Ethic and the Spirit of Capitalism*, trans. Talcott Parsons (1985).

1

✧✧✧✧✧

The decline of Mary's motherhood
1: Visual images

The divine motherhood in the twelfth and thirteenth centuries

In the Essex village of Great Canfield, the parish church, which is dedicated to St Mary, retains an early thirteenth-century wall-painting of the Virgin and Child (Plate 3). The painting is simple in its construction, although the figures have a bearing of great dignity. The Virgin is enthroned and wears a crown. The Child is depicted not as a baby, but as a child-sized boy of almost adult proportions. He is seated on the Virgin's knee, and is held secure with her left hand, while he raises his right hand as if about to give a blessing. With her own right hand, the Virgin offers the Child her breast, as though she is going to suckle him. The painting is above the high altar, so that the image forms a focal point for reflection or devotion. It was covered over after the Reformation, but may have been continuously visible from the thirteenth until the sixteenth century.

The motif of the Virgin enthroned and suckling her Child is not the most common iconographic type from this, or any other, period of Christian history, but examples of it can be found intermittently in medieval representation. The image of the Virgin Mary as a woman who is both heavenly Queen and nursing mother is one which encapsulated almost to perfection the Christian doctrine of the Incarnation; and together with its doctrinal significance, the image proclaimed the corresponding ethic which elevated the qualities of lowliness and poverty to the status of virtues of the highest order. For

Mary was the sign of God's incarnation in the man Jesus, and she also typified the Christian ideal of humility. Therefore, if we are to understand the iconographic form of the Canfield Virgin, it is necessary to know what is being stated in the doctrine of the Incarnation, and what role is played by Mary in this central aspect of the Christian story of salvation. Indeed, not only in the medieval period, but wherever Mary is depicted in Christian art, the artist expresses some understanding of Mary's part in God's redemption of the world. A brief account of the Christian story will throw into relief Mary's role in the drama.

Christian faith is concerned centrally with the man Jesus, who is believed to have saved the world from sin. God created the world in a state of goodness, as a work of *grace*, but sin entered the world when Adam and Eve, the first man and woman, disobeyed the Lord God in the Garden of Eden (Genesis 3); and according to most ancient and medieval accounts, it was the entry of sin into the world which brought about death and all kinds of hardship. Thus, nature had fallen from grace. But God did not wish his creation to continue in this state of suffering and estrangement from him, and he therefore sent Jesus into the world to save it from sin and death. And paradoxically, Jesus' own death, by crucifixion, was the only sacrifice which was sufficient to atone for the sins of the world, and to restore humanity to its right relationship with God: to overcome death itself. This conquest over death was realized in Christ's resurrection from the dead on the third day after his Crucifixion, and it is the Resurrection which constitutes the most fundamental tenet of the Christian faith. This resurrection will one day be shared by all those who have been redeemed by Christ, when he returns in glory on the Last Day. Indeed, Jesus continues to offer all humanity the possibility of salvation from their sins, and hence the ultimate possibility of eternal life in a state of heavenly bliss.

Now, the reason why the Crucifixion and Resurrection of Jesus is able to have the universal redemptive significance which Christians attribute to it lies in Jesus' identity. Since sin entered the world by human action, it was necessary that a human being should atone for that sin. Yet only God has the power to effect atonement adequately – to redeem the world from sin and death. Therefore, if Christ's saving work is truly effective, he must be both God and human. So Jesus Christ is God incarnate, that is God made flesh. To be more precise, since the one God is also Trinity, it was the eternal Word of God, the Second

27

Person of the Blessed Trinity, who became flesh in Mary's womb for the salvation of the world. Thus, the means by which God chose to save the world from its sins was that he himself should take human flesh – that the Creator should be one with a creature, that he who is immortal should take on mortality – and that he should suffer and die for the sake of his creation.

So Jesus' unique salvific power derives from his unique identity as true God and true man, and it is for this reason that Mary is central to the Christian account of God and creation. For in the union of God and humanity, it is Mary who imparts the humanity: eternally begotten of the Father, Christ was born on earth of his mother Mary. This belief is expressed in the teaching that Mary conceived Jesus by the power of the Holy Spirit when she was still a virgin. Furthermore, in order to make clear the fact that in Jesus humanity and divinity were perfectly united, Mary was given the title 'Mother of God'. The Greek term for this is *Theotokos*, which literally means 'Godbearer', or 'the one who conceived God', and it is rendered in Latin as *Dei Genitrix*, *Deipara* or *Mater Dei*. The title *Theotokos* occurs in the earliest known prayer to the Virgin, which dates from the fourth or fifth century, but the title was almost certainly in use before this time.[1] The title was proclaimed a doctrine of the whole Church at the Council of Ephesus (AD 431), and it makes clear, on the one hand, that Jesus was not solely human (or Mary's motherhood would not have been 'of God') and, on the other hand, that Jesus was nonetheless a real man, and not a divine apparition with no bodily substance (in which case, he would not have had a human mother). The title *Theotokos* thereby indicates that Mary was the mother of a son in whom humanity and divinity were undivided.[2]

Moreover, for many authors of the patristic and medieval periods, the Incarnation was not merely the necessary condition for the accomplishment of human salvation: it was in itself a salvific work. For by uniting himself to human flesh, the eternal Word of God made possible the restoration of all human flesh to its original glory. Thus, Cyril of Alexandria (d. 444), defending the title *Theotokos*, writes:

> [The Word] united to himself hypostatically the human and underwent a birth according to the flesh from [the Virgin's] womb. This was ... in order that he might bless the beginning of our existence, in order that seeing that it was a woman that had given birth to him, united to the flesh, the curse against the whole race should thereafter cease, which was consigning all our earthly bodies to death, and in order that the removal

through him of the curse, 'In sorrow thou shalt bring forth children' [Genesis 3:16], should demonstrate the truth of the words of the prophet: ... 'God has wiped every tear away from all faces' [Isaiah 25:8]. It is for this cause that we say that in his economy [of salvation, i.e., the Incarnation] he blessed marriage ...[3]

St Anselm (1033–1109) also teaches a high doctrine of the Incarnation, and for this reason attributes the greatest importance to Mary's part in the work of salvation. In a prayer addressed to her, he writes:

> O woman, uniquely to be wondered at,
> and to be wondered at for your uniqueness,
> by you the elements are renewed, hell is redeemed,
> demons are trampled down and men are saved,
> even the fallen angels are restored to their place.
> O woman full and overflowing with grace,
> plenty flows from you to make all creatures green again.[4]

It is because of Mary's contribution to the Word becoming flesh that these things can be said of her.

If we return, then, to the thirteenth-century Virgin of Great Canfield, we can see how admirably the image articulates Christian faith in the Incarnation. For the figure of the relatively mature Christ, his head surrounded by the cruciform nimbus and his hand raised, is an image which indicates that he is ruler of the universe, through whom God the Father created all things. And in one sense, this is why he is not depicted as a baby. Yet he is nevertheless only a boy in his mother's lap, being offered her breast, thus indicating that the all-sufficient Creator of the cosmos took on the dependent form of a creature who required bodily nourishment to sustain him: he became a helpless infant who needed a mother's milk for his survival. He also has bare feet, which signify his humanity. Early Christian authors, such as Eusebius and Maximus the Confessor, state that scriptural references to Christ's head refer to his divinity, whilst references to his feet are speaking of his humanity;[5] and consequently, medieval representations of the Virgin and Child nearly always show the infant with his feet exposed. The painting thus conveys in a single image the notion that Christ is Creator and creature, omnipotent and dependent – in short, that he is both God and man.

However, the painting says more than this. After all, the idea of the Incarnation as such could have been conveyed quite well if Mary had been portrayed as a peasant woman; but instead, she is depicted as a queen. So what does it mean that she is crowned and seated on a throne? To understand this, it is necessary in the first place to grasp more fully the Catholic understanding of Mary's unique and decisive contributions to the Incarnation.

In the first place, Mary is physically the mother of God incarnate. It was her flesh which became the body of Jesus Christ: which is to say that her flesh was united to the Word of God in the Incarnation within her own body, and that the body which was formed from her was the same body which suffered, died and rose from the dead for the salvation of the world.

The art historian Yrjö Hirn has drawn attention to another aspect of Mary's physical motherhood which has been important within Catholicism since the early centuries of the Church, namely, her condition of being the sacred vessel which, like the Ark of the Covenant, was incomprehensibly the bearer of the true God.[6] In contemporary Europe it is common to regard a vessel as something which is purely functional. For example, people buy milk in cartons, and when the milk is finished, the carton is thrown away as rubbish. Yet until recently in Britain, milk always came in glass bottles which were returned to the dairy to be used again, an action which already suggests a more respectful attitude towards milk-bearing vessels than is expressed by throwing cartons into the bin. And there will be people reading this book who remember a time when they took their own china or earthenware jug to the milk cart, to have it filled from a churn. That jug may have been cared for through many generations, and may have been of great sentimental value – a simple container which was a small treasure. Beyond this secular example, the awareness that vessels have the capacity to be infused with holiness has permeated Catholic consciousness for many centuries, and was certainly a dominant motif of liturgical piety at the time when the Canfield Virgin was painted, remaining so throughout the Middle Ages and Renaissance. Reliquaries containing the remains of saints, and altars, which themselves are vessels containing relics, are among the most obvious examples of sacred containers; but eucharistic chalices and patens, which must be lined with the most precious materials and purified with cloths set aside for that purpose, have perhaps been the most common. The font, likewise, is the precious bearer of the waters of rebirth for all who are baptized into Christ. All these things are holy objects in themselves, because of the precious contents which they may bear. Mary's body, therefore, which carried God incarnate, and part of whose very substance became God's flesh, is necessarily the most sacred of all vessels.

In the case of the Canfield Virgin, the importance of Mary's physical motherhood is underlined by the fact that the painting is placed above the altar, so that she is seen immediately above the eucharistic elements during the celebration of Mass. This is probably a deliberate device which is intended to remind the worshipper that the bread and wine on the altar are truly the body and blood of Christ. During the eleventh century, the Western Church had settled on a realist interpretation of the consecrated elements of the Eucharist: that is to say, the bread and wine over which the priest proclaimed the words, 'This is my body', and 'This is my blood', were truly the body and blood of God incarnate. The bread and wine did not have a purely mystical relationship to the body and blood of Jesus of Nazareth, but were turned into those very things.[7] During the late twelfth century, it also became common for the priest to elevate the chalice (containing the wine) and the paten (containing the bread) after he had spoken the words of consecration.[8] Now, the image of the Virgin and Child is an image of the original incarnation of Christ, and the placing of such an image above the altar therefore provided a strong visual reminder that the bread and wine of the Mass became the body and blood of that same Christ who took his human flesh from his mother Mary – that the eucharistic elements participate in the original incarnation.

During the twelfth and thirteenth centuries Christians universally believed that, in addition to these physical aspects of Mary's motherhood, there was also a strong moral element to her participation in the Incarnation: that she became Jesus's mother through an act of her own free will, so that God did not force her to be the mother of Christ, but sought her consent. Mary is not merely the instrument of God's will in the world, nor simply the vessel through whom he realized the beginning of the world's salvation, but is also a participant who actively agreed to co-operate with God's plan. Now this view of Mary's part in the drama of salvation is one which dates back to the early centuries of the Christian Church. Irenaeus, in the second century, took up St Paul's motif of Christ as the second Adam, and extended it to render Mary the second Eve. He contrasted Eve's disobedience to God with Mary's free obedience, the former having brought death to the world, whilst the latter restored life.[9] This view of Mary is the one which held sway throughout Christendom until the time of the Protestant Reformation. It is based upon the story of Jesus' conception as it is recounted in the first chapter of Luke's Gospel (1:26–38), in which the angel Gabriel appears to Mary and tells her that she is to conceive the Son of God, and Mary responds with the words: 'Behold the handmaid of the Lord; be it unto me according to thy word.' Thus, the Incarnation is a consequence of Mary's deliberate action. This is seen most vividly in one of St Bernard's homilies on the Annunciation. The Marian devotion of St Bernard of Clairvaux (1090–1153) had great influence on subsequent Catholic devotion to Mary, and in the fourth of his homilies 'In Praise of the Virgin Mother', he lays the greatest possible emphasis on the contingency of Mary's response to the angel, and consequently, on the dependence of the world's salvation upon the Virgin's word. Addressing Mary, Bernard says:

> Since you have heard joyous and glad tidings, let us hear the joyous reply we long for ... The angel is waiting for your reply. It is time for him to return to the one who sent him ... The price of our salvation is being offered you. If you consent, we shall immediately be set free ... Doleful Adam and his unhappy offspring, exiled from Paradise, implore you, kind Virgin, to give this answer ... For it the whole world is waiting, bowed down at your feet.[10]

Mary is therefore a moral as well as a physical agent in the Incarnation, and so is doubly active in the process of humanity's redemption from sin and death. It is for this reason that she is honoured above all other saints. In part, Mary's regal status can therefore be read as a sign of her supereminent position among the saints of the Church – a position of such central importance that she can be portrayed as holding the office of highest authority after that of Christ.

In addition to indicating Mary's personal merits and the dignity of the divine motherhood, however, the portrayal of her as Queen of Heaven also reflects something of the Christian Church's under-standing of its own nature and mission in the world. As far back as St Ambrose (339–397), Mary is explicitly said to be the *type* or *figure* of the Church, which in effect means that she is the Church's pattern or model, both actual and ideal.[11] Mary's willing co-operation with God's plan of salvation is the model for the Church's own relationship to her Maker. The Church, like the Virgin, is bride of Christ;[12] each is mother of Christians and bearer of Christ to the world.[13] Indeed, sometimes it seems that the Christian imagination has in some sense rendered the

Virgin and the Church almost identical with one another, and in painting, this identity seems to date back to the second century, to the art of the catacombs.[14] The authority attributed to Mary is in part an expression of the power wielded by the institutional Church.[15]

In high medieval England, the power of the Church was felt in many areas of social and economic life and, by the time of the Canfield Virgin, the cult of Mary's queenship was firmly established and flourishing in Western Christendom. The many visual representations of Mary as queen bear witness to this. At the beginning of the thirteenth century, references to Mary's queenship include Pope Innocent III calling her 'Empress of Angels' and 'Queen of Heaven',[16] whilst in the same period, the anthem *Salve Regina* was becoming increasingly popular throughout the Latin Church.[17]

Nevertheless, the Canfield Virgin should not be seen as expressing naked power and triumphalism. The image is too complex to convey such a brash message. In particular, the gesture of the Virgin's offering her breast to the Child serves to qualify the connotations of institutional power that are suggested by the crown and the throne. It reminds the worshipper that the Church not only exercises legal and juridical power, but that both she and the Blessed Virgin offer nourishment and solace to the faithful. St Hildegard of Bingen (1098–1179) wrote of the Church's teaching as milk which suckled even the woods and the hills; and she chastised negligent clergy as those 'who have breasts and will not suckle God's children'. She also refers to mercy, truth and holiness as foods which nourish the faithful when they suck the breasts of God.[18] Alan of Lille (d. 1203), in his commentary on the Song of Songs, states that the Song refers to the Church in her relationship with Christ, which had been the dominant theme of earlier commentators. But Alan considers that the Song's female figure also signifies the Virgin; and unlike earlier authors, for whom this had been a more minor motif, it is the Marian meaning which he makes the principal theme of his own commentary.[19] Of Mary, he writes:

> For just as the Virgin was mother of Christ by conception, so she is mother of the faithful by doctrine and by the instruction of her example. However, there were in the Virgin two patterns of goodly living – chastity and humility – which she proposed to us by way of example. By means of them, as by means of breasts, she suckles the faithful people as a mother suckles her son.[20]

St Bernard of Clairvaux likewise used nursing as a metaphor for instruction, seeing the role of an abbot towards his community as that of a mother towards her children in this regard. However, in addition to offering the milk of instruction, the abbot had also to offer maternal care and affection to the men under his authority, and according to the evidence presented by Caroline Walker Bynum, in the writings of twelfth-century Cistercians it is this affective element which the image of the nursing mother most commonly signifies.[21] It is not unreasonable, therefore, to see implications of tenderness as well as nourishment in the nursing Virgin at Great Canfield.

In addition to this, we must not overlook the simple ordinariness of a mother offering her breast to her child. Indeed, there is a paradox in the image of a queen who nurses her own infant. From the eleventh century onwards, it is likely that increasing numbers of wealthy and noble families employed wet-nurses in preference to maternal suckling, so that by the thirteenth century it was mainly women of the lower and middle classes who would have nursed their own infants.[22] This being the case, the Canfield Virgin is engaged in an activity which is socially humble, in spite of the fact that she bears the trappings of political power. She thus conveys messages which might appear to be contradictory.

The perception that it is inappropriate for a queen to nurse her own child is alluded to in Wolfram von Eschenbach's *Parzival* (c.1200–10), a work which may be more or less contemporary with the painting of the Canfield Virgin. Parzival's mother, Queen Herzeloyde, is in late pregnancy when she hears of the death of her husband, Gahmuret. In her distress, she prays for the birth of her baby and presses milk from her breasts.[23] Then, after the baby Parzival is born, Herzeloyde nurses him herself. Eschenbach makes it clear that this behaviour is unusual for such an aristocratic lady, yet he expresses approval for her actions:

> She had carried him in her womb and was now herself his nurse. This lady who shunned the failings of her sex reared her child at the breast. It was as though her prayers had restored Gahmuret to her arms again. Yet she did not give way to frivolity: humility stood by her. 'The Queen of Heaven gave her breasts to Jesus,' she said ... [24]

Herzeloyde is presented as more truly 'noble' than other ladies of noble birth who do not nurse their own infants. That is to say, Herzeloyde is noble in a moral and not just a social sense, since the actions of the noblest queen of all bestow the mark of ultimate authority upon a practice which was often repudiated by earthly ladies.

34

The fact that maternal suckling was uncommon amongst the upper ranks of the nobility means that the image of an enthroned queen nursing her child is incongruous. But paradox is at the heart of the medieval appreciation of the Christian gospel, and it is by means of a visual paradox that the Canfield Virgin reminds her devotees of a central Christian virtue: that of humility. For Mary's elevation to the most exalted position in heaven is the just, if ironic, consequence of her perfect humility whilst on earth. Her perfect co-operation with the will of God, in agreeing to be the mother of Christ, is the principal manifestation of this humbleness of heart, and it is also the virtue which is extolled in the *Magnificat*, Mary's song of rejoicing over her miraculous pregnancy. In this canticle, she proclaims that the Lord has 'put down the mighty from their seats and exalted the humble and meek' (Luke 1:52). Indeed, God's preference for the humble and meek is a popular theme in the teachings both of the Old Testament Prophets and of the Gospels (see, for example, Amos 6:4–7; 8:4–8; Luke 6:20–6; Matthew 20:1–16), and it also pervades much medieval spirituality, amongst which is included devotion to the Virgin. In this understanding of divine action, it is precisely the poor and the weak whom God uses to manifest his glory; hence, poverty and humility incur divine favour, whilst wealth can bring spiritual benefit only when it is charitably dispensed to the needy. And pride, of course, is a deadly sin.

Now, this view of weakness and humility had a particular consequence with regard to gender. Medieval theologians in general regarded women as being in most respects weaker than men and inferior to them. For example, Prudence Allen's summary of the theory of sex identity held by St Albert the Great (1193–1280) indicates that Albert believed women to be generally weaker in the cardinal virtues, more inclined towards evil, and more suited to obedience than men were.[25] Similarly, Ian MacLean's study of the notion of woman in medieval and Renaissance scholarship cites Alexander of Hales and St Bonaventure (1221–73) as proponents of the idea of women's inferiority to men.[26] Yet this belief in the inferiority of the female sex ironically provided a special route by which women could become channels of God's grace and his agents in the world. In the words of MacLean, 'God delights in confounding the mighty by the agency of the weak', as is exemplified by the heroic women of the Bible; and 'scholastic writers dwell on this paradox of strength in weakness.'[27]

The paradox was firmly established in twelfth-century Christianity.

Barbara Newman has argued that it played a part in contemporary perceptions of St Hildegard, and in Hildegard's own understanding of her role in the world. Hildegard was a visionary, poet and preacher whose wisdom was greatly sought after by devout men and women of her own age; and because this divine wisdom had been bestowed upon a woman, rather than a man, it was seen as an example of God's exaltation of the humble. Indeed, it was partly in virtue of her lowly estate as a woman that Hildegard had been elevated by God through his spiritual gifts to her. Some Cistercian monks who corresponded with Hildegard compared her to Mary, who, Newman points out, 'typified for them a central paradox of Christianity: all who humble themselves will be exalted'.[28] Allen's presentation of the thought of Peter Abelard (1079–1142) concerning the relative status of the two sexes likewise suggests that he held women to be weaker than men by nature, but superior to them in their response to God's grace.[29]

The demand for humility – a virtue seen as more natural to women and supremely exemplified in the Virgin Mary – was the ethical counterpart to the doctrine of the Incarnation. St Paul, writing to the church at Philippi, had tried to induce his readers to serve one another, in the words of a canticle:

> Though Jesus Christ was in the form of God, he did not count equality with God a thing to be grasped, but emptied himself, taking the form of a servant, being born in the likeness of men … [H]e humbled himself and became obedient unto death, even death on a cross. Therefore God has highly exalted him and bestowed on him the name which is above every name … (Philippians 2:5–9)

In similar vein, St Bernard exhorts his hearers to humility, with the words: 'Your Creator was obedient to … Mary and Joseph … God stoops down in humility and you exalt yourself? God is obedient to men, and you, anxious to lord it over men, set yourself up as your own authority?'[30] In a movement of mirroring, Christ humbles himself for the sake of humanity, so that men and women who are humble come to be glorified by God. Hence, we may suppose that at Great Canfield, the Queen of Heaven who nurses her Son is reminding the viewer not only of the Incarnation by which God humbled himself to become human, but also of the doctrine's ethical counterpart, by which humans who are humble of heart will attain a place with God in Heaven.

The loss of the nursing Virgin in Christian art

Despite the devotional and doctrinal richness of such images as the Canfield Virgin, the motif of Mary suckling Christ is one which has hardly been depicted at all for the past two hundred years. It attained its greatest popularity during the fourteenth and fifteenth centuries, and continued to be reproduced, although in smaller numbers, until the eighteenth century, when it more or less died out. The extinction of the nursing Madonna in Christian art is in part the product of changes in the cultural significance of the female body; for the circumstances under which it is now acceptable to portray the naked female breast are defined according to criteria very different from those which obtained during the Middle Ages. The fact that the Virgin could be portrayed with a naked breast is evidence in itself that it was possible for a woman's breast – at least in the context of nursing a child – to be incorporated into an image which was essentially sacred. This possibility arose from the fact that a mother's breast carried a variety of connotations which were appropriate to the Christian sensibilities of the Middle Ages. The notions of humility and spiritual sustenance in connection with suckling have already been alluded to, but there are other qualities to be found in depictions of the Virgin's breast.

Margaret Miles' study of the image of the nursing Virgin in fourteenth-century Italy lays emphasis upon people's need for actual nourishment: that in periods of poor harvest and famine, a good supply of breast milk was essential to the survival of infants, so that the nursing Virgin reminded her viewers of their own physical dependency and of the spiritual source from which all their needs might ultimately be met.[31]

In England during the same century, representations of the Last Judgement quite commonly include an image of Mary interceding with Christ by baring her breasts to him (Plate 4). There are examples from classical antiquity in which the sight of a woman's naked breasts arouses feelings of compassion in the viewer. In these instances, the breasts are exposed in the interests of securing mercy for the woman herself, who might otherwise be subject to harsh judgement against her. Thus, the Athenian hetaira Phryne was charged with blasphemy; and in court, when it seemed certain that she would be condemned to death, her advocate, Hypereides, tore off her clothes to reveal her breasts. Whereupon the court was moved to compassion for her, and the death sentence was not imposed.[32] In fourteenth-century iconography, Mary's breasts are revealed in order to turn Christ away from a judgement of death upon sinful humanity. A variant of the same theme is found in the widespread representation of Mary interceding for a petitioner by showing one of her breasts to Christ, who in turn shows the wound in his side to God the Father. The breast and the wound are emblems of Christ's humanity and reassurances of his mercy.

Overall, then, the image of a woman offering her breast to her child was one which for several centuries carried a changing, and perhaps accumulating, wealth of social and emotional significance, well suited to incorporation in Christian devotion. In the nineteenth and twentieth centuries, by contrast, the social significance of the female breast is confined to a far smaller number of spheres of human experience, and is almost never represented in works of Christian art. Most notably, the breast's significance is overwhelmingly sexual. According to Marilyn Yalom's history of cultural interpretations of women's breasts, the tendency to see the breast in a predominantly erotic light seems to have begun during the Renaissance period, among the early shoots of modernity, and generally to have intensified thereafter.[33] In the public sphere, the breast's sexual connotation now takes precedence over its function in nursing infants. As Susan Brownmiller points out, there are women who will expose the greater part of their breasts in a low-cut dinner dress, and yet would be disturbed by the sight of a mother breast-feeding her baby.[34] The nursing breast is now generally designated a place within the sphere of the medical and scientific, and at best, is viewed as 'wholesome'.[35] The richness of the medieval vision has well-nigh vanished, as has the possibility of depicting a nursing breast as something sacred. Indeed, I suggest that it is precisely in consequence of the breast's association with the narrowly sexual and the medical that it is no longer possible for it to feature in Christian art; for Christianity has always excluded from the realm of the sacred that which is understood to be predominantly sexual, while scientific medicine is a practice which is not itself sacred, and its imagery would have no meaning in works of a devotional or theological nature. A nursing Virgin in the twentieth century would be either shockingly sexual, or inappropriately medical.

Yet the period which witnessed the demise of the nursing Virgin did not see the complete elimination of the motif of women's bare breasts in Christian art. It was with a new connotation, however, that the exposure of the female breast started to occur in the religious painting of the modern period. Instead of belonging to the sinless Virgin Mother of God, it was depicted on the penitent Mary Magdalene, who from the seventeenth century started to be presented with one or both breasts exposed, or else completely naked. The significance of this type of representation lies in the belief that Mary Magdalene was a penitent whore, and the naked breast is thus associated with lost virginity and sexual immorality.[36] Throughout the Middle Ages, the Magdalene was represented as fully clothed, and her identity was indicated by the alabaster jar containing the ointment with which she anointed the feet of Christ. In the modern period, by contrast, her reputation as a prostitute came to be given precedence over her act of charity, and it was in the exposure of her breasts that this emphasis was often realized. Indeed, Susan Haskins points out that not all modern paintings of Mary Magdalene can properly be classed as 'religious': many were intended for the drawing room, rather than the church, and were not intended to encourage Christian devotion. But this in turn is symptomatic of the exclusion of the female human breast from the field of modern religious sensibility.

Modern images of the Virgin

Modern devotional representations of the Virgin do not generally draw attention to any particular aspect of her body. The statue of Our Lady of Lourdes (Plate 2), which dates from the mid-nineteenth century, is commonly reproduced in photographs and in three-dimensional figures for personal use, and is also copied in the larger statues placed for public devotion in the churches of France, Britain and other countries both in Europe and around the world. The Lourdes image is based upon Bernadette Soubirous's account of the apparition that she saw in the grotto where the statue now stands.[37] Subsequent miraculous visions of the Virgin have also been commemorated by pale images of a mild-featured young woman who is dressed in a long robe and stands in an attitude of prayer. These include, for example, the images of the Virgin as she appeared at Banneux in Belgium, Knock in Ireland, and Pellevoisin in France. This style of representation could scarcely be more dissimilar from the medieval forms that have been referred to so far. For the modern Mary has neither the authority of the medieval Virgins, nor any visible sign of her motherhood.

The greater and lesser shrines of Marian devotion in the Middle Ages contained images of a regal mother, such as those found at Chartres (France), Walsingham (England), and 's-Hertogenbosch (Netherlands). All these shrines were accorded miraculous powers. In the modern era, the two most popular Marian shrines have proved to be those of Our Lady of Lourdes, in southern France, and Our Lady of Guadalupe in Mexico,[38] and these shrines, like the medieval ones, are associated with miraculous events, such as cures for serious ailments. However, the images of the Virgin at these two sites are neither regal nor maternal, since in both instances Mary is represented simply as a young woman standing alone and at prayer. The close association which exists between Mary and the Church suggests that the absence of signs of institutional authority – such as the crown and the throne of the Queen of Heaven – might be partly attributable to the fact that the Church itself does not carry the political and economic power that it did in the Middle Ages. However, I shall argue that the decline in visual indicators of Mary's authority is a factor which is also related to the changing significance of her position as mother of Christ.

It is evidently the case that Mary's physical motherhood does not provide a visual focus for meditation or devotion in the iconography of either Lourdes or Guadalupe. My contention is that Western Christianity has moved away from a culture in which a maternal body, carrying several layers of meaning, could be incorporated into religious devotion, and has moved instead towards a culture in which a woman's breasts have primarily sexual significance, in which physical motherhood is an object principally of medical investigation, and in which, moreover, neither the sexual nor the medical can be represented in religious art. Accordingly, the medieval representations of the Virgin as physical mother and bearer of God have been gradually supplanted in Catholic devotion by images of a prayerful young woman whose body had no ostensible association with maternal functions.

Furthermore, the doctrinal significance of the modern image is expressly different from that of the medieval one. For where the Virgin in Majesty, or the wall-painting at Great Canfield, represents the Incarnation and divine motherhood, images in the tradition of Our Lady of Lourdes are associated with the Immaculate Conception, that is, the teaching that Mary was conceived without original sin. As it stands, this shift betokens a change of emphasis away from Mary's bodily processes and their sacred significance, and towards her purely moral qualities. However, the representation and interpretation of the Immaculate Conception has itself changed over the centuries, and this transformation will be examined in Chapter 4.

Notes

1. The prayer is written in Greek on a fragment of Egyptian papyrus which is now in the possession of the John Rylands Library, Manchester. (C. H. Roberts (ed.), *Catalogue of Greek and Latin Papyri in the John Rylands Library, Manchester* vol. III, *Theological and Literary Texts (Nos. 457–551)* (1938) no. 470. It is a Greek version of the prayer which occurs in Latin as the *Sub tuum praesidium*. The papyrus dates from the fourth or fifth century, and may be reconstructed to yield the following translation: 'Beneath your compassion we take refuge, Mother of God. Do not ignore our supplications in our necessities, but deliver us from danger: alone chaste, alone blessed.'

    See Th. Koehler, 'Maternité spirituelle, maternité mystique' in Hubert du Manoir (ed.), *Maria* tom. VI (1961), pp. 571–2, n. 77; Michael O'Carroll, *Theotokos: A Theological Encyclopedia of the Blessed Virgin Mary* (1982), p. 336.

2. The dispute surrounding Ephesus was in fact more complicated than this, since both parties to the debate held that Christ was truly God and truly human. The difference between Cyril of Alexandria, the principal protagonist in favour of the title *Theotokos*, and Nestorius of Constantinople, the main opponent, was concerned with the nature of the union between Christ's divinity and humanity. See J. N. D. Kelly, *Early Christian Doctrines* (1977), pp. 310–30. The texts which the Church finally accepted are given in *DEC*, pp. 40–62.

3. Cyril of Alexandria: *Third Letter of Cyril to Nestorius*, *DEC*, p. 58.

4. *The Prayers and Meditations of Saint Anselm*, trans. Benedicta Ward (1973), pp. 119–20.

5. E.g. Maximus the Confessor, *Liber Ambiguorum*, PG 91:1379C. Other references are given in Leo Steinberg, *The Sexuality of Christ in Renaissance Art and Modern Oblivion* (1983), pp. 143–4.

6. Yrjö Hirn, *The Sacred Shrine: A Study of the Poetry and Art of the Catholic Church* (1958).

7. Miri Rubin, *Corpus Christi: The Eucharist in Late Medieval Culture* (1991), pp. 14–28

8. Miri Rubin, *Corpus Christi*, pp. 55–7.

9. Irenaeus of Lyons, *Adversus Haereses* III, Ch.22:4 in *PG* 7:958–60. The comparison had already been suggested by Justin Martyr (d. *c*.165).
10. St Bernard, 'Four Homilies in Praise of the Virgin Mother', IV:8 in Bernard of Clairvaux and Amadeus of Lausanne, *Magnificat: Homilies in Praise of the Blessed Virgin Mary*, trans. Marie-Bernard Saïd and Grace Perigo (1979), pp. 53–4.
11. Ambrose of Milan, *De Institutione Virginis* 1:XIV:89, in *PL* 16:326C.
12. Examples given in Marina Warner, *Alone of All Her Sex: The Myth and the Cult of the Virgin Mary* (1978), pp. 121–4. Two modern theologians who have developed the theme of Mary as bride are Matthias Scheeben, *Mariology*, trans. T. L. M. J. Geukers (1946), esp. vol. 1, pp. 154–83; and Otto Semmelroth, *Mary Archetype of the Church*, trans. Maria von Eroes and John Devlin (1964).
13. Mary's spiritual motherhood (i.e., her motherhood of Christians) was becoming a popular doctrine in the high Middle Ages. See O'Carroll, *Theotokos*, pp. 254–5.
14. Maurice Vloberg, 'Les types iconographiques de la Mère de Dieu dans l'art Byzantin' in Du Manoir (ed.), *Maria* tom. II (1952), pp. 486–93.
15. For a detailed discussion of the relationship between the development of Marian iconography and ecclesial politics, see Daniel Russo, 'Les représentations mariales dans l'art d'Occident: essai sur la formation d'une tradition iconographique' in D. Iogna-Prat, E. Palazzo and D. Russo (eds), *Marie: Le Culte de la Vierge dans la Société Médiévale* (1996), pp. 173–291.
16. G.-M. Roschini, 'Royauté de Marie,' in Du Manoir (ed.), *Maria* tom. I (1949), p. 604.
17. Hilda Graef, *Mary: A History of Doctrine and Devotion* vol. 1 (1985), p. 229. One popular tradition has maintained that the *Salve* was sung by the Crusaders on their way to the Holy Land.
18. Barbara Newman, *Sister of Wisdom: St Hildegard's Theology of the Feminine* (1987), pp. 231–5.
19. Alan of Lille, *In Cantica Canticorum*, PL 210:53B.
20. Alan of Lille, *In Cantica Canticorum*, PL 210:54C.
21. Caroline Walker Bynum, 'Jesus as mother and abbot as mother' in *Jesus as Mother: Studies in the Spirituality of the High Middle Ages* (1982), pp. 113–25. Newman's work on Hildegard indicates that she too presented tenderness as an element in maternal nursing, although not to the same extent as the Cistercian men did (see n.18).
22. Valerie Fildes, *Breasts, Bottles and Babies* (1986), pp. 47–8.
23. Wolfram von Eschenbach, *Parzival*, trans. A.T. Hatto (1980), p. 65. After she presses the milk from her breasts, Herzeloyde says, 'Milk, how loyal of you to have come! Were I not baptized already, you would have marked my christening!' According to the narrative, Gahmuret had previously had a

devoted lover who was a Moorish woman. Von Eschenbach describes her as being very virtuous, even though she was not a Christian. She too had borne Gahmuret a son. This context suggests that the significance of Herzeloyde's remark is that for a woman to bear the child of a noble Christian knight may bestow upon her something similar to baptismal grace.

This is particularly interesting in the light of the iconography of the Canfield Virgin, since observers often comment that the Virgin's throne seems to be a font. If this is correct, then its immediate purpose is probably to point to the fact that those who are baptized are incorporated into Christ, or 'christened', so that rebirth from the womb of the font is an incorporation into Christ's birth from Mary. However, the fact that the breast and the font are shown together in an image which is contemporary with *Parzival* leads to the suspicion that there is deliberate association being made between breast milk and the waters of baptism. It may be significant that some early Christian writers refer to the conception of Christ in Mary's womb as being equivalent to her own baptism (see Sebastian Brock, 'Mary in Syriac Tradition' in Alberic Stacpoole (ed.), *Mary's Place in Christian Dialogue* (1982), p. 190). Mary herself is also spoken of as a 'fount' of life or love, as in the thirteenth-century *Stabat Mater*.

24. Von Eschenbach, *Parzival*, p. 66.
25. Prudence Allen, *The Concept of Woman: The Aristotelian Revolution, 750 BC–AD 1250* (1997), p. 363.
26. Ian Maclean, *The Renaissance Notion of Woman: A Study in the Fortunes of Scholasticism and Medical Science in European Intellectual Life* (1983), pp. 10–11.
27. Maclean, *The Renaissance Notion of Woman*, p. 21. The paradox may, of course, serve to perpetuate women's subordination to men.
28. Newman, *Sister of Wisdom*, p. 2.
29. Allen, *The Concept of Woman*, pp. 271–92.
30. St Bernard, 'Four Homilies in Praise of the Virgin Mother', I.8, in Bernard of Clairvaux and Amadeus of Lausanne, *Magnificat*, p. 11.
31. Margaret Miles, 'The Virgin's one bare breast: female nudity and religious meaning in Tuscan early Renaissance culture' in Susan Rubin Suleiman (ed.), *The Female Body in Western Culture* (1986), pp. 193–208.
32. Example from Athenaeus, cited in Marilyn Yalom, *A History of the Breast* (1997), pp. 19–20.
33. Yalom, *A History of the Breast*, pp. 49–90. Klaus Theweleit identifies the eighteenth century as the time when women's bodies came to be presented overwhelmingly as sexual, and he associates this with the consolidation of bourgeois culture and the rendering of women as objects for men's possession (*Male Fantasies* vol. 1, trans. Stephen Conway, *et al.* (1987), pp. 332–50).

34. Susan Brownmiller, *Femininity* (1986), p. 28.
35. Barbara Sichtermann, *Femininity: The Politics of the Personal*, trans. John Whitlam (1986), p. 55.
36. Examples are given in Susan Haskins, *Mary Magdalen* (1993), esp. Chapters VIII and IX, pp. 297–365.
37. René Laurentin, *Bernadette of Lourdes*, trans. John Drury (1979), pp. 116–21.
38. Victor Turner and Edith Turner, *Image and Pilgrimage in Christian Culture: Anthropological Perspectives* (1978), p. 77.

2

୧୬୧୬୧୬୧

The decline of Mary's motherhood
2: Written texts

Visual representations of Mary are by no means the only source of evidence for the development of the cult of the Virgin. Another important medium which can reveal changes in the character of Marian devotion is the written word. In the present chapter, I draw upon written sources to complement the iconography which was described in the previous chapter. These indicate that in the modern period there has been a trend away from the veneration of Mary's divine motherhood, especially in its physical aspects, in favour of a concentration upon her assent to God's will as an example for imitation.[1]

Maternal authority in the Middle Ages

It is sometimes said that the changes which occurred in Marian devotion around the thirteenth century are marked by a tendency to see Mary less as a powerful queen and more as a tender mother.[2] It is undoubtedly the case that in both visual art and written prayer she became in a certain sense less distant and in some respects more intimate with the worshipper during this period, and that this trend continued throughout the Middle Ages. Yet this change should probably not be read as a move from seeing Mary as a queen to seeing her instead as a mother; rather, what might be at issue is a change in the perception of Mary's motherhood itself. That is to say, the representation of and appeal to Mary as a figure characterized chiefly by power and authority is an expression of the way in which Mary's status as Mother of God was understood. The development of a more intimate picture of her signifies not the introduction of a newly maternal element into her cult, but rather, a change in the interpretation of her maternity, and perhaps also of motherhood in general.

In her study of Christian ideas about motherhood in the Middle Ages, Clarissa Atkinson considers that the rise of the urban middle classes during the high Middle Ages brought to Christianity a new appreciation of motherhood, since religious reflection on the subject was no longer confined to monastic institutions in which virginity alone was valued as the most elevated condition for the Christian life.[3] However, Atkinson also notes that the term 'Mother' could be a highly honorific one amongst monks and nuns of the early Middle Ages, particularly when it was used to refer to the 'spiritual motherhood' of women religious superiors. For example, St Bede (673–735) writes of St Etheldreda, the founding abbess of the monastery at Ely, that she became 'the virgin mother of many virgins vowed to God'.[4] Similarly, Bede praises St Hilda, abbess of Whitby, 'whom all her acquaintances called Mother because of her wonderful devotion and grace'.[5] Atkinson oberves: 'The term "Mother" carried overtones of profound respect, almost awe, in the writings of men whose stories celebrated holy virgins who presided over communities of women, and even of men.'[6] Such reverential use of the term 'Mother' seems to reflect a similar sentiment about motherhood to that which finds expression in the Romanesque image of the Virgin in Majesty.

Textual evidence suggests that at the Carolingian court in the ninth century, an empress would be crowned as such only after giving birth to a child, thus making motherhood, and not marriage alone, the condition for the emperor's wife to hold full imperial status. Furthermore, the rites for the crowning of empresses made allusion to the Virgin Mary, who herself was queen and empress in virtue of her motherhood.[7]

St Bernard, in the twelfth century, also held Mary's physical motherhood in high esteem. Bernard's most famous Marian homily is probably that written for the feast of the Nativity of the Virgin, in which he calls her an 'aqueduct'. It is the Lord who is 'the fountain of grace', and Mary the favoured channel by whom the Lord chose to offer that grace to humanity.[8] The primary sense in which Mary acts as a channel is in bearing God incarnate to the world.

Elsewhere, Bernard exhorts his audience to imitate Mary's virtues:

> You are told that she is a virgin. You are told that she is humble. If you are not able to imitate the virginity of this humble maid, then imitate the humility of the virgin maid. Virginity is a praiseworthy virtue, but humility is by far the more necessary.[9]

The motif of instruction, however, is subordinate to the praise of Mary's motherhood:

> A soul in whom humility embellishes virginity and virginity ennobles humility finds no little favor with God. Imagine then how much more worthy of reverence must she have been whose humility was raised by motherhood and whose virginity consecrated by her childbearing.[10]

> But in Mary there is something else still more admirable [than her humility]; her childbearing allied with her virginity. Never since the world began has it been known for any woman to be at once a mother and a virgin. If you just think whose mother she is, surely you must be astounded at such marvellous greatness. Who could ever admire enough? ... should she not be exalted above all the choirs of angels, she who bore the Son of God?[11]

Moreover, although Mary often came to be seen in less majestic and more intimate ways in the later centuries of the Middle Ages, she always remained a figure who wielded great authority. Sometime around the year 1260, the Dominican James of Voragine composed *The Golden Legend*, and for the next three hundred years it was published in numerous editions both in Latin and in vernacular languages. *The Golden Legend* is a book which gives a calendar of saints' days with explanations of the feasts, together with legends concerning the various saints.[12] Amongst these, the feasts of the Virgin receive extensive treatment, consisting of legends pertaining to the feasts themselves, and of accounts of miracles which Mary has worked on behalf of those who appealed to her for assistance in time of trouble. Eamon Duffy observes that in Caxton's English edition of *The Golden Legend*, published towards the end of the fifteenth century, the Latin *mater misericordiae* is rendered not '*mother* of mercy', but '*lady* of mercy'. Duffy considers that Caxton's translation illustrates the extent to which the older conception of Mary as Queen of Mercy continued to underlie the title Mother of Mercy.[13] This suggests that the notion of 'mother' carried sufficient connotations of dignity and authority that the gracious term 'lady' was an appropriate translation of the Latin *mater*, at least when applied to the mother of Christ.

Throughout the later Middle Ages, it was widely believed that Mary held great power to intervene for the alleviation of every kind of human distress; but most importantly, she had the power to save souls from damnation. The miracles of the Virgin which are recounted in *The Golden Legend* and in the many collections of *Miracles of the Virgin*[14] include any number of examples of this. The oldest such legend is probably the story of Theophilus, a layman who works for the Church and makes a contract with the devil in exchange for promotion to a higher office. Theophilus subsequently regrets his action, and fearing that he is now cut off from any means of salvation, he appeals to Mary to rescue him. In response to his prayer, she goes down to hell and wrests back from the devil his half of Theophilus' contract. Theophilus' soul is thus redeemed from damnation.

In the story of Theophilus, Mary seems to act on her own, without reference to Christ. But in other places it is made clear that Christ, who is the Lord of all things, will not refuse Mary any request. Thus, St Bridget of Sweden (1303–73) had a vision in which Christ addressed Mary with the words: 'Ask of me whatever you please, nothing shall be refused, and all sinners who implore mercy through your intercession will sure obtain it, if they have a firm resolution to amend.'[15] Mary goes on to ask for mercy for the souls in purgatory, and Christ lessens their pain.[16] In another vision, Mary intervenes on behalf of a soul who comes before Christ for judgement. She is presented as being sovereign over the powers of hell, and her intercession with Christ obtains the man's salvation and the alleviation of his sufferings in purgatory.[17] Mary then says, 'I ask not that he should at this moment be delivered from any other pains he endures; for I know the laws of Thy justice, and cannot go beyond the limits prescribed by Thy mercy.' The Judge replies that he can refuse his mother nothing.[18]

The basis of Mary's overriding influence with Christ is not always stated, but on at least some occasions it is clear that it is her motherhood which is the source of her power. In the eighth century, St German of Constantinople, whose Marian writings carried authority in both the Eastern and Western Churches, addressed Mary with the words: 'You cannot fail to be heard, since God, as to everything, through everything, and in everything, behaves towards you as his true and unsullied

48

mother.'[19] The commandment to 'honour your father and your mother' was taken to include filial obedience, and since Mary would not have asked for anything that would be against God's will, Christ would have no grounds for refusing her requests.

In modern Britain, people may assume that when a man attains the age of majority, or even before then, he is freed from any childhood obligation to obey his parents. He has become an adult in his own right and can now meet his parents as his equals. However, this attitude towards relations between parents and children is by no means universal, and may even be rather uncommon. In his study of present-day Andalusia, the anthropologist Timothy Mitchell observes that Andalusian peasants typically assume that Christ will grant his mother's wishes, and that this reflects the Andalusian ideal of the relationship between a mother and her adult son.[20] It is assumed that the obligation of filial obedience remains for as long as both parties survive, and that the well-behaved man will obey his mother's requests, regardless of his age. The evidence of medieval Marian devotion indicates that a similar attitude may have prevailed in much of medieval Europe, suggesting that changes in expectations concerning kin relations could account in part for changes in attitudes towards Mary, and in particular, for the challenge to Mary's authority which occurred during the later fifteenth and sixteenth centuries.

Challenges to maternal authority

The authority of Mary's motherhood came to be seriously challenged at the time of the Reformation.

Erasmus of Rotterdam's colloquy *A Pilgrimage for Religion's Sake* was first published in 1526. The greater part of the colloquy takes the form of a letter in which the Virgin Mary herself defends the Church's veneration of her against the more extreme Protestant reforms, but in which she also attacks certain aspects of popular Marian devotion which Luther has succeeded in abolishing. Under the title *Maria a Lapide*, the Virgin states:

> Up to this time I was all but exhausted by the shameful entreaties of mortals. They demanded everything from me alone, as if my Son were always a baby (because he is carved and painted as such at my bosom),

still needing his mother's consent and not daring to deny a person's prayer; fearful, that is, that if he did deny the petitioner something, I for my part would refuse him the breast when he was thirsty.[21]

Just over a century later, the same complaint was levelled against the Jesuits in a tract by an English author, 'C.W.':

> She is always set forth as a woman and a mother, and he as a child and an infant, either in her armes, or in her hand, that so the common people might have occasion to imagine that looke, what power of overruling and commanding the mother hath over her little child, the same hath she over her son Jesus ... the mother is compared to the son, not as being a child or a man, but as the saviour and mediator, and the paps of a woman equalled with the wounds of our Lord, and her milke with his blood ... But for her the holy scriptures speake no more of her, but as of a creature, a woman ... saved by Faith in her Saviour Jesus Christ ... and yet now after 1600 yeares she must still be a commanding mother and must show her authority over him ... she must be saluted as a lady, a Queen, a goddesse and he as a child.[22]

These objections to the veneration of Mary, or to aspects of her cult, are particularly interesting for the light in which they cast her office as mother. They assume that the influence of a mother ought to be confined to the nursery, and simultaneously deny that there is any theological or devotional merit in attributing to Christ the characteristics of a dependent baby. Mary's motherhood is thereby stripped of any authority. In contrast to the sense of intimacy and vulnerability which is conveyed in much Marian devotion of the later Middle Ages, and the numinous authority which is accorded the Mother of God in the earlier period, the objections of the Reformers could hardly be more dramatic. They are couched principally in terms of theological error and orthodoxy; but they occurred at a time during which new economic and social relationships were giving rise to changes in notions concerning the family and gender.

Alice Clark's study *Working Life of Women in the Seventeenth Century* argues persuasively that the economic position of women in most social classes in England weakened during the seventeenth century, through a variety of factors, including land enclosure, the system of poor relief, and more restrictive practices on the part of craft guilds. These developments were accompanied by a decline in the standard of education for many women, and by a decline in both the economic and social status of motherhood. Clark observes:

The ridicule with which Peter Heylin treated the worship of the Virgin Mary in France seems to have been pointed more at the notion of honouring motherhood, rather than at the distinction given to her as a woman, for he wrote, 'if they will worship her as a Nurse with her Child in her arms, or at her breast, let them array her in such apparel as might beseem a Carpenter's Wife, such as she might be supposed to have worn before the world had taken notice that she was the Mother of her Saviour. If they must needs have her in her state of glory as at Amiens; or of honour (being now publikely acknowledged to be the blessedness among Women) as at Paris: let them disburden her of her Child. To clap them both together, is a folly equally worthy of scorn & laughter.[23]

There might seem to be a certain irony here, since the leaders of the Reformation had generally been keen to emphasize the important role of the woman as mother of her family. Indeed, for some of them, this was the only true vocation that a woman could have.[24] However, the position of the Christian mother was subordinate to that of the Christian father, and she was considered to occupy an integral place within an expressly patriarchal household. Motherhood was essential for women, but was not to be elevated too highly.

The bourgeois patriarchal family was both lived and praised by Catholics as well as Protestants.[25] Erasmus' friend Thomas More described such a family in his vision of *Utopia*.[26] It is fair to note that in More's Utopia, women's subordination to their husbands is only partial, and that men are to some degree constrained by the wishes of their wives. But his vision is not one which could generate or sustain a cult of the powerful mother such as had existed in the Marian devotion of the Middle Ages. Yet Catholics continued to venerate Mary. It is probably true to say that there were differences between typical family structures, as well as between the economic circumstances, of those parts of Europe which were most affected by the Reformation and those which remained Catholic, and that both these sets of factors contributed to the continuation of Marian devotion within the Catholic Church.[27] It is also the case that the Catholic Counter-Reformation encouraged certain types of devotion to Mary, such as the rosary, because they could be universally practised and were therefore seen as encouraging unity and cohesion amongst all sections of the Church. But over time, devotion to the Virgin changed its emphasis in that it became less interested in Mary's authority and glory as Mother of God and more concerned with her spiritual role as mother of Christians, and subsequently with her moral example as the recipient of God's Word. This transformation was not immediate, but it has become substantial.

The subordination of Mary's motherhood

When C.W. attacked devotion to Mary on the grounds that it attributed to her an authority over Christ which she no longer possessed, he nonetheless allowed that a mother had power of command over her child during its infancy. It is striking, then, that notions of command or governance can be entirely lacking from more recent accounts of her motherhood.

The Jungian analyst Nor Hall cites the work of C. G. Jung's colleague Toni Wolff, who started to develop a psychology of women based upon her own analytical practice. Wolff formulated an understanding of women's consciousness as constructed upon four dominant archetypal images. The four images are designated 'Mother', 'Hetaira', 'Amazon' and 'Medium', and are configured differently in different individual women.[28] The theologian Jennifer Dines has tried to use Hall's account to understand how these archetypes have appeared in the Christian understanding of Mary. She describes the Mother archetype in the following words:

> This kind of woman can be summed up as 'the nurturer', whether of child or adult. She will be most herself in promoting life: conceiving it, giving birth to it, feeding it, protecting it, being always there for it, completely geared to its needs ... the one who creates stability and gives confidence, both inside and outside the home.[29]

Of Mary as mother, Dines writes, 'Mary is depicted with all the expected warmth, tenderness, care and selfless devotion.'[30] This description fairly sums up Mary's motherhood as it is presented in much contemporary devotional material. But it in no way does justice to the commanding authority which was assumed to be part and parcel of her motherhood for the best part of a thousand years of Christian history.

Dines does refer to Mary's queenship, although within the context of a different archetype, namely, the Amazon, or 'Companion'. This 'type of the feminine' is the one who engages in 'co-creative relationships based on affective equality'. Dines considers that 'queenship suggests

52

the role of consort, of co-ruler, and in fact Mary is often depicted in this way, seated on the same throne as the glorified Christ, in the act of being crowned by him'.[31] Dines ignores the fact that Mary's queenship is a consequence of her divine motherhood, and the power and authority which attend Mary's regal office are subordinated to her companionship with Christ.

In contemporary Marian theology and devotion, Mary's humble assent to God's will predominates over other motifs, including her physical motherhood. The Belgian Dominican Edward Schillebeeckx wrote in the 1950s: 'Mary was all openness. Her very being was a waiting for God.'[32] In the Introduction to the present work, I cited Caryll Houselander's book *The Reed of God* as an example of a piece which is concerned with Mary's 'emptiness' before God. A similar concern with Mary's complete openness to the will of the Lord was expressed in Adrienne von Speyr's work *Magd des Herrn*, which was published in Switzerland in 1948 and apparently remains popular since its publication in the United States in 1985.[33] Von Speyr's Mariology might in certain respects be described as 'high', since she associates Mary with the whole of Christ's saving work and refers to her in terms such as 'mediatrix'. Von Speyr considers that Mary mediates for humanity in her subordinate office as bride of Christ, which identifies her with the Church.[34] But the mystery of the divine motherhood is presented neither as a source of authority nor as a cause for veneration and praise. Even Mary's human motherhood is cut off at a moment when traditional devotion has tended to emphasise it, namely, at the Crucifixion.

Throughout the late Middle Ages, and continuing through the seventeenth century and in some places down to the present day, the relationship between mother and son at the Crucifixion was a focus for intense reflection. Poetic laments of the Virgin at the Cross would often include moving exchanges between mother and son, as in these stanzas from the English folksong 'The Seven Virgins':

> 'O peace, mother, O peace, mother,
> Your weeping doth me grieve;
> O I must suffer this,' he said,
> For Adam and for Eve.'

> 'O how can I my weeping leave
> Or my sorrows undergo,
> Whilst I do see my own Son die,
> When sons I have no mo'?'

'Dear mother, dear mother, you must take John,
All for to be your son,
And he will comfort you sometimes,
Mother, as I have done.'

'O come, thou John Evangelist,
Thou'rt welcome unto me,
But more welcome my own dear son,
That I nursed upon my knee.'

Then he laid his head on his right shoulder,
Seeing death it struck him nigh:
'The Holy Ghost be with your soul, –
I die, mother dear, I die.'[35]

In contrast to this maternal–filial exchange, Von Speyr presents the
relationship between Christ and Mary during the Passion as one in
which this type of intimacy would have come to an end:

> When she had carried the Child in her arms, she could say: 'I am your
> mother, and you are my little child.' The one turning her away now is no
> longer a child, but an independent adult. To him she may no longer say:
> 'I am your mother.'[36]

Like Erasmus and C.W., Von Speyr believes that the proper relationship
of a mother to her grown-up son is that of one 'independent adult' to
another. Yet human adults are not 'independent': on the contrary, they
depend upon other people and upon the natural world – air, earth and
water, for example – for their continuing survival. In much medieval
devotion, the image of Christ with his mother told the viewer of the
Lord's dependent humanity, since it was she who had given him his
mortal flesh. For Von Speyr, that relational image of human weakness is
no longer tenable for the whole span of Christ's earthly life, because it has
been superseded by the modern belief in adult independence.

Moreover, the general tone of *Handmaid of the Lord* is not one of awe.
A key term for Von Speyr is the word 'assent'. This word signifies Mary's
entire attitude to God throughout her life, and has its paradigm in her
response to Gabriel's annunciation and her conception of Christ in her
womb. Mary's assent is undergirded by her 'surrender' of everything to
God, and her 'renunciation' of anything for herself. Both these terms are
employed frequently. Furthermore, Mary's relationship with the Holy
Spirit is cast in such a way that it seems to be one of wife in relation to
husband, and to provide an example for Christian marriage:

when the woman truly surrenders herself to the man she loves, she not only gives herself on one isolated occasion to one isolated man but she affirms his whole circle of life ... In this perfect disposition of marriage Mary's spirit lives, as she surrendered herself physically and spiritually to the Holy Spirit in boundless trust and placed herself at the service of the family from Nazareth within her allotted task ... As she is a glowing example of purity and grace to the virgin, Mary also introduces the future mother to the responsibility-filled surrender to the divine will, which is embodied for the married woman in her spouse.[37]

Humanity's relationship with God is thus confounded with the relationship between one human being and another. Von Speyr's Mariology is a topsy-turvy world in which the unique miracle of Mary's encounter with Gabriel is treated as though it were the ordinary marriage of a man and a woman, whilst the proper attitude of a wife to her husband is declared to be that of creature to Deity.

A striking contrast to Von Speyr's anthropology comes from the fifteenth century, in the writings of the scholar and bishop Nicholas of Cusa (1401–64). Nicholas's theological writing is filled with the sense both of God's immediate presence and of God's utter transcendence: the approach to God is through created things, and it is possible for men and women to come eventually into the fullness of his presence; yet God is always beyond anything that the human mind can conceive of. In the course of the series of meditations entitled *De Visione Dei*, Nicholas writes:

Whoever ... merits to see your face sees all things openly and nothing remains hidden to this person. Whoever has you, O Lord, knows all things and has all things. For no one sees you unless one has you. No one can approach you because you are unapproachable. No one, therefore, will be possessed of you unless you give yourself to this person. How can I have you, O Lord, I who am not worthy to appear in your sight? How will my prayer reach you, who are unapproachable by any means? How will I beseech you, for what would be more absurd than to ask that you give yourself to me, you who are all in all? And how will you give yourself to me if you do not at the same time give me heaven and earth and all that are in them? And, even more, how will you give me yourself if you do not also give me myself?

And when I thus rest in the silence of contemplation, you, Lord, answer me within my heart, saying: 'Be your own and I too will be yours.'

O Lord, the Sweetness of every delight, you have placed within my freedom that I be my own if I am willing.[38]

Nicholas goes on to explain in Augustinian fashion that this self-possession comes about when sense is governed by reason, and reason is guided by the divine Word.

Nicholas's understanding of the soul's relationship with God is characterized not in terms of 'surrender' and 'renunciation', but of God's self-giving and the soul's self-possession. This description of such a relationship might stand well as an account of Mary's experience at the Annunciation. Certainly, according to orthodox Christian teaching, at the conception of Christ God gives himself to Mary in a manner which exceeds anything that has been known by anyone else. And when Nicholas writes explicitly about Mary, it is to ponder upon and praise her divine maternity:

> No one ... should doubt that this mother, who was so full of virtue and provided the material [for Christ's body], surpassed all virgins in the complete perfection of virtue and received a more excellent blessing than all other fertile women ... Had she not been most holy and blessed most highly by the Lord, how would she have been made the sacristy of the Holy Spirit, in which the Spirit would form a body for the Son of God?[39]

Because Nicholas does not confuse the Creator with creatures, he does not reduce the Holy Spirit to the confines of created masculinity, and consequently he cannot fail to stand in awe of the miracle of the Incarnation whereby the uncreated Word is bound to flesh in the Virgin's womb. Yet at the same time, the mark of divinity is imprinted upon every detail of the creation,[40] so that the acquisition of union with God is spoken of not as a process of self-negation, but as one of God-given self-possession.

The increased separation of Christ from Mary

When Christians speak of God incarnate, it is common for them to speak also of Mary, because it was she who gave the eternal Word his human flesh. Conversely, the devotion which venerates Mary most highly tends to be that which is centred upon her office as Mother of God, since this is the most honorific and remarkable of her privileges, and lies at the foundation of all the others. In both these cases, Christ and Mary are kept together – understood in relation to one another. Modern Catholicism, however, has been marked by an increasing tendency for Christ and the

Virgin to be represented separately. This trend can be seen by comparing the Marian writing of the Counter-Reformation period with that of the decades since the Second Vatican Council.[41]

During the period immediately following the Council of Trent (1545–63), Catholic theologians had the twofold task of opposing Protestantism and reforming Catholicism. They needed to eliminate those aspects of Catholic practice which they saw as untrue or unhelpful to the Church's central tradition, and at the same time to articulate and assert that tradition in opposition to those who wished to abolish Catholic practice *in toto*. The work of repudiating error on two fronts, combined with the renewal and honing of fundamental principles of Catholicism, gave rise to a brief period of very fine theological writing – writing that was both clear and profound. The Mariology and Marian devotion of the late sixteenth and early seventeenth centuries often exemplify these qualities.

In 1573, the Jesuit Gaspar Loarte published a book of meditations on the rosary. Rosary beads had been used in different forms for many centuries, but by this time they were most commonly used in their modern form, consisting of fifteen mysteries from the lives of Mary and Jesus, with the '*Hail Mary*' as the prayer most requently recited as the background to the meditations.[42] In the Preface to his rosary book, Loarte explains to the reader that his original intention had been to write a work on the life of Christ; but when he realized that meditations on the complete mysteries of Christ's life would be too long, he decided instead to write only upon the mysteries of the rosary, since the chief points of the life of Christ are contained in them.[43] Loarte thus chose a Marian devotional practice as the vehicle for meditations upon the Lord. Furthermore, Loarte's concluding prayers for each of the meditations are addressed to the Virgin, even when she does not take any physical part in the particular mystery concerned. This suggests that for Loarte, meditation upon the Mother of God is something which is undivided from meditation upon God incarnate – that Christocentric and Mariocentric devotion go hand in hand. Nevertheless, the present-day Jesuit historian John O'Malley, in his study of the first Jesuits, seems anxious to play down the extent of early Jesuit devotion to the Virgin, and he comments: 'Loarte's meditations on the rosary ... dealt more explicitly with the life of Christ than with Mary.'[44] This observation presupposes an opposition between the figures of Christ and Mary which is quite alien to the character of Loarte's own work.

Yet the notion of some theological or devotional opposition between Christ and Mary would not have been unknown to Loarte, for Protestants had long been complaining that Catholics elevated Mary too highly in relation to Jesus. In 1577, the vast *Opus Marianum* of Peter Canisius was published. This work was written in defence of Catholic teaching on the Virgin Mary, as a response to Lutheran propaganda.[45] It is frequently concerned to demonstrate that Catholic teaching about Mary means not that she eclipses Christ but, on the contrary, that her graces and privileges reveal the extent of his goodness, since it is from him that these gifts are bestowed upon her.[46] Thus, the praises which are heaped upon Mary are in no way a diminishment of her son.

An assumption that the praise of Mary and that of Christ are in some kind of competition with one another may underlie a certain Protestant emphasis on Mary's lowliness. Martin Luther wrote in his commentary on the Magnificat:

> The masters who so depict and portray the blessed Virgin that there is found in her naught to be despised, but only great and lofty things – what is it they do but contrast us with her instead of her with God? Whereby they make us timid and afraid, and hide the Virgin's comfortable picture, as the images are covered over in Lent.[47]

Mary, Luther says, should be an example of the grace of God, encouraging us to believe that he will regard us also as he once regarded her. The phrase 'they . . . contrast us with her instead of her with God' reveals the relationship which Luther assumes to exist between God and humanity: it is one of distance and separation. There is a gulf between God and ourselves which was once crossed in the life, death and Resurrection of Jesus Christ, but which otherwise remains present. Mary must therefore be either on God's side or on ours, so those who greatly elevate Mary necessarily make her too distant from us. Yet in much Catholic devotion of the later Middle Ages and Renaissance, Mary is precisely the figure who assures the Christian that in Christ, the gulf between God and humanity has been permanently overcome – that the way is always open. To illustrate this, they use the medieval image of Mary as the bridge between God and humanity, or as the neck between the head, which is Christ, and his body, which is the Church. Canisius calls Mary our Mediatrix because she constitutes the connection between Christ and ourselves. The bond between God and humanity is established in Christ: but in this union of divinity and creation, it is Mary who gives Christ his flesh and thus ties us to God in her son. For centuries, the marvel of the Incarnation had meant that when people looked at Mary they saw God's glory active and manifest within the created order. For Luther, when we look at Mary we see principally a moral example of someone who 'leaves herself out and ascribes everything to God alone'.[48]

An implicit sense of competition between the veneration of Mary and that of God or Christ is perhaps found even more surely in present-day Catholicism than it was in early Protestantism. For example, Hilda Graef's important work *Mary: A History of Doctrine and Devotion* has at its beginning, as its keynote, a quotation from Pope John XXIII: 'The Madonna is not pleased when she is placed above her Son.'[49] Graef's concern is always to make clear that Mary's place is lower than Christ's; but we need to ask whether the relationship between Christ and the Virgin should be expressed in terms of rank at all. For according to Christian doctrine, the Word of God is uncreated and cannot be grasped by any human notions of time or space, whereas the Virgin is a creature who participates in the limited condition which is proper to the created order. This is the difference between Christ and the Virgin, but it is a distinction in the order of being, or ontology, and not strictly one of rank. What deeper anxiety are modern authors expressing in their concern that Mary might be placed 'above' Christ?

The English Catholic Michael Evans, in a document on Mary which was commissioned by the British Methodist/Roman Catholic Committee, writes: 'Mary is nothing apart from the grace of God.' Here again, the observation is odd, because from the standpoint of Christian orthodoxy, it is true not only of Mary, but of everyone and everything that exists. Apart from the grace of God, everything would be nothing. So why bother to specify this of Mary? Well, here as elsewhere, there is an implicit suggestion that attributing glory to Mary in some way detracts from that which is due to God, for Evans continues, 'Everything in her says to God, "Not to us, Lord, not to us, but to your name give glory"'.[50] This deployment of a scriptural quotation subtly creates the impression that the glorification of the Mother of God is not itself an act of praise in honour of the Blessed Trinity, but might in some way be a distraction from the proper object of Christian devotion. So rather as John O'Malley assumes that a devotional focus upon Mary is in opposition to such a focus upon Christ, Michael Evans seems to suspect that the act of praising Mary is in competition with praising God.

Where Catholic writers once assumed that the Mother of God was bound by both nature and grace to God incarnate, so that the praise of Mary was the praise of her Creator, it is now assumed that mother and son are separate to such an extent that the veneration of Mary might prove a threat to the proper worship of Christ.[51]

Conception and childbirth: attitudes to bodily processes

The current tendency to keep Christ and his mother well away from one another is in part a consequence of an underlying change which has occurred in Mariology between the Counter-Reformation and more recent theology, namely, a change in attitude towards the physical conception of Christ and the flesh of God incarnate.

Every published history of Marian doctrine and devotion claims that the founder of modern, systematic Mariology was the Spanish Jesuit Francisco Suárez (1548–1617).[52] If we turn, then, to look at the work of Mariology's founding father, and see what he considers to be important about the Virgin, we find that she is placed next to Christ because she is a pivotal figure in the whole economy of salvation. Since God chose the Incarnation as the means for salvation, the woman who gave Christ his humanity is of key importance for our redemption. Suárez's Mariology derives entirely from the doctrine of the divine motherhood, that is, the fact that Mary is Mother of God. Modern authors are sometimes careful to point out that the term 'Mother of God' signifies more than physical conception and childbearing. They consider that the condition of motherhood entails caring and educative functions, and that in Mary's case it might also be taken to include her assent to Gabriel's message. In Suárez's writing, however, although he frequently uses the term *Mater Dei* (Mother of God), the sense in which he uses it means that it cannot always be distinguished from the terms *Dei Genitrix* and *Deipara* (Conceiver and Bearer of God). That is to say, Suárez attaches great importance to Mary's physical conception of Christ, and to the fact that Christ's flesh was the flesh of the Virgin. He quotes words of Gregory of Nazianzus: 'If anyone does not believe St Mary to be the Godbearer, that person is without divine understanding.' For this reason, says Suárez, the Fathers call the Virgin 'throne, bridal chamber, tabernacle and temple of God'.[53] He goes on to lay great emphasis upon the dignity which accrues to Mary because her flesh was shared with Christ, and because her blood and milk nourished him and thus were united to the Word of God. He concludes by saying that the Virgin retains a supreme and excellent degree of dignity, because of her singular union with and closeness to God.[54] Elsewhere, he enumerates three ways in which the Blessed Virgin has assisted in our salvation, of which the third is 'by conceiving Christ, the author of our salvation'.[55]

Suárez raises a doubt – a *dubium* – about the merit of Mary's physical conception of Christ. He says: surely what counts is Mary's voluntary action of accepting the word of the Lord and keeping it, rather than her physical maternity? To the woman in the crowd who cried out, 'Blessed is the womb that bore you and the breasts that gave you suck,' Christ replied, 'Blessed rather are those who hear the word of God and keep it.' And in this respect, Mary is surely no different from any other saint? All the saints have done God's will in their own lives, and Mary's virtue likewise resides in her acceptance of God's word. In reply to this, Suárez insists that the divine motherhood is of a different order; for while all the saints are adopted children of God, Mary alone is his mother, and divine motherhood is a condition which is outstandingly different from adoptive filiation. He allows that the saints also conceive Christ in a spiritual manner by hearing the word of God and keeping it,[56] but Mary has a unique part to play in the work of objective salvation. Her divine maternity is an unparalleled honour.

Yet even during Suárez's own lifetime, a quite different understanding of the human condition, and consequently of the Incarnation, had taken root in European thought – an understanding in which flesh was accorded a lower status. In 1618, the Spanish theologian Hernando Chirino de Salazar – an influential Mariologist who also became an important figure at the court of King Philip IV[57] – published a work which included a discussion of Mary's co-operation in the work of redemption. We have already seen that Suárez had argued that conceiving Christ was one of the ways in which she contributed to our salvation. But Salazar rejected this, stating that this act of engendering was of itself 'a work of nature, and consequently neither free nor meritorious'.[58] Now this opinion was not new. The notion that a physical condition could not be regarded as being of intrinsic moral worth is found in medieval philosophy; but a physical action could gain moral significance from the intention underlying it, or from its consequences, and was taken to be united with that intention or those consequences.[59] However, in modern times, the opinion that

Mary's physical conception of Christ was, in the words of Salazar, 'a work of nature, and consequently ... [not] meritorious' has become well-nigh universal and is accompanied by a loss of any sense that Mary's conception of Christ and her pregnancy are events of grandeur and wonder. The importance of the Annunciation is now considered to reside largely in Mary's acceptance of God's will, as is exemplified in Adrienne von Speyr's emphasis on her assent.

It is true that Catholic theologians of the present century generally agree that Mary's free consent to become Christ's mother and the physical motherhood itself must be understood as a single event. It is the consent which makes the conception come about, but without the conception the consent would be of no salvific value (except perhaps for Mary herself). Thus, Edward Schillebeeckx writes:

> Mary had this particular Child [the Redeemer], and the bearing of this Child, coupled with her free acceptance ... was for her both the objective gift of redemption and the appropriation of this gift, for she 'conceived in faith' ... This event was in history the real gift of the Redeemer and Mary's free acceptance of this Redeemer and thus of the Redemption ... Mary's sublime subjective redemption thus coincided with her motherhood of the Messiah and formed one single event. She was active conception in the bodily sense and active receptivity in the spiritual sense.[60]

Likewise, Karl Rahner writes: 'Mary is blessed because she believed; and she is blessed because her sanctified womb bore the Holy One.'[61] But these authors are clear in their conviction that the physical conception of Christ is not in itself a cause for praising Mary. It is subordinated to her *fiat*, her free acceptance of God's will, which is considered to be of the highest moral worth. Thus, Schillebeeckx writes:

> Mary was redeemed by her faith, here externally represented in her bodily reception of the primordial sacrament – the conception of Christ himself. This can be put another way, namely that Mary was redeemed by her faithful reception, embodied in bodily conception or mother-hood.[62]

This seems to be saying that Mary's motherhood is the 'outward and visible sign of an inward and spiritual grace', where every sort of priority is given to the 'inward and spiritual'. Rahner, by contrast, sees the physical motherhood of Christ as partially constitutive of, rather than merely representative of, her redemption,[63] yet he still gives pride of place to her free acceptance of God's will.[64]

Joseph Ratzinger, writing of Mary's identity with the Church, has tried to overcome the dichotomy between the spiritual and biological aspects of Mary's motherhood by speaking of the relationship between Christ and his mother as a 'theological reality'. He says:

> Doubtless, [Mary] is the concretization of the Church by physically becoming the Mother of the Lord through her *Fiat*. But this biological fact is theological reality in that it realizes the most profound spiritual content of the Covenant which God wished to make with Israel. Luke indicates this marvellously by relating 1:45 ('Blessed is she who believed') and 11:27 ('Blessed are those who hear the word of God and keep it').[65]

But does this not amount to the subsuming of Mary's divine motherhood under ecclesiology, as had already occurred in Otto Semmelroth's *Mary Archetype of the Church*? In this case, our attention is turned away from the divine miracle of the flesh-and-blood by focusing not on Mary's assent but on the Church.

The modern aversion from Mary's physical motherhood is expressed not only in the high evaluation of her assent to God's will, but also in a certain embarrassment on the part of some commentators in the face of descriptions of pregnancy and parturition. Giovanni Miegge, an Italian Protestant theologian, wrote in 1950 a perceptive critique of Catholic Marian doctrine. During the course of his study, Miegge cites favourably the christological commentary of Tertullian (*c*.160–*c*.220) on Psalm 22:9, 'Thou hast drawn me from my mother's womb', which is intended to show the real humanity of Jesus:

> What is drawn away if it is not that which is adhering, fixed and immersed in that from which it is drawn from outside? If there was no adhering to the womb how was there a drawing away from it? And if that which was drawn away adhered, how did it adhere if not by means of the umbilical cord? ... And when a distinct thing has been amalgamated to another distinct thing it becomes at that point one flesh only, *ita concarnatur et convisceratur*, with that to which it is so amalgamated, so that when it is drawn away from it, it takes with itself something of the body from which it is drawn.[66]

Despite his support for Tertullian's theology of the Incarnation, Miegge comments that Tertullian 'was glad to show the reality of the forming of the body of Christ in the womb of his mother, with expressions the crudeness of which must appear excessive today'.[67]

Like Miegge, Hilda Graef expresses a certain unease concerning the physical details of Mary's motherhood. Writing of the French theologian Pierre de Bérulle (1575–1629), she observes that on a number of occasions he 'considers the state of Jesus in the womb of Mary', and that 'he frequently recommends [this theme] as a subject for meditation'. Graef herself, however, finds the topic of Jesus in his mother's womb to be 'a somewhat embarrassing preoccupation'.[68]

This coyness with regard to Mary's physical motherhood may already have been emerging in devotional writings of the nineteenth century. Although in 1855 a Dutch *Life of Mary* could still include a chapter of meditation on Mary's 'holy breasts',[69] Anne Catherine Emmerich's visions of the life of the Virgin, published in 1833, had already displayed a surprising degree of reserve on this matter. One of Anne's visions showed her the birth of Jesus in Bethlehem. One of the earliest surviving written sources for the details of this narrative is the apocryphal Gospel of James, or *Protevangelium*, which is thought to date from the second century.[70] According to this account, as soon as the child appeared, 'it came and took the breast of its mother Mary'.[71] When St Bridget of Sweden, in the fourteenth century, had a vision of Christ's birth, she provided a more elaborate rendering of the drama, thus: 'His Mother took him in her hands and pressed him to her breast, and with cheek and breast she warmed him with great joy and tender maternal compassion.'[72] Mary then caught her son's umbilical cord in her fingers, and the cord was cut off.[73] St Bridget herself subsequently appeared to Anne Emmerich;[74] but when Anne gave the account of her own vision of the Christmas story, she was more guarded about the details of intimacy. Anne's account retained the action of Mary taking Christ to her breast, but it then said, more cautiously, '[Mary] sat there enveloping herself and the child completely in her veil, and I think Mary suckled the Redeemer.'[75]

Discussion of Mary's *in partu* virginity has shown a similar movement away from anatomical frankness and towards reticence. *Virginitas in partu* is the term for the doctrine which holds that Mary gave birth to Christ without loss of her physical virginity. This means that Christ's birth did not cause his mother any injury, and it has usually been interpreted to mean that her hymen remained intact during labour. It usually also entails the belief that she gave birth without pain. The earliest authoritative record of such a belief seems to be that contained in the apocryphal Gospel of James. Although it was disputed within the early Church, it was affirmed in the letter of Pope St Leo the Great, known as the Tome of Pope Leo, which was approved at the Council of Chalcedon (451).[76] By the early Middle Ages, the *in partu* virginity was almost universally believed by Christians, and has continued to be the standard teaching of the Catholic and Orthodox Churches down to the present day. Modern authors sometimes object to the doctrine on the grounds that it makes Mary's childbearing less than fully human, or that it seems to be influenced by a philosophical outlook which despises the physical world and cannot accept normal bodily processes as a part of God's good creation. The question of the relationship between Mary's childbearing and that of other women will be addressed in Chapter 6. For the present, a comparison between Suárez's literal understanding of the doctrine of Mary's virginal childbearing and Rahner's revised interpretation of the doctrine will suggest that contemporary theologians have at least as much difficulty in addressing the facts of parturition as their forebears did.

As one would expect, Suárez's Mariology accepts the doctrine of the *in partu* virginity.[77] He raises the question of whether Mary would have suffered labour pains, and then asks whether she would have expelled an afterbirth and other matter following the birth of Christ. In reply to the first question, Suárez points out that earlier authors agree that Mary would not have suffered labour pains. They give several reasons for this conclusion, of which the most important is that the pain of childbirth is caused by division, violent movement and widening of the body,[78] and since the Virgin's bodily integrity was unaffected by Christ's birth, she would not have suffered pain. With regard to whether or not Mary would have expelled an afterbirth, Suárez cites authors such as the fifteenth-century Dominican Cajetan, who argued that there would have been an afterbirth. Cajetan taught that the infant was contained in a membrane and nourished with blood. When the child was born, the membrane and blood were expelled since they were no longer needed, and it is this membrane with the blood which constitute the afterbirth. Since Christ was gestated in the Virgin's womb in the normal way, an afterbirth would have followed his own birth in the usual manner.[79] Against this view, Suárez cites other authors who consider that the afterbirth is a consequence of insemination by male seed. According to them, since Mary conceived Christ without insemination, there would have been no afterbirth following her parturition.[80] After further discussion of the matter, Suárez takes the view that there would have been no afterbirth. He thus has no anxiety about presenting a detailed consideration of the physiology of childbirth. It is true that he comes down strongly on the side of Mary's being different from other women in this regard, but he can scarcely be accused of a refusal to think frankly about the bodily processes involved.

A sharp contrast to Suárez's approach is provided by Karl Rahner, in two essays which he wrote on the *in partu* virginity.[81] He is not keen to interpret the doctrine as meaning that Mary's hymen was unbroken, partly because this cannot be proven, and partly because it is an idea which seems too mythological for modern believers to accept. Instead, he takes the primary meaning of the doctrine to be that Mary's childbirth was painless, and argues that this might be understood as referring to a spiritual attitude on Mary's part. He writes:

> ... the birth of a human being, at least as first and foremost an act on the mother's part, is an event affecting the *whole* of human nature, and hence ... depends to a large extent upon the particular disposition and attitude of the individual mother concerned. ... [p]ain (regarded as a physiological occurrence) can be experienced in different ways, according to whether the individual subject is in a position positively to integrate this 'pain' into the totality of his active living or not. Pain as lived through is from the outset pain that is interpreted by the free and intelligent subject, and so true is this that under certain circumstances one and the same physiological process ... constitutes a pain (in the popular sense of the term) for one individual and not for another.[82]

In the Blessed Virgin's case, says Rahner, her sinlessness and personal integrity mean that what we call 'pain' would be experienced differently than would be the case for the rest of us. Rahner suggests that this is 'a starting-point for a true interpretation of the phrase "virginitas in partu".' He considers that Catholics are therefore not bound to believe that Mary's virginal hymen remained unbroken.[83]

Whatever one considers to be the merits and defects of Suárez's and Rahner's arguments concerning Mary's parturition, it is evidently the case that Suárez's thoughts tend to be down with the blood and entrails whilst Rahner's prefer to inhabit the realm of mind and spirit. Once again, then, we see that contemporary authors, far more than their predecessors, shy away from the topic of Mary's physical childbearing.

From mother to disciple

The changes in Catholicism that have followed the Second Vatican Council have included a more drastic rejection of the veneration of Mary's physical motherhood. The work of Von Speyr which has been quoted above is typical of the type of devotion which has received official encouragement during the past twenty years. But in addition to this, there has arisen a body of literature which explicitly rejects Mary's motherhood as the foundation of Mariology. Thus, the Spanish theologian Joseph Paredes has written:

> It has been traditionally held that the divine maternity is the *fundamental principle* of Mariology, and that everything that can be theologically predicated of Mary is summed up and derived from that principle. Nevertheless, on the basis of recent exegetical studies on Mary in the New Testament, some theologians have proposed Mary's perfect discipleship as 'a paradigm for mariology' for the present time.[84]

Paredes provides a substantial bibliography in support of this claim;[85] and he continues: 'The paradigm of "Mary, the perfect disciple and follower of Jesus", which we are proposing here, is viewed by us to be the key to a unified understanding of all ecclesial truths concerning Mary.'[86]

At first sight, the claim that Mary is primarily a disciple, rather than a mother, can feel like a breath of fresh air to women who have had foisted upon them the job of being mother in a patriarchal household, and who have been offered the figure of Mary as an example to imitate in the performance of their duties. For the claim that Mary's most fundamental relationship with Christ is one of discipleship suggests that a Christian woman's identity and vocation in life can be founded upon something other than her specifically female biology, and that she need not feel constrained to devote her life exclusively to the welfare of her children and their father. But any such welcoming of this new emphasis in Mariology has itself emerged out of a society in which motherhood is not highly valued, and in which a mother has restricted authority and few spheres of freedom of action. Furthermore, the welcoming of Mary as a disciple rather than a mother seems to be the product of a Christian culture in which the presentation of Mary as a moral exemplar has come to take almost complete precedence over the honouring of the Mother of God who signifies the presence of divinity within the very fibres of the material creation.

Notes

1. There has also been a tendency for greater emphasis to be placed upon Mary's spiritual motherhood, that is, her motherhood of all Christians. This seems to be another example of a shift from the physical to the moral in modern Catholicism.

2. E.g., Clarissa Atkinson, *The Oldest Vocation: Christian Motherhood in the Middle Ages* (1991), p. 115; Penny Schine Gold, *The Lady and the Virgin: Image, Attitude and Experience in Twelfth-Century France* (1985), pp. 66–7.

3. Atkinson, *The Oldest Vocation*, pp. 64–100 and 144–93 *passim*, esp. pp. 144–5.

4. Bede, *A History of the English Church and People*, trans. Leo Sherley-Price (1955) IV:19, p. 239.

5. Bede, *A History of the English Church and People* IV:23, p. 248.

6. Atkinson, *The Oldest Vocation*, p. 95.

7. Dominique Iogna-Prat, 'La Vierge et les *ordines* de couronnement des reines au IXe siècle' in D. Iogna-Prat *et al.* (eds), *Marie: Le Culte de la Vierge dans la Société médiévale*, pp. 100–7.

8. St Bernard, 'Sermon for the Feast of the Nativity of the Blessed Virgin' in *St Bernard's Sermons on the Blessed Virgin Mary*, trans. A Priest of Mount Melleray (1984), pp. 82–3.

9. St Bernard, 'Four Homilies in Praise of the Virgin Mother', I:5 in Bernard of Clairvaux and Amadeus of Lausanne, *Magnificat: Homilies in Praise of the Blessed Virgin Mary*, trans. M.-B. Saïd and Grace Perigo (1979), p. 9.

10. *Ibid.*

11. St Bernard, 'Four Homilies in Praise of the Virgin Mother', I:7 in *Magnificat*, pp. 10–11.

12. Jacobus de Voragine, *The Golden Legend: Readings on the Saints*, trans. William Granger Ryan (1993).

13. Eamon Duffy 'Mater Dolorosa, Mater Misericordiae', *New Blackfriars* vol. 69, no. 816 (May 1988), pp. 210–27. Contrary to my own argument, Duffy seems to assume that there is a certain tension between these two titles.

14. Modern editions include: Johannes Herolt, *Miracles of the Blessed Virgin Mary*, trans. C.C. Swinton Bland (1928); Nigel of Canterbury, *Miracles of the Virgin, in Verse: Miracula Sancte Dei Genitricis Marie, Versificie*, ed. Jan Ziolkowski (1986); Wynkyn de Worde's edition of *The Myracles of Oure Lady*, ed. Peter Whiteford (1990); Jean le Marchant, *Miracles de Notre-Dame de Chartres*, ed. Pierre Kunstmann (1973).

15. *The Revelations of St Bridget, Princess of Sweden* Book I (1873), p. 43.

16. *The Revelations of St Bridget* Book I, p. 43.

17. *The Revelations of St Bridget* Book IV, pp. 148–61.

18. *The Revelations of St Bridget* Book IV, p. 161.
19. St German of Constantinople, *Sermo II in Dormitionem B.V. Mariae*, PG 98:351/352A.
20. Timothy Mitchell, *Passional Culture: Emotion, Religion, and Society in Southern Spain* (1990), p. 115.
21. Erasmus, 'A pilgrimage for religion's sake' (from the *Colloquies*, 1526, trans. Craig R. Thompson) in D. Englander *et al.* (eds), *Culture and Belief in Europe 1450–1600: An Anthology of Sources* (1990), p. 69. *Maria a Lapide* is the Latin name of the Marian shrine known in German as Mariastein, in Switzerland.
22. C.W., *The Bespotted Jesuite* (1641), cited by Alice Clark, *Working Life of Women in the Seventeenth Century* (1919), pp. 238–9.
23. Clark, *Working Life of Women in the Seventeenth Century*, p. 239, quoting Peter Heylin, *The Voyage of France* (1673), p. 29.
24. Atkinson, *The Oldest Vocation*, pp. 194–220.
25. Atkinson, *The Oldest Vocation*, pp. 220–9.
26. Thomas More, *Utopia*, trans. Paul Turner (1965).
27. Timothy Mitchell's *Passional Culture* suggests that there is a connection between kinship structure and the fact and character of Marian devotion. Michael Carroll has provided evidence which indicates that the development of popular Catholicism, including Marian cults, in different parts of Italy has been strongly influenced by a nexus of eonomics, politics and church organization: see *Madonnas that Maim: Popular Catholicism in Italy since the Fifteenth Century* (1992).
28. Nor Hall, *The Moon and the Virgin* (1980), pp. xiv and 32–4.
29. Jennifer Dines, 'Mary and the archetypes', *The Month*, August/September 1987, p. 289.
30. Dines, 'Mary and the archetypes', p. 290.
31. Dines, 'Mary and the archetypes', p. 291.
32. E. Schillebeeckx, *Mary, Mother of the Redemption* (1964), p. 85.
33. Adrienne von Speyr, *Handmaid of the Lord*, trans. E.A. Nelson (1985).
34. Von Speyr, *Handmaid of the Lord*, pp. 103–9. The idea that Mary's mediation is grounded, at least in part, on a spousal relationship with God is found in the Mariology of Jean-Jacques Olier (1608–57), although for Olier, Mary's spouse is God the Father (*Vie Intérieure de la Très-Sainte Vierge* tom. I (1866), pp. 59–60).
35. A number of versions of this song have been collected from around the country. This set of words is included in the *Oxford Book of Carols* (© 1928 Oxford University Press). A similar version was published in a Staffordshire collection of 1837, and included by Sir Arthur Quiller-Couch in the *Oxford Book of English Verse, 1250–1918* (1939), no. 392.
36. Von Speyr, *Handmaid of the Lord*, p. 114.
37. Von Speyr, *Handmaid of the Lord*, p. 174.
38. Nicholas of Cusa, *On the Vision of God* 7: 25, in *Nicholas of Cusa: Selected*

Spiritual Writings, trans. H. Lawrence Bond (1997), pp. 246–7 (translation amended). An older translation, by Emma Gurney Salter, was published in 1960 (reprinted 1978) under the title *The Vision of God*.

39. Nicholas of Cusa, *On Learned Ignorance* III, 5: 212, in *Selected Spiritual Writings*, p. 182. A consideration of this section of Nicholas's writing on Mary's part in the Incarnation will be given in Chapter 6.

40. This is seen most clearly in Nicholas's work *On God as Not Other* (Nicholas of Cusa, *On God as Not-Other: A Translation and an Appraisal of De Li Non Aliud*, ed. and trans. Jasper Hopkins (1979)).

41. Some of the material in this section and the next has previously appeared in a paper presented to the conference of the Catholic Theological Association of Great Britain, 1996: 'Mary at the margins: Christology and ecclesiology in modernity', published in *The Month*, December 1996, pp. 463–75.

42. Eithne Wilkins, *The Rose-Garden Game: The Symbolic Background to the European Prayer-Beads* (1969), pp. 40–1; Anne Winston-Allen, *Stories of the Rose: The Making of the Rosary in the Middle Ages* (1997), pp. 65–80.

43. Gaspar Loarte, *Instructions and Advertisements, how to Meditate upon the Misteries of the Rosarie of the Most Holy Virgin Mary* (1613), pp. 18–19.

44. John W. O'Malley, *The First Jesuits* (1994), p. 270.

45. James Brodrick, *Saint Peter Canisius SJ* (1938), pp. 664–765.

46. This is one of the arguments used in defence of the Immaculate Conception. Peter Canisius, *De Maria Virgine Incomparabili, et De Genitrice Sacrosancta* Lib.1, Cap. VI (1677), p. 39. Reproduced in J.-J. Bourassé (ed.), *Summa Aurea de Laudibus B.V.M.* vol. 8 (1862), cols. 694–5.

47. Martin Luther, 'The Magnificat translated and explained' (trans. A.T.W. Steinhaeuser) in *Works of Martin Luther* (1982 [1930]) vol. III, pp. 156–7.

48. Luther, 'The Magnificat translated and explained', p. 138.

49. Hilda Graef, *Mary: A History of Doctrine and Devotion*, p. v.

50. British Methodist / Roman Catholic Committee, *Mary, Mother of the Lord: Sign of Grace, Faith and Holiness* (1995), p. 6.

51. From the seventeenth until the early twentieth century devotional writers gave considerable space to the union of Christ and Mary at the Cross and at other times in Jesus' life. But this union was a moral, not a substantial, one, and was apparently not so well grounded that it could withstand the tendency to separation.

52. E.g., Heinrich Stirnimann, *Marjam: marienrede an einer Wende* (1989), p. 134; Michael O'Carroll, *Theotokos: A Theological Encyclopedia of the Blessed Virgin Mary* (1982), p. 334; Graef, *Mary: A History of Doctrine and Devotion* vol. 2, p. 21; Warner, *Alone of All Her Sex*, p. 39.

53. Francisco Suárez, *De Mysteriis Vitae Christi: Commentarii et Disputationes in Tertiam Partem D. Thomae*, Disp. I, Sec. I:9 in *Opera Omnia*, ed. Charles Berton (1860), vol. XIX, p. 5.

54. Suárez, *Commentarii*, Disp. I, Sec. II:2, pp. 7–8.

55. Suárez, *Commentarii*, Q. XXXVIII, Art. IV, Disp. XXII, Sec. I:4, p. 331.
56. Suárez, *Commentarii*, Disp. I, Sec. II:3–5, p. 8.
57. René Laurentin, *Marie, l'Eglise et le Sacredoce:1. Essai sur le Développement d'une Idée Religieuse* (1952), pp. 232–3.
58. Laurentin, *Marie, l'Eglise et le Sacerdoce:1*, p. 244. Quotation from *In Proverbiis*, 1618 (ed. Paris, 1619), vol. I, VIII:206–7, p. 621.
59. This subject will be taken up again in the discussion of the history of the doctrine of the Immaculate Conception, Chapter 4.
60. E. Schillebeeckx, *Mary, Mother of the Redemption*, trans. N.D. Smith (1964), pp. 92–3.
61. Karl Rahner, 'The Immaculate Conception' in *Theological Investigations* vol. 1, trans. Cornelius Ernst (1961), p. 203.
62. Schillebeeckx, *Mary, Mother of the Redemption*, p. 94.
63. Karl Rahner, 'Le principe fondamentale de la théologie Mariale', *Recherches de Science Religieuse* 42 (1954), p. 511, n. 61.
64. Rahner, 'The Immaculate Conception' and 'Le principe fondamentale de la théologie Mariale', *passim*.
65. Joseph Cardinal Ratzinger, 'On the position of Mariology and Marian spirituality within the totality of faith and theology', trans. Graham Harrison, in Helmut Moll (ed.), *The Church and Women: A Compendium* (1988), p. 75.
66. Tertullian, *De Carne Christi* cap. 20, quoted in Giovanni Miegge, *The Virgin Mary: The Roman Catholic Marian Doctrine*, trans. Waldo Smith (1955), p. 39.
67. Miegge, *The Virgin Mary*, p. 39.
68. Graef, *Mary: A History of Doctrine and Devotion* vol. 2, p. 33.
69. Cited in Els Maeckelberghe, ' "Mary": maternal friend or virgin mother?' trans. David Smith in A. Carr and E.S. Fiorenza (eds), *Motherhood: Experience, Institution, Theology* (*Concilium* 206:6 [1989]), pp. 123 and 127.
70. *The Protevangelium of James* in J.K. Elliott (ed.), *The Apocryphal New Testament*, (1993), pp. 48–67.
71. *The Protevangelium of James*, p. 64.
72. *Revelations* VII, 21:16 in Birgitta (of Sweden), *Life and Selected Revelations*, trans. Albert Ryle Kezel (1990), p. 203.
73. *Revelations* VII, 21:17, p. 203.
74. *The Life of the Blessed Virgin Mary from the Visions of Anne Catherine Emmerich*, trans. M. Palairet (1970), p. 85.
75. *The Life of the Blessed Virgin Mary from the Visions of Anne Catherine Emmerich*, p. 194.
76. DEC, p. 77.
77. Suárez, *Commentarii*, Q. XXVIII, Art. III, Disp. V, Sec. II, pp. 83–8.
78. Suárez, *Commentarii*, Q. XXXV, Art. VIII, Disp. XIII, Sec. II:2, p. 214.
79. Suárez, *Commentarii*, Q. XXXV, Art. VIII, Disp. XIII, Sec. II:1, p. 214.

80. Suárez, *Commentarii*, Q. XXXV, Art. VIII, Disp. XIII, Sec. II:4, p. 215.
81. Karl Rahner, 'Virginitas in partu' in *Theological Investigations* vol. 4, trans. Kevin Smyth (1966), pp. 134–62; 'Human aspects of the birth of Christ' in *Theological Investigations* vol. 13, trans. David Bourke (1975), pp. 189–94.
82. Rahner, 'Human aspects of the birth of Christ', p. 193.
83. Rahner, 'Human aspects of the birth of Christ', p. 194.
84. Joseph Paredes, *Mary and the Kingdom of God: A Synthesis of Mariology*, trans. Joseph Davies and Josefina Martinez (1991), p. 154.
85. Paredes, *Mary and the Kingdom of God*, p. 169.
86. Paredes, *Mary and the Kingdom of God*, p. 154.

3

∾∾∾∾∾

The cult of the Virgin in the rationalization of Western civilization

The previous chapters have described with broad brush strokes some of the changes which have occurred in the cult of the Virgin Mary between the high Middle Ages and the twentieth century. This chapter will present a wider cultural background to these changes and propose the beginnings of a theory for their interpretation.

Within Christian theology and devotion, Mary represents creation in its right relationship with the Creator. Christian understandings of the relationship between God and creation correspond to aspects of humanity's relationship with the 'natural' world, and this latter relationship has changed dramatically over the past millennium with the invention and deployment of new technology. Humanity has exercised increasing domination over both human and non-human nature, and this domination is tied also to the domination of one human group by another. Christian understandings of the relationship between God and creation have altered accordingly. The fact that Mary stands for creation in relation to God, taken together with the correspondence that exists between the Christian presentation of God's relationship to creation and that of humanity's relationship to 'nature', mean that major changes which have occurred in Marian devotion act as an index of humanity's domination of nature, and of social relations of domination in general. Yet at the same time, the cult of the Virgin is founded upon notions of incarnation and perfect humanity which are constant reference points by which to criticize domination of every kind. The transformations described in the previous chapters are indicators of widening and intensifying domination; but they contain points at which there is a vision of potential liberation.

Mary as representative of creation in relation to God

Although all the major trends of Christianity hold that Jesus was both God and man, and that Mary is therefore properly endowed with the paradoxical title of Mother of God, the interpretation of her role in salvation varies amongst the different Christian denominations. Most notably, Orthodox and Catholic Christianity attribute to Mary an active part in bringing about the redemption of the world, whilst the principle strands of Protestantism regard her as the passive instrument of God's will. A comparison of these two attitudes will suggest that what Christians believe about Mary tends to typify their beliefs about creation's relationship to its Creator.

The differing views of Mary's significance are all interpretations of Luke 1:26–38, the narrative of the annunciation by the angel Gabriel to Mary, in which he tells her that she is to be the mother of the Saviour. As was shown in Chapter 2, the ancient understanding of this dialogue holds that Mary's words are the assent of a free agent: she willingly agreed to accede to the word of God. She is therefore a moral as well as a physical agent in the Incarnation. Thus, Nicolas Cabasilas, the fourteenth-century Orthodox theologian, wrote:

> The incarnation was not only the work of the Father, by His power and by His spirit, but it was also the work of the will and faith of the Virgin. Without the consent of the Immaculate, without the agreement of her faith, the plan was as unrealisable as it would have been without the intervention of the three divine Persons themselves.[1]

This position has been reiterated over and over again in Catholic and Orthodox teaching. The modern theologian Karl Rahner wrote that 'this Motherhood is a free act of the Virgin's faith', as well as being a biological fact.[2] Elsewhere, he writes: 'This divine motherhood occurs, by God's grace, as a freely-willed conception, receiving for the world the grace that the Incarnation brings; it is a true partnership with God's action for mankind.'[3]

The phrase 'for the world' indicates another important aspect of the Catholic interpretation of the story of Gabriel's annunciation to Mary,

74

namely, that she acts here not simply on her own behalf, but both represents and acts in the interests of all humanity. As Rahner says, Mary's consent is not 'merely ... a fragment of the Blessed Virgin's private biography';[4] it is an integral element in the story of God's plan for the world: 'for us and for our salvation she opened the way into our flesh of sin for the Eternal Word'.[5] The Orthodox theologian Vladimir Lossky states: 'In the person of the Virgin, humanity has given its consent to the Word becoming flesh and coming to dwell amongst men.'[6] Mary signifies and embodies humanity co-operating with God and overcoming the sin which causes the fatal separation of humanity from its Creator.

One of the most profound changes in the outlook of the Reformation as compared with the Catholicism which preceded it concerned the understanding of the relationship between Creator and creation. Whilst Catholic devotion had in certain respects emphasized the presence of the divine within the created order – in sacraments, relics, or sacred springs, for example – and had concentrated upon the possibility of creaturely co-operation with the will of God, much Protestant teaching insisted upon the strongest possible interpretation of the radical discontinuity between Creator and creation, and attributed all goodness directly to God without allowing for any human or other created intermediaries. From this, it is clear that the Catholic and Orthodox approach to the interpretation of the annunciation story is firmly rooted in a particular sort of theology of creation and grace, and that its concern with willing co-operation between humanity and God will not be acceptable to all branches of the Christian Church.

Yet the Catholic belief in the active participation of creatures in the work of salvation does not rest upon a claim that creatures are set apart from the need of God's grace, or that a creature is ever an equal participant in its co-operation with God's work. The very possibility of such co-operation is itself an act of God's grace upon which the creature's own contribution is entirely dependent. Hence, Rahner can write of Mary that her obedience 'is itself a pure grace of God'.[7] Lossky writes that in the Incarnation, God acted freely and wished that Mary also should do so;[8] and Catholic authors have contended that it is the grace of God which makes Mary's choice truly free, since it releases her from the sin which normally is able to cloud human judgement.[9] And in this there is nothing which would be considered offensive to some of the main lines of Protestant theology. However, a clear difference between Protestant and Catholic thought emerges in the conclusions which are drawn with regard to the moral status of the creature which has been blessed with God's grace in this way. For in Catholic eyes, a creature which has been honoured highly by God is worthy also of the veneration of humanity. Moreover, if that creature is a human being who has co-operated with the grace of God as an act of free will, then he or she is all the more to be thanked and praised for such an action. In Calvinist and much Lutheran theology, by contrast, attention is directed only to God himself, since he is the author of all grace and goodness: the notion that a creature could be anything more than the passive instrument or vehicle of that grace is viewed as too close to the heresy of Pelagius, whilst the veneration of a creature on the grounds that she is a helper in the work of redemption is too close to idolatry, that is, the adoration of a created being rather than the Creator.

When Protestant commentators of the twentieth century address the question of Catholic Mariology, this fundamental difference between the two traditions is made especially clear. For example, the Waldensian Giovanni Miegge writes: 'The young woman affianced to Joseph, in the account of the annunciation and birth of Jesus, has the subordinate role of the chosen instrument and faithful witness of the great event.'[10] He attacks

> the Catholic theology of the period since the Council of Trent, with its rigid definition of the collaboration of human liberty with divine grace – in antithesis to the '*sola gratia*' of the Reformation – and the human capacity to deserve *de congruo*, and with appropriate acquiescence, the grace that saves.

Miegge seems to question the idea that Mary had even the free will which Christian theology attributes to all human beings, since he continues:

> There is no shadow of evidence that Mary is consulted in the angelic annunciation; or that the divine plan depends for a moment upon her '*fiat* – so be it': or that 'speaking absolutely' – that is abstractly – she could have refused.

Gabriel's message is simply 'the communication of a sovereign decision'.[11]

It is clear from this that a classical Protestant understanding of Mary's interaction with the angel at the Annunciation implicitly reveals the corresponding view of creation's relationship to its Creator, just as the Catholic interpretation of the same story articulates Catholicism's view of the same relationship. Moreover, just as Catholic theologians have viewed Mary as representative of humanity in its relationship to God, so the Protestant theologian Karl Barth likewise views Mary as holding this position in Christian anthropology – except that in Barth's case, it is Mary's receptivity, rather than her co-operation, which is the focus of attention. Barth writes of Mary: 'She is simply man to whom the miracle of revelation happens.' Mary, 'in conceiving the Lord, can only represent man (both Old Testament and New Testament man alike) in his reception of God'. It is true that she is an indispensable figure in the history of salvation, but

> every word that makes her person the object of special attention, which ascribes to her what is a relatively independent part in the drama of salvation, is an attack upon the miracle of revelation, because it is, after all, an attempt to illumine and to substantiate this miracle from the side of man or of his receptivity.[12]

'The "Mother of God" of Roman Catholic Marian dogma is quite simply the principle, type and essence of the human creature co-operating servantlike (*ministerialiter*) in its own redemption on the basis of prevenient grace',[13] and the elevation of the creature is precisely what Barth opposes. He refers favourably to Luther's perception that the greatness of the New Testament figure of Mary resides in the fact that she always turns attention away from herself and towards the Lord.[14]

From this it can be seen that in different types of Christian theology, Mary signifies humanity in its right relationship with God: the difference in attitude between Protestants and Catholics on this matter lies in the determination of what constitutes that 'right relationship'. Furthermore, the difference in question concerns not only humanity, but any aspect of creation, in its relationship with its Maker. The theological distinction that is at issue is the distinction between Creator and creation, and not that between different orders within creation. Although not every creature has free will, any creature may become a channel or instrument of God's self-communication, and as such, may be viewed either as an object of veneration, or else as an essentially profane tool whose value is expended when it has performed its particular, temporally limited function. In medieval and Tridentine Catholicism, Mary's physical union with Christ and the act of bearing him in her womb rendered her flesh the supreme example of consecrated matter, except for the body of Christ which was itself taken from his mother. In most of the Reformed churches, on the other hand, the kind of adoration which is offered by Catholics to the Blessed Sacrament, or the veneration which is shown before statues and relics, is quite unknown, and Mary's childbearing is similarly the object of little attention.

Mary as creation in the condition of its fulfilment

It has been observed that Mary represents not only the created order in general, but also a specific state of creation, namely, creation in its proper, undistorted relationship to the Creator. This perception has been manifested not only in interpretations of the Annunciation but in many other teachings about Mary. The doctrine of the Immaculate Conception is a good example of this, stating that Mary is the object of perfect redemption since she possesses that justice which was God's original gift to creation.[15] But the Immaculate Conception is by no means the only example.

There has always been a tendency to attribute to Mary a variety of blessings which show her to be exempt from some of the consequences of the sin of Adam. This is seen strikingly in the belief that Mary gave birth without pain and without loss of her physical virginity. After Adam and Eve had eaten the fruit of the tree of the knowledge of good and evil, the principal curse that was laid upon Eve was that she should have pain in childbirth (Genesis 3:16). This, then, is one of the most obvious signs of the Fall from grace, so that painless childbearing is a corresponding sign of preservation or redemption from the effects of that Fall.

As we have seen above (p. 64), the belief that Mary gave birth without any noticeable change in her physical condition has one of its earliest surviving literary witnesses in the apocryphal *Gospel of James*, which probably dates from the second century. The idea that Mary remained a virgin *in partu* was challenged early on by Tertullian, since it seemed to cast doubt upon the real humanity of Jesus.[16] However, by the late patristic and early medieval period, the miraculous childbirth was a widely held belief, although the precise nature of Mary's parturition remained an object of speculation.[17]

The doctrine of Mary's Assumption into heaven is also significant in this context. Like the Immaculate Conception, this teaching has been known for centuries but was dogmatically defined only in modern times. It states that at the end of her earthly life, Mary was assumed into heaven, body and soul. This is frequently said to mean that she has already obtained the state of glory which all the elect will possess on the last day.

From early centuries the Church has known two different traditions concerning the Dormition or Assumption of the Virgin.[18] One of these maintains that after her death, Mary's soul was taken to heaven by Christ, while her body was taken by angels to paradise (on earth), where it will remain until the resurrection of the dead at the end of time. The alternative tradition claims that her soul and her body were reunited, so that Mary is now a complete and perfect person in heaven. In general, the former tradition was that which was taught in the East, whereas the latter was widely disseminated in the West. It is the latter tradition which was formulated in the Bull *Munificentissimus Deus*, when the Assumption was proclaimed an article of faith by Pope Pius XII in 1950.[19]

Within the Western Church itself there have been many variations and disagreements concerning the nature of the Assumption. Over the centuries, a number of different opinions have been brought to bear on the subject of how many days elapsed between the transition of Mary's soul into heaven and the assumption of her body. Some theologians have taught that Mary's body and soul were assumed into heaven simultaneously; and this belief is suggested by many Renaissance and later paintings of the subject.[20] The more ancient teaching, however, is that Mary's soul was taken to heaven first, and was followed some time later by her body.[21] Within this tradition there have also been variations in opinion as to the exact duration of the period between the two events and the location of Mary's body during that time.[22]

Another area of disagreement concerns whether or not Mary actually died at the end of her earthly life or whether she only fell into a sleep and was preserved by God from death. The authors of *Munificentissimus Deus* deliberately refrained from defining this point, because there was no clear agreement on the subject amongst Catholic theologians.[23]

Yet in spite of all the differences of view over details of the Assumption, one point which has remained constant in the doctrine, regardless of the time or place at which it has been taught, is the belief that Mary's body remained incorrupt. This is held to be true as much by those who believe that her body was taken to paradise as by those who believe that it was assumed into heaven; and it is taught by those who believe that she died, as much as by those who believe that she merely fell asleep. The belief that Mary's body has remained uncorrupted, and is either in paradise or heaven, indicates that she has been utterly preserved from the decay which accompanies the mortality that is the consequence of sin. In fact, Mary's sinlessness is sometimes referred to as one of the reasons for her assumption.[24] Sinlessness in life and bodily integrity after death are both examples of what a common Catholic understanding has held to be humanity's ideal condition.

In the thought of many Catholic and Orthodox Christians, to co-operate in the redemption of one's own soul and of the rest of the world is the highest achievement that anyone can attain, so that Mary's uniquely necessary contribution to salvation is the most complete and glorious example of the human capacity for recovering the image of God which was imprinted upon man and woman in the beginning, but which was tarnished by sin. When Rahner writes of Mary as 'perfectly redeemed', and therefore as 'type of the Church', he asserts that what this means concretely is that she is the Mother of God. That is to say, if we ask the question, 'What would it mean to be perfectly redeemed?' the answer would be: 'To conceive Christ in faith and in the flesh'.[25] Mary's sinlessness and bodily assumption are further indications of this state of perfect redemption and thus of her being in a right relationship to her Creator.

Mary as the foundation of the new creation

From the eighth century until the Second Vatican Council, Old Testament texts concerning Wisdom were used in the Marian liturgies of the Western Church.[26] The attribution of Wisdom texts to Mary (especially Proverbs 8:22–31) can create the impression that she plays an active part even in the creation of the universe; and this impression seems to be undergirded by the belief that she plays an active part in the world's salvation and that the work of salvation is closely associated with that of creation. Since the liberation of the world from sin means that creation is restored to its original condition – or to an even superior condition[27] – Christian writers have often drawn a parallel between God's acts of creation and redemption and have understood Mary to play a central role in this work of fundamental restoration. An elegant example of this is found in Anselm's third prayer to St Mary. Anselm draws a parallel between God's act of creation and Mary's contribution to salvation:

> All nature is created by God and God is born of Mary.
> God created all things, and Mary gave birth to God.
> God who made all things made himself of Mary,
> and thus he refashioned everything he had made.
> He who was able to make all things out of nothing
> refused to remake it by force,
> but first became the Son of Mary.
> So God is the Father of all created things,
> and Mary is the mother of all that is re-established.
> For God gave birth to him by whom all things were made
> and Mary brought forth him by whom all are saved.
> God brought forth him without whom nothing is,
> Mary bore him without whom nothing is good.
> O truly, 'the Lord is with you'
> to whom the Lord gave himself,
> that all nature in you might be in him.[28]

The lines of this prayer which were quoted in Chapter 1 (p. 29) express the notion that through Mary, creation is restored to its original glory. Moreover, this renewal is still more delightful than was the original condition of creation:

> Heaven, stars, earth, waters, day and night,
> and whatever was in the power or use of men was guilty;
> they rejoice now, Lady, that they lost that glory,
> for a new and ineffable grace
> has been given them through you.
> They are brought back to life and give thanks.[29]

Thus, by virtue of the salvation which is wrought in the Incarnation, Mary is the instrument and partner by whom the original state of grace is returned to the creation.

In accordance with the general principle that participation in God's salvific work is not only possible for creatures but required of them in so far as they are capable of it, Mary's contribution to the restoration of the created order does not place her outside that order, but leads to her being compared to aspects of the creation before the Fall. For example, early Christian and medieval writers compared Mary to the ground from which Adam was made. Irenaeus, taking up the motif of Christ as the second Adam, states that the creation of Adam from the virgin earth is a type, or foreshadowing, of the virgin birth. The sense in which he considers the earth to be 'virgin' is that 'God had not rained' and 'there was no man to till the soil' before Adam was made.[30] Tertullian uses the same motif when he refers to Mary as 'that virgin earth, not yet watered by the rains nor fertilized by the showers'.[31] Ephraim of Syria (306–73) likewise declaims: 'The virgin earth gave birth to that Adam, head of the earth, today the virgin gave birth to Adam, head of heaven.'[32] Elsewhere, Ephraim writes of Mary's body as simultaneously the earth and the Church:

> Just as, because the bodies which themselves have sinned, themselves must also die, and the earth their mother was cursed, so because of this body, because it is itself the church, which is not corrupted, the earth was blessed from the beginning. For the earth is the body of Mary, the temple which received the seed.[33]

In the fourteenth century, the mystic Bridget of Sweden had a revelation in which Christ himself took up the same imagery in answer to the question as to why he had chosen a virgin, rather than some other woman, to be his mother. Bridget writes his words as follows:

> Just as the first man was made from the earth when it was, in a way, virgin – for it had not yet been polluted with blood – and because Adam and Eve sinned while their nature was still healthy, so too I, God, willed to be received by the purest receptacle so that through my goodness all things might be reformed.[34]

The examples given so far show Mary as one who enjoys a state of pre-lapsarian glory and through whom others also have the possibility of restoration. Yet her association with the beginnings of the created order runs more deeply even than the virgin earth of Genesis 2, for there is an ancient, if intermittent, tradition of a correspondence between Mary and the prime matter of creation.

Maria d'Agreda, a Spanish nun of the seventeenth century, wrote one of the most popular works of Marian devotion in the history of Western Christianity. It is entitled *The Mystical City of God* and is claimed to have been written from divine revelations concerning the Virgin. During the discourse concerning the Virgin Mary's conception, Maria draws a comparison between the formation of the Virgin in her mother's womb and the creation of the world by God. According to Maria, the Virgin's body was conceived on a Sunday, and although – according to Aristotelian biology – it normally takes eighty days for a girl's body to be prepared to receive its soul, in the case of the Blessed Virgin, this period was reduced to just seven days.[35] Mary was thus ready to receive her soul on the Saturday following her conception, and it was on this day that her soul was created.[36] Maria comments: 'God maintained a mysterious correspondence in the execution of this work with that of creating all the rest of the world in seven days, as is related in the book of Genesis.' She observes that this must have been a day of rest and paschal feasting, because it was the beginning of the work of redemption.[37] Maria claims that this is why Saturday is consecrated to the Virgin, and she further explains:

> During the other seven days preceding the vivification of the inanimate body, it was disposed and organised by the divine power, in order that this work might correspond with the account that Moses gives of the Creation of all things, comprising the formation of the whole world at its beginning.[38]

Although this account of the formation of the Virgin is unusual, it contains strands which can be found in other Christian writings. The notion that Mary was made after the pattern of the world's creation could be viewed as an elaborate extension of the idea that she is the earth from which the New Adam is formed; and this passage articulates clearly some parallel between Mary and the created order as such. Moreover, in comparing the formation of Mary's body with the creation of the world, Maria implies that the stuff of which Mary's body was formed was in some measure analogous to the prime matter of creation, or the waters from before the creation of heaven and earth (Genesis 1:1–2), and this idea also is one which seems to draw upon earlier Christian teaching.

Several New Testament scholars have claimed that the Gospel writers themselves intended the conception of Jesus to be understood in the light of the biblical account of the creation of the world. Ethelbert Stauffer put forward this argument with regard to the Gospel of Matthew. He considered that Matthew saw the birth of Jesus as something which resulted from the operation of the same Spirit who brooded over the waters on the first day of creation; the birth of the saviour is the new creation in whom all things will be restored to their original condition.[39] Miegge takes up Stauffer's idea and suggests that Luke's intention is the same as Matthew's: that is, that in the narrative of the Annunciation, there is 'an allusion ... to the creator Spirit of the beginning, an allusion to the "power of the All Highest" that initiates our creation'.[40]

René Laurentin, a leading Mariologist of the twentieth century, supports the same interpretation of Luke when he writes:

> Luke ... suggests that the new creation announced by the prophets begins thus: the Spirit of God who presided at the first creation (Gen. 1:2) and was to inaugurate the second (Is. 11:2), comes to rest upon Mary in whom the new world begins (Lk. 1:35).[41]

Raymond Brown, the American biblical scholar, also favours this understanding of Luke's intention, and discusses its theological importance at some length. He points out that there is no Old Testament precedent for a virginal conception, and that it is 'more startling' than a conception in a woman who is barren (as were Sarah, Hannah and Elizabeth when they conceived their sons: Gen. 18:9–14, 21:1–2; 1 Sam. 1:1–20; Lk. 1:5–25, 27).[42] Because it is completely new, a virginal conception 'would be consonant with a theology of a new creation wherein God's Spirit, active in the first creation of life (Gen. 1:2), was active again'.[43] Further on, Brown makes the following observation:

> The begetting is not quasi-sexual as if God takes the place of a male principle in mating with Mary. There is more of a connotation of creativity. Mary is not barren, and in her case the child does not come into existence because God co-operates with the husband's generative action and removes the sterility. Rather, Mary is a virgin who has not known man, and therefore the child is totally God's work – a new creation.[44]

The Spirit which comes upon Mary is similar to the Spirit of God in Genesis 1:2: 'The earth was void and without form when that Spirit appeared; just so Mary's womb was a void ... until through the Spirit God filled it with a child who was His son.'[45]

This comparison of the Virgin at the Annunciation with the waters of chaos at the creation of the world is one which has appeared intermittently during the history of Christian mystical thought. Hildegard of Bingen (1098–1179), for example, wrote of Mary:

> so you are that luminous matter
> through which the same Word
> breathed forth all virtues,
> as in prime matter
> it brought forth all creatures.[46]

In similar vein, the twelfth-century abbot Rupert of Deutz wrote: 'The Holy Spirit, who in the beginning was borne over the waters, came upon the blessed Virgin and ineffably overshadowed her womb, like a bird warming an egg beneath with its longed-for brooding.'[47] This sentence seems to have a parallel in another piece by Hildegard, which is cited by Barbara Newman as a further example of 'the Annunciation as a second genesis', thus:

> The Virgin bore a Son by the warmth of the Holy Spirit brooding over her; and as a chick would never hatch from an egg without the warmth of the hen, so the Virgin would never have borne a Son without the warmth of the Holy Spirit.[48]

The image of the Annunciation as a new creation is also familiar to Eastern Orthodox Christianity. In a commentary on the place of Mary in the calendar of the Orthodox Church, Lothar Heiser writes:

> As God's Spirit swept over the waters at the beginning of the first creation (Gen.1:2) of which it would be said: God saw that all that he had made was very good (Gen.1:31), so the Spirit of God comes over Mary and shapes in her and with her the new creation, which in its dignity is still more elevated than was the original one.[49]

In the West, however, the use of this motif fell into decline during the modern period, although it has been taken up again in recent mystical writings.[50]

The comparison of Mary with the waters of creation makes vivid her role as a figure for the matter of creation in relation to the Creator. This particular representative or symbolic function governs many aspects of the development of Mary's cult.

'As Mary is to God, so nature is to humanity'

If Mary stands for creation in relation to God, or rather, for creation in its right relationship with God, then there is an ambiguity as to the precise significance of this. For on the one hand, the state of creation in its right relationship with the Creator can be understood principally as a condition to which the whole created order may aspire, so that Mary is a sign of hope, showing the potential of all things to reach harmony and fulfilment. But on the other hand, the image of creation in its right relationship with the Creator can serve to throw into relief the apparent wickedness of other creatures, so that Mary becomes predominantly a sign of what is lacking in that which is unredeemed and of its condemnation by God. During the past millennium, Mary has performed both these functions within the imagination of Western Christians. But over the centuries, and especially within the last three hundred years, the Catholic perception of Mary seems to have shifted from being one in which she was typically a sign of hope for all creatures to one in which she appears more frequently as the representative of that which is already good in the created order, cast in opposition to that which is evil. This change corresponds to other changes in the Virgin's cult, and all these developments can be understood in part by reference to humanity's changing relationship with the natural world.

When Karl Barth writes that humanity can be only the recipient of God's grace, and not a co-operator in God's work of redemption, he is depicting men and women in a condition of the most intense humility and powerlessness before their Creator. In a world in which humanity is bent ever more on the pursuit of power over other creatures – that is, both human and other members of the physical universe – Barth can be read as providing a timely reminder of the need for such humility. Yet there is an irony here; for the history of the Christian presentation of the relationship between God and creation, including humanity, suggests that this relationship has been understood largely as a grander reflection of humanity's own relationship with 'nature', where this signifies the physical world in which men and women participate. In the light of this consideration, one might suspect that, whatever Barth's intention, his presentation of the relationship between God and humanity functions not so much to attack the actions of people who arrogate to themselves too great a right of technical command over the world, as to project the image of that arrogant command on to God. And since one of the actual (if unnecessary) consequences of greater technical control has been an increased sense of powerlessness on the part of men and women, one might similarly suspect that Barth's account of divine power and human impotence implicitly misrepresents in terms of ontological necessity a malaise which is really caused by human society. If one were to read Barth's theology in isolation, such a judgement might appear to be unfair; but when set against a more general background of the development of Western Christianity, this interpretation seems plausible. From the time of the high Middle Ages, the civilization of Western Europe has been increasingly concerned with technical control and with a form of economic development which depends upon the evolution of new technology and its ever wider application. Christian representations of God have changed over the same period, as people's understanding of God's creative activity has corresponded to their own changing modes of engagement with, and aspirations to dominate, the natural world. And since Mary stands for creation in its right relationship with the Creator, the way in which Christian culture construes her is also indicative of technological and economic conditions: as Mary is to God, so nature is to humanity.

Catholic Marian devotion has existed in a geographical area and historical period which have been marked by the greatest technological and economic change that human society has ever known. From the eighth century down to the present day, through inventions ranging from the spinning wheel to the microchip, humanity has gained a progressive mastery over a variety of natural forces, and at the same time has developed its self-understanding in such a way that men and women (but perhaps men more than women) perceive themselves to be the potential controllers of all physical nature. The present study attempts to understand the transformation of Marian doctrine and devotion in relation to these changes, which involve both humanity's domination of 'nature' and the domination of one human group by another. There are two broad historical periods which have seen the greatest advances in technology, with corresponding changes in other areas of society. These periods are the high Middle Ages, especially the twelfth century, and the modern era, beginning in the sixteenth and seventeenth centuries, with more rapid change occurring in the nineteenth and twentieth. This chapter will pay particular attention to these two periods of European history. I argue that if the perceived relationship between God and creation is closely correlated with humanity's relationship to physical nature, then changes in the cult of the Virgin Mary must be understood in connection with technological change. Scholarly discussion of the relationship between God and creation has taken place under the auspices of theology, which in the Middle Ages was a highly influential discipline. I shall therefore take note of some medieval theologians' ideas about God and creation, as well as technological and other cultural change which was contemporary with their work. The relationship between humanity and nature is realized largely in technology, which since the nineteenth century has become entirely intertwined with science. These disciplines have the kind of dominance in the modern world which theology had in the Middle Ages, and I shall therefore consider aspects of science and technology in order to gain some understanding of people's perception of their relationship with nature in modernity.

God and creation in medieval theology

There are several respects in which the relationship between God and creation is understood as analogous to humanity's relationship with physical nature. One of the most enduring of these is the characterization of both relationships in terms of gender, such that God is presented as male in relation to a female creation, and humanity as male in relation to female nature. Notions of this kind help to explain why a female figure, Mary, comes to stand for creation in relation to God, and I draw on feminist theory to articulate more thoroughly her position in Christian world-views.

In their accounts of relations of domination, feminist authors have employed the concept of *dualism*. Their principal concern is usually the domination of women by men, but a number of feminist writers have contended that the dualistic nature which pertains to men's domination of women can be seen also to characterize those social and psychological relations of domination which take place between actors who are not necessarily of opposite sexes.[51] Thus, it is argued, first, that in general a relationship of domination is constructed as a set of interactions and attitudes between two partners of whom one is relatively powerful and the other correspondingly subordinate; and second, that different relationships of domination are structurally analogous to one another. Specifically, a member of the superior group in a (dyadically constructed) relationship of domination will act, on the one hand, as though he or she has nothing in common with the subordinate group in the relationship, and on the other hand, as though all members of the subordinate group are substantially similar to one another, so that members' individual characteristics go unrecognized. A white racist, for example, will fail to take account of the shared humanity which characterizes both white and black people and will simultaneously fail to recognize the personal differences between individual black people, seeing them all as 'the same'. The members of the subordinate group may be idealized, rather than spurned, but the structure of the relationship is similar. The dualist sees the world in terms of pairs of opposites, and thereby misses both the unity and the diversity of the world which he or she inhabits. To spell out this phenomenology of dualism identifies a dynamic which pertains to a variety of relationships of domination whose interconnections will be described more precisely in the remainder of this chapter and in Chapter 5.

Feminist concern with dualism dates back at least as far as Simone de Beauvoir's *Le Deuxième Sexe*, which the author begins by observing that woman is understood as 'the Other' in relation to man who is 'the Subject . . . the Absolute'.[52] When Christians think and act dualistically, Mary occupies the position of 'other' in relation to an 'I' which is projected on to God, and there are grounds for supposing that Mary's female sex is not accidental to her constitution as 'other'. This may be seen from an examination of the way in which dualism has affected some Christian thinking.

Christian monotheism became an integral aspect of the dualistic thought and practice of Western Europe. This seems ironic, since Christians claim that the metaphysics of their faith are not dualistic, and since orthodox Christianity has always been opposed to the dualism taught by such groups as Manichees and other Gnostics. The Christian faith does not teach that the universe is torn between ultimate forces of good and evil in opposition to one another, or that the world of the spiritual is in a state of irreconcilable tension with the world of matter. What it does teach is that there is only one God, and that he is the sole creator and sustainer of the universe. There is literally nothing which is outside God's creation and governance. There is, however, a kind of second level in the Christian world-view, in which dualist categories frequently operate. In John's Gospel, for example, oppositions are drawn between good and evil, light and darkness, and even God and the devil (e.g., John 8:41–4). But in an orthodox Christian interpretation of this Gospel, the choices between these opposing forces are not choices between ultimate forces which are evenly balanced, but are choices between the Creator himself and an aspect of his creation. If there is any sense in which Christianity can be said to be fundamentally dualistic, then that dualism lies in this radical distinction between Creator and creation, whereby creation constitutes an intrinsically ambivalent category, such that when it behaves in accordance with the Creator's will it is placed in a favourable light, but equally, when it is disobedient, it takes on the character of sinfulness. This, then, is a conceptual scheme which can be referred to as *Christian dualism*. It is the construing of the world in terms of God on the one hand, and some aspect of creation on the other: in the case of a rational creature (such as a human being), the creature has the possibility of choosing to accept or reject the Creator's will, and is judged accordingly; in the case of a non-rational creature, it may be used either in the service of the Lord or to some opposing purpose.

There is also a less orthodox type of dualism which creeps into both theology and devotion, and which has a crucial influence on the dualism described above. This occurs when God is spoken of in language which is used also of some aspect of the created order, in such a way that there is confusion between divine and created attributes. God thus takes on the appearance of certain created beings, while the created beings correspondingly appear to be especially Godlike. God and the creatures which he is supposed to resemble then constitute a group which is distinguished from, and may be opposed to, the rest of creation. Mary occupies a position within each of these dualistic constructions.

Superficially, there does not seem to be any connection between Christian dualism and gender. Christian theology teaches that God is without gender, since God is perfect – that is, complete, without restriction of any kind – while gender is a created attribute which limits its possessor. However, historical and anthropological findings suggest that the Christian understanding of God and creation have in practice been frequently bound up with notions of what it means to be male and what it means to be female.[53]

From the time of the later Greek philosophers, and through the philosophy of the Middle Ages and Renaissance, the qualities of spirit, activity and rationality were frequently regarded as masculine, and the qualities of physicality, passivity and emotion as feminine.[54] Most writers considered both sets of qualities to be present to some degree in members of both sexes, but the masculine qualities were seen as stronger and more natural in men, and the feminine qualities as stronger and more natural in women. Moreover, the masculine qualities tended to be considered superior to the feminine ones and more desirable than them, while the feminine qualities were viewed as correspondingly inferior.[55] The attributes which were characteristically masculine were also those which could be ascribed to God with the least inaccuracy, whilst the supposedly feminine attributes were seen as being confined to the created order.[56] This can be seen in the work of Thomas Aquinas. Aquinas considered that human likeness to God resided primarily in intelligence, or capacity for understanding,[57] and that humanity's 'intelligent nature' was equally present in both men and women. However, he stated, 'God's image is found in man in a way in which it is not found in woman; for man is the beginning and end of woman, just as God is the beginning and end of all creation.'[58] The association of God with maleness and creation with femaleness is also implied elsewhere in Thomas's writing. He holds *materia prima*, or prime matter, to be that which is furthest from God. *Materia prima* is the original matter from which all things are created by God. It is entirely passive, and merely awaits the reception of form from the Creator, since, in Aquinas's words, 'matter in itself neither exists nor can be known'.[59] God is characterized in terms of active intellect, and is as unlike passive matter as possible.[60] Ostensibly, the relationship between the Creator and prime matter is not concerned with gender. However, it is more or less analogous to the interaction which Thomas believes takes place between a man and a woman in the conception of a new life. Using Aristotelian biology, Aquinas teaches that the male partner provides the active seed in human generation, whilst the female partner provides the passive 'soil' in which the seed can grow. As if in imitation of God's creation of the world out of prime matter, the female provides the 'formless matter of body' and the male provides the 'formative power' through which the matter receives its 'rational soul'.[61]

Aquinas was by no means alone in his thinking on these matters, and a general statement indicating the association of ideas about creation with notions of gender is given by the scholastic philosopher Roger Bacon, who draws a clear distinction between 'the active potency of God' and the 'passive potency of matter'.[62] He says one should not think that matter has

> a kind of active potency which, under the stimulus of an external agent, activates itself and becomes form. The potentiality of matter truly is its craving for perfection which, as Aristotle says, it loves as the female loves the male and as the ugly loves the beautiful.[63]

In this example, the scholastic understanding of Creator and creation is

91

articulated in such a way that the dyad God/creation corresponds to the dyad male/female respectively.[64]

Thus, it seems to be the case that in Christian philosophy, the divine Creator could be perceived as an immaterial being who was most appropriately referred to as male, while the matter of which creation was formed was lacking almost all the qualities of the Deity, and was perceived in terms which were typically associated with the female. Clusters of attributes were gathered around two poles of God and creation, respectively, in such a way that maleness and divinity were accorded a special similarity to one another, and stood in contrast to the couple comprised of femaleness and creatureliness .

Taking account of this implicitly gendered view of God and creation in the work of Christian philosophers might cast light on why it is that a figure who stands for the matter of creation is female.[65] The examples given above also indicate something else which is relevant to the later development of the cult of the Virgin. The possibility of a creature doing God's will, and thus doing good, or of opposing God's will, and thus doing evil, shows more precisely what is involved in the ambiguity which I have said follows from Mary's standing in a 'right relationship' with her Creator. We have seen that she may show the salvation which is possible for all created beings, including those who have formerly disobeyed God's will by doing evil. St Anselm holds that through Mary, 'even fallen angels are restored to their place'. But a more dualistic version of Christianity will present Mary as the paradigm of those who do God's will, and present her in opposition to creatures who disobey, thereby drawing attention to the latter's condemnation. In this view, Mary is the perfect creature on its best behaviour, which is to say that she is the 'other' who, like Thomist prime matter, is entirely formed according to the will of a characteristically masculine master.

Yet the grounds for a critique of such a view exist already within the Christian tradition. For orthodox doctrine holds that God is neither male nor female, and any account of God which renders him intrinsically more like one gender than the other cannot but present him as too similar to creatures. God's transcendence of created categories stands in antithesis to any 'masculinity' which men and women may project on to him.

We have seen that some twentieth-century theologians regard the relationship of God to creation explicitly as that of male to female, and that this resonates with images of abusive domination. In the thirteenth century, however, the dualism was not yet so rigid, and a strong sense of the material world's capacity for holiness continued to characterize Christian sensibilities for several centuries. Although Christianity maintains that there is an ontological distinction between God and his creation, its central teachings are equally concerned with the union of creation with its Creator, and with the overcoming of the gulf between nature and grace.[66] The doctrine of God's incarnation in Jesus, the divine and the human natures united in one person, declares that notwithstanding the ontological distinction between God and creation, God has become one with a creature. This is the means by which God has chosen to redeem the world from sin and from the separation which sin has engendered. So the restoration of an original closeness and harmony between God and the world is a fundamental concern of Christian teaching.

It is probably true to say that in the daily life and worship of medieval Catholicism, there was as much emphasis on the operation of God's grace in created things as there was on his separation from them. A quasi-magical attitude to the Church's sacraments, the belief in the power of church officials to convey both physical and spiritual benefits, and the cults of images and relics, all indicate faith in the operation of the divine within the physical.[67] Furthermore, since most of the important feasts and rituals of the agricultural year had been given Christian significance, and since the craft guilds were strongly associated with Christian saints and celebrations, the tasks of daily labour were likewise imbued with a sense of sacred meaning.[68]

Caroline Walker Bynum has argued that the late medieval emphasis upon the Incarnation and upon God's presence within the physical world had a particular consequence for women. Since materiality was commonly associated with the female and spirituality with the male, religious women would identify themselves with matter and rejoice that it was in this very condition that God would unite himself with them. So although matter was deemed inferior to spirit, it was the temple in which God would come to dwell and thereby unite the worshipper to himself.[69]

Much of medieval Catholic practice might therefore be characterized as strongly 'sacramental', that is, tending to focus upon the physical world's potential for sanctity rather than on its distance from that which is spiritual or divine. Mary's particular dignity of being the one in and by whom God was perfectly united to creation ensured that she occupied a central position in Christian devotion.

Medieval sacramentalism was rejected by many theologians of the Reformation, who placed a new emphasis on the separation of nature from its Creator. Calvinism in particular stressed the distance which existed between God and creation.[70] Protestants did not initially reject the notion that God communicated with humanity through natural and social phenomena,[71] but they did not believe that humanity could manipulate God's power in the world by means of special prayers or sacraments, and they interpreted many Catholic practices as being attempts to do precisely that.[72] Many Reformers also considered the veneration of saints, relics and holy objects to be idolatrous, on the grounds that it accorded to mere creatures a status and power which belonged only to the Creator himself. The Reformation (and in England, subsequent reforms in the seventeenth century) therefore saw the abolition of many practices which had been at least the weft of the fabric of medieval daily life, as the Reformers attempted to leave people with a far less magical view of the world which they inhabited.

The new theology indicated a change in humanity's attitude towards its natural environment, since it abolished the notion that there were sacred powers which were immanent to the natural world and which should be venerated in their proper physical phenomena. Instead, it was now possible to consider intervening in the physical universe in a manner which would have been forbidden by the sacred or magical prohibitions of an earlier age, although we shall see that the origins of such ideas had been laid many centuries before the Reformation.

Male and female in the dualism of science: recent research

In the Aristotelian philosophy employed by medieval scholastics, the term *nature* had usually signified the active principle of change in things; but during the seventeenth century, a new mechanistic conception of nature arose which depended upon the assumption that 'matter is passive', so that change comes about through the impact of external forces.[73] Evelyn Fox Keller has connected this transformation to 'the rhetorical shift in the locus of essential secrets from God to Nature'.[74] Whereas earlier empiricists had once sought initiation into the 'secrets of God', by which they would acquire privileged knowledge that had to remain hidden, the new scientists sought to expose the 'secrets of nature' by 'dissolving, or ripping open, the veil of secrecy'.[75] Concomitantly, says Keller,

> the terms God and nature had themselves to undergo subtle transformation as they came to mark a different – simultaneously more distant and more authoritarian – relation between God and the natural world ... [b]y the beginning of the eighteenth century, Nature had given way to nature: devoid of both intelligence and life.[76]

These changes were expressed by corresponding transformations in the language of gender which was used to describe the activities of science and technology.

The medieval understanding of matter tended to associate it with that which was female, whilst God the Creator was thought of in terms which were commonly associated with the male. More generally, the dyad comprised of spirit and matter was often described as being analogous to male and female, respectively.[77] This manner of conceptualization was on occasions continued and intensified in language used to describe modern science.

Carolyn Merchant[78] charts attitudes towards the natural world at the time of the scientific revolution. Her work indicates that there was a movement away from regarding the earth as a bountiful mother who should be treated with gratitude and respect, and towards regarding the earth as an object of rape and pillage. Opposition to mining, for example, was supported by two different kinds of argument. The first of these, found in Pliny's *Natural History*[79] and in other ancient and medieval sources,[80] regards the earth as a generous giver of vegetation whom it is ungracious and improper to assault. But this reverential attitude was not universal, and by the time of Edmund Spenser and John Donne, a more common view, and one expressed by both these writers, was to regard avarice for precious metals as being equivalent to lust for women, and hence as base and degrading.[81] In these texts, the earth is still female, but is wickedly tempting, rather than bountiful. However, the protagonists for scientific and technological development of this kind did not generally oppose the comparison of technology to sensual desire: on the contrary, they themselves came to speak of science and technology in terms of sexual advances towards a female Nature. Yet this was not necessarily because they regarded Nature as a delightful mistress. Rather, she was often viewed as the potential object of sadistic assaults, whose secrets were to be extracted by means of torture.[82]

What we thus see is a transition from viewing aspects of the physical world as a female subject and an object of reverence, to seeing Nature instead as a female object of male domination. The relationship of the human mind to the physical universe, like the relationship of God to matter, was conceptualized as the activity of a transcendent male mind upon passive female nature. Moreover, this view has continued, and possibly intensified, over the centuries following the scientific revolution, as the following examples illustrate.

Keller has described the cultural battle going on in the seventeenth century between the followers of Paracelsus and the followers of Francis Bacon, with each group striving for ascendancy over the other. Their different views of science included different views of gender. In the older, Paracelsian thinking, woman was certainly not seen as all good; but God was nonetheless believed to be immanent in the material world, in woman, and in sexual activity. Furthermore, Paracelsian philosophy placed central importance upon the notion of the union of masculine and feminine principles in Nature. In the Baconian view, by contrast, it was held that science consisted in the subjugation of the feminine Nature by virile, masculine intellect. This view is more rigidly dualistic than is the Paracelsian understanding, since it has the tendency to polarize clusters of attributes, including those of gender. In the end the battle was effectively won by the Baconians when the Royal Society was established in England in 1662.[83]

The same trend was continued in the medical science of the eighteenth century, when, according to Ludmilla Jordanova, the 'capacity for scientific prowess was [increasingly] conceptualized as a male gift', whilst 'nature was the fertile woman'.[84] Jordanova's research suggests that medical scientists worked with clear pairs of dichotomies, such as nature/culture, woman/man, and physical/mental. There was also a tendency for these dichotomies to be grouped into two classes along the lines already established in medieval and Renaissance thought. However, they were not unswervingly attributed to actual men and actual women; rather, they were tendencies which could be identified within each individual, or within society as a whole. But Jordanova considers that by the middle of the nineteenth century, the psychological distinction between the sexes had been made rigid, so that attributes which had previously been regarded as merely more characteristic of one sex than the other were now regarded as constitutionally inevitable features of being male or being female.[85]

Thomas Laqueur's study of the evolution of anatomical drawings from the Middle Ages until the nineteenth century also indicates a polarizing of the attributes associated with men and women respectively. He writes that in the medieval period 'there was only one sex, and that was male'.[86] Religious thinkers of the Middle Ages seem also to have pointed out the similarity and continuity between the sexes, as much as their differences.[87] Laqueur's presentation of medieval scientific ideas about gender has been qualified by more recent research in the history of medicine, indicating that there was a greater variety of opinion about such matters than is given in the single-sex model which Laqueur describes.[88] But it was in the eighteenth and nineteenth centuries that medical authors came to present women as radically different from men, and taught that a woman's whole nature was dictated by her sexual and reproductive organs. Both Laqueur and Jordanova have noted an increase in the dissection and illustration of women's genitals which occurred between the seventeenth and nineteenth centuries, and Jordanova has observed a tendency to both violence and voyeurism in these activities.[89] In the same essay, Jordanova has given examples of eighteenth-century medical science in which women's anatomy is presented in a manner which is entirely concerned with sexual attraction, reproduction and the nervous system, while other parts of the human body are associated with the male.[90] Londa Schiebinger has similarly indicated that anatomists of the early nineteenth century associated women with 'feeling and instinct', and the (male) scientist with 'reason and truth'.[91] This type of distinction was maintained in the gynaecological practice of early nineteenth-century England, according to Ornella Moscucci. She argues that gynaecology as a distinct field of medical practice arose in the context of the belief that woman's nature was dominated by her organs of reproduction, whereas man's nature was determined principally by his brain.[92] Gynaecology helped in the maintenance of this system of ideas. It was a system which claimed that a woman's proper sphere of activity was 'private', whilst a man's was 'public',[93] and it thus militated against the emancipation of women in political and professional life.

The continuing application of an association between masculinity and intellect on the one hand, and femininity and reproductive or sexual functions on the other, seems to have occurred in physics as well as medicine. In his study of the origins of the nuclear arms race, Brian Easlea has emphasized the extent to which physicists think of their work in terms of the male mind 'penetrating' female nature. Scientific activity tends to be seen by physicists as a competition in masculinity, in which the winner is the man whose mind penetrates the most deeply into the inner recesses of the natural world.[94] Theoretical physicists therefore claim their discipline as the most prestigious science, since it is the purely mental 'unveiling' of nature's deepest secrets.[95] Writing during the Cold War, Easlea suggested that this ethos of aggressive masculinity could be one of the factors which would account for the origin and maintenance of the nuclear arms race.[96]

These studies show that notions of gender, including motherhood, have been employed to describe human endeavours which have been central to the evolution of Western civilization. The descriptions tend to show an increasing hostility on the part of a putatively 'male' mind towards a supposedly 'female' object of study, and this corresponds to a deepening and widening domination of the natural world on the part of the sciences concerned. We can see from this that the opposition of Erasmus, Peter Heylin and 'C.W.' to the notion of Mary's possessing specifically maternal authority comes at the beginning of a historical movement of increasing hostility towards motherhood. It is during the same historical period that devotional representations of Mary have shown her increasingly often as a figure alone, without her child. Where Christians once venerated the powerful mother with her divine infant, who together signified the union of God with the material creation, modern Catholics have transferred their affections to a girl who is the icon of the creature subordinated to a remote Lord. For the conviction that sacred forces are manifest in earth and water has been all but lost to the project of world-mastery.

Yet the doctrines of the Incarnation and divine motherhood remain a foundation of Catholic doctrine, and this may be the cornerstone on which to construct an immanent critique (i.e., criticism of a practice by appeal to an ideal which is supposed to underlie or be embodied in that practice) of much contemporary theology and devotion, including a reappraisal of Christian approaches to nature.

Cultural change in the twelfth and thirteenth centuries

The enthusiasm of Western Europeans for the scientific investigation and technological control of their natural environment had some of its strongest roots laid during the high Middle Ages. This can seen dramatically in the sphere of engineering, that is, in the human enterprise which is most obviously concerned with the acquisition of mastery over natural forces. The most famous accomplishments in this regard are those which were achieved in the development of Gothic architecture.[97] Formerly, the possible height of a building had been restricted by the fact that the ceiling was constructed of barrel vaulting, which could be increased in height only by increasing the thickness of the walls that supported it, in order to avoid their being pushed outwards by the load of the roof. Western Europeans had already developed a taste for ever higher ceilings in their churches, and the old mode of construction was becoming extremely laborious and expensive because of the amount of stone which was needed for the walls. The ogival arch may have been introduced into Europe from Buddhist India, where it performed a decorative function, and within decades it had begun to transform the construction of larger churches:[98] this was not, however, because of its aesthetic merits, but because the first engineers of Gothic architecture realized that the pointed arch directed the load of the ceiling downwards, rather than outwards, to a far greater extent than round arches had done, so that it was now possible to raise the height of a building with the use of slimmer walls than had previously been possible. The construction of a large building was therefore cheaper and quicker than had formerly been the case, and the height of churches could be increased considerably.[99] These advantages were enhanced by the introduction of flying buttresses, which made use of the technical possibilities that had been introduced by the pointed arch.

The origins of the new passion for building lay in the monasteries, but, as with other cultural developments of the period, it was taken up with enthusiasm by the secular middle class. It was common for the burghers of medieval towns and cities to endow the building and improvement of great churches, since the church was the symbol of the town; and throughout the twelfth and thirteenth centuries, the naves of churches were built to ever greater heights as one record was broken by another.[100]

The advances made in the technology of building, moreover, had parallels in other areas of technical expertise. The rapid spread of the watermill and the invention of the spinning wheel are particularly obvious examples; but in general, the twelfth and thirteenth centuries witnessed the introduction of new agricultural and industrial machinery which was to become the bedrock of the changing economy of Western Europe, and which was not to be surpassed until the Industrial Revolution.[101]

This extraordinary mastery over natural forces depended in part upon the natural phenomena of mineral, wind and water being viewed as profane resources for human exploitation. Yet the situation was by no means as simple as this. The builders of Gothic churches were trying to create in the material world, by means of number and geometry, an imitation of heavenly reality. They may not have considered the stone they used to have been intrinsically sacred, but it carried the potential to be the bearer of sanctity when subject to human craft. And it is striking that nearly all the great Gothic cathedrals are dedicated to the Virgin: each one is a palace for the Queen of Heaven.

Greater insight into the nature of the great cultural changes of the Middle Ages can be gained when we take account of the fact that these changes were not confined to technology. The scholastic philosophy represented by Thomas Aquinas and Roger Bacon was a new movement in the twelfth century, and was part of a much wider transformation which was taking place in Western European culture at this time. The Dominican scholar M.-D. Chenu has written:

> The encounter between man and nature becomes complete only when man has subdued nature to his service; the order of nature demands man's mastery and, for the Christian, so too does the command given man by the Creator on the first pages of the Bible. The twelfth century followed this command.[102]

The intention to subdue nature was accompanied by a more critical and managerial approach to many aspects of human life. The new mendicant religious orders, the Franciscans and Dominicans, rationalized preaching techniques, and aids to the construction and delivery of sermons became widely disseminated.[103] Chenu refers to instances of secularization in a number of institutions during the twelfth century, such as the limiting of certain secular rights of the clergy and the substitution of rational proofs for trial by ordeal in courts of law.[104] People also began to be sceptical about the authenticity of the relics of saints.[105]

There was a renewed interest in classical philosophy during this period, and a rapid growth of interest in the varieties of study of natural phenomena, such as physiology.[106] Scholars were reading classical works such as Seneca's *Quaestiones naturales*, and were searching for the causes of things in the world around them: 'an activity proper to science, and one which clashed violently with religious consciousness, which ... was willing to engage in its characteristic activity of looking immediately to the Supreme Cause, at the expense of disregarding secondary causes'.[107] Chenu describes this as a 'desacralizing of nature – and of the outlook men brought to nature'.[108] He also observes that during the twelfth century there was a great increase in theologians' 'perception of the universe as an entity'; it was not any longer a collection of fascinating parts, but a unity in which everything together was harmonious,[109] and designed by a rational Creator. These intellectual trends became enhanced during the thirteenth century, with the growth of Aristotelianism in place of Platonic philosophy, and they reflected the movement of theology away from the monasteries and into the schools.[110]

Yet notwithstanding Chenu's remarks about the subduing of nature in the twelfth century, this early rationalization of the intellectual life of Western Europe was in no way a crude attempt to gain mastery over the physical world, for the scholars of the high Middle Ages were not trying to devalue the worth of God's creation when they began subjecting it to analytical scrutiny. On the contrary, the religious order in which were found the leading exponents of natural science in the thirteenth century was that of the Franciscans: the very order who most emphasized the moral worth of non-human creatures and who preached the venerable nature of that which is most humble.[111] It was not antagonism, but devout affection, which moved the Franciscan scientist to desire greater knowledge of the physical creation.

An interest in the fine details of natural phenomena may have existed in some form in the earlier Middle Ages, but if so, then it seems that no clear indications of this interest have remained for modern scholars. In contrast to this, the twelfth and thirteenth centuries have bequeathed a wealth of artistic representations which reveal an intense concern to imitate nature as accurately as possible. Whereas the carvings associated with Romanesque architecture had been highly stylized, and served the functions of symbol and decoration at the expense of likeness to nature, the figurative work of the Gothic period became ever more accurate in its rendering of the characteristics of people, plants and animals, both as species and as individuals.[112] The philosophy embodied in this type of art is that which holds that art is the imitation of natural forms, a principle which dominated the art of the West until at least the nineteenth century.

101

The new naturalism of the Gothic period had a striking impact on the representation of the Virgin. The characteristic Romanesque image of a woman in Roman dress, enthroned and looking austerely ahead of her, with an adult child upon her knees, was supplanted in the manufacture of church art (though perhaps not in general devotion) by a woman standing in contemporary dress, with a slight smile upon her face, and looking not at the viewer but at a child who was now a lifelike infant. Famous examples of the new style of carving include the Vierge Dorée at Amiens Cathedral, the gilded virgin and child of Jeanne d'Evreux and the Vierge à l'Oiseau at Riom (Plate 5). No longer a commanding authority whose gaze draws the devotee into her service, Mary is now entirely occupied with her child, so that the viewer looks at but is not communicating immediately with the figures in the image. They are the objects of our gaze. The Virgin wears a crown to signify her royalty, but her likeness has started to undergo a process by which, over the centuries, it will become progressively more humble.

If Chenu is right, in the twelfth and thirteenth centuries men and women in Western Europe were taking up the study of natural phenomena to understand how they worked and to represent them as accurately as possible. The natural world was becoming less a harbinger of sacred power and more an object of investigation. And as human beings were experiencing themselves as increasingly separate from a world which they were trying to comprehend as a unity, so God also was pictured more frequently as the rational Creator of an ordered whole. Under these circumstances, devotional representations of the Virgin Mary, who stands for creation in relation to God, start to lose the air of authority which images made from the tenth to the twelfth centuries had possessed.

The concept of rationalization

The development of relations of domination[113] has been integrally connected to the social process of rationalization, a process which erupted with great flourish in the medieval culture described in the previous section. Rationalization is a concept taken from the work of Max Weber (1864–1920), one of whose central interests was the phenomenon of Western rationalism and its growth within the cultures of Western Europe and North America. Broadly speaking, Weber wrote of 'rational' action with reference to *instrumental rationality*, that is, goal-orientated action which is taken according to the criterion of calculability, and not, say, on grounds of tradition or religious regulation.[114] According to this typology, it is rational to adopt, for example, a particular agricultural technique on the basis of experience which indicates that the technique in question offers a higher crop yield than do other practices; but a technique is described as non-rational if it is adopted on the grounds, say, that this technique is the one which has always been employed by the agriculturalist's ancestors, or that it is the one which is most respectful of the Corn Deity.

The term *rationalization* was employed by Weber to refer to the application of rational principles to human activities which had previously been governed by considerations of a traditional, magical, or religious nature, or other principles which were not greatly concerned with precise calculation. The invention of the bar-line in music and of naturalistic perspective in drawing are examples of the rationalization of the respective arts. The development of Gothic architecture constituted a rationalization of building procedures, and it began to be accompanied by attempts to rationalize the administration of construction works. For example, in 1264 the municipality of Douai proclaimed that all stone building blocks which entered the city should be of standard dimensions.[115] Weber argued that the process of rationalization had attained its greatest sophistication in modern Western society, where it had increasingly encroached upon areas of life which in other cultures had been governed by non-rational considerations. He saw the rationalization of Western society as the 'disenchantment' of the world – the substitution of the logical and the predictable for the mysterious and the magical.[116]

Furthermore, Weber saw Western rationalism as being centrally a project of world-mastery, directed towards the ever-increasing domination of the natural and social environment. The application of instrumental rationality is manifested in the sort of capitalist economy that is characterized by the calculated production of ever-increasing quantities of goods, and correspondingly, by the planned accumulation of capital. It is seen also in the development of forms of science and technology which are successfully bent upon the perpetual pursuit of increasing practical knowledge about the world, and upon the transformation of the world through the application of that knowledge. This process of rationalization depends upon, and helps to generate, a particular sort of attitude towards the world on the part of those who participate in the process. In the words of the sociologist Wolfgang Schluchter, 'The disenchantment of the world, its demagification, presupposes its "devaluation", the denial of its intrinsic value.'[117] That is to say, the rationalism of world mastery implicitly rejects the world as it is, since it seeks to change and 'improve' it. This transformation, moreover, is to be implemented not according to divine law or to imagined ideals of human perfection, but according to principles derived from empirical investigation and logical inference.

Weber regarded the increasing bureaucracy and mechanization of modern society as tendencies which would inevitably continue, although he certainly did not contemplate this aspect of rationalization with any enthusiasm. He considered the disenchantment of the world to be in some sense a *de-humanizing* of the world; and unlike Marxists, who believed that the increasing application of scientific and technological methods to the production of commodities could in principle help liberate humanity to live lives that were fulfilled because they were not bound by sheer economic necessity, Weber saw the expansion of instrumental rationality as a source of spiritual impoverishment, in spite of its practical advantages.[118]

The rationalization of Western civilization – especially in the growth of science, technology and industry – has generated and depended upon certain radical transformations in the values held by those who are involved in the process. One of the most important preconditions and consequences of rationalization is humanity's attitude towards nature, because the rational mastery of natural forces requires that the physical world be viewed as a potential object of control, and not as a venerable source of sacred power. The conviction that the world was rationally constituted and that it was subject to an overarching plan of divine origin, depended upon a radical distinction being drawn between a divine Creator and a dependent creation. If natural phenomena were themselves deities, then the world could not be subject to the absolute authority of a single God, and hence could not be certain to operate in accordance with any plan or rational direction. The monotheism inherited by Christianity from ancient Judaism in effect placed a limit upon the extent of the possible sanctity of the natural world.[119] The absolute distinction between God and creation, and the corresponding limit to the holiness of nature, were beliefs shared by both traditions. For a study of the Christian understanding of Mary, this teaching about

God's relationship to creation is important because it lays unmoveable bounds which Marian doctrine and devotion cannot transgress. Yet within these bounds, very flexible parameters have come into play. If we ask the question, 'what in fact is the limit to the sanctity of the natural world?' the answer is that the natural world is not itself the Deity and cannot be holy in precisely the same sense in which God is holy. On the one hand, this makes it possible to regard the created order as lacking any kind of sanctity, but equally, it allows that created things may be filled with God's grace or in some other manner hallowed by him. The extent to which Western Christians have believed in the sanctity or profanity of nature is related to the rationalization of European society and is expressed in the development of the Virgin's cult.

The belief that the natural world is rationally ordered and the conviction that humanity is entitled to investigate and manipulate it, are ideas which have been central to the rationalization of Western society, and particularly to the growth of science and technology. The engineers and philosophers of the Middle Ages must already have seen themselves as men set over against the natural world, and when artists represented the Virgin less as a celestial monarch and more as a lifelike woman, they were celebrating the glory of the human condition. Yet they were also giving expression to a perceived loss of divine power from within the physical creation, and in doing so, they created a sign which indicated nature's increased subjection to human domination.

A changed relationship with the soil as the basis for further domination

Amongst the many technological advances made during the high Middle Ages, some of the earliest occurred in the area of military equipment. It was the technical superiority of the West which ensured the successes of the Crusades, and much of this military engineering had itself been made possible by technical improvements in agricultural and industrial processes, since these had generated surplus wealth and cheaper goods, thereby freeing the time and resources required for military preparation.[120] However, the fact that time and resources were available does not account for what it was that motivated the rulers of medieval Europe, and especially the Franks, to pursue the particular

105

project of conquering the Holy Land. White has suggested that the aggression of the Latin West in this period was one of a number of manifestations of a profound anxiety which permeated almost the whole society of north-western Europe. He points out that the concept of a Holy War – 'a necessary presupposition of the Crusades'[121] once their goal was extended beyond a minimal protection of pilgrims to Jerusalem – did not seriously emerge in Christianity until the middle of the eleventh century, but that it grew quickly thereafter. This was also the period which saw the introduction of the doctrine of purgatory and indulgences.[122] Moreover, the early part of the eleventh century saw the beginning of widespread persecutions of Jews, as well as the renewal of the practice of executing heretics.[123] It was also during this period that the persecution of witches began to get under way.[124] All this, White suggests, points to a 'dreadful anxiety' in the West in the eleventh century.[125]

The coincidence of these phenomena is of particular interest to the present study because several of them seem to be examples of the kind of dualistic action which has been mentioned above, with the casting of social and economic relationships in terms of a dominating 'self' and an 'other' who must be subdued or banished. The relationship between these developments and the cult of the Virgin is not straightforward, and it seems that for some time she retained the awe-inspiring imperial authority of an earlier age. Yet the period of dramatic change in the high Middle Ages may be an important moment in the process by which, in the Christian imagination, that authority ceased to be wielded in respect of the whole creation and instead became aligned with an 'us' constituted of orthodox Christians against a 'them' comprising heretics and infidels.

What, then, are the connections between the new developments in technology and changes in social and devotional behaviour? At least part of the answer to this question may be provided by Lynn White in his attempt to address a number of questions concerning the advance of technology in the Middle Ages. White argues that underlying many developments in Western civilization was a major change in the technology and economy of agriculture, namely, the spread of the heavy plough in northern Europe from the eighth century onwards.[126] Up until this time, the plough which had been available was the light 'scratch' plough (aratrum), which was capable of tilling only light, sandy soils. For this reason, the only land which was put to agricultural use in northern Europe before the Middle Ages was on high ground with soil which is easily turned. The heavy plough, by contrast, could be used on the heavy, alluvial soils that are found on lower, damper ground; and since these soils are in fact more fertile than those which had formerly been worked, the new plough provided an immediate advantage over the old one for those farmers who lived in regions – most notably in the north of Europe – where the heavier soils are common. Most importantly, though, the new plough enabled the introduction of a three-field, rather than two-field, rotation of crops, and this massively enhanced productivity.

However, the use of the heavy plough required changes in the social organization of the communities who used it. The scratch plough had been drawn by only a single yoke of oxen, which would have been in the possession of the person or household who used them. The heavy plough, on the other hand, required several yokes of oxen to pull it, so a co-operative plough-team had to be created by peasants who had previously worked, in this specific regard, separately from one another. This entailed a complete rearrangement of the system of land allocation; for under the old system, the principle of allocation had been based on the notion that each household should have the land necessary to support it (thus, Domesday Book describes the Anglo-Saxon hide as *terra unius familiae*);[127] now, however, the combining of teams of oxen owned by different farmers necessitated a change away from farming which was centred on the household, and led instead to the introduction of the open-field system of strip farming, in which each strip was assigned to a particular peasant. Different peasants were able to make different sizes of contribution to their team (e.g., some would own more oxen than others), and the distribution of strips of land to the farmers in a given team was proportionate to their respective contributions to that team. The co-operative system which this method of ploughing generated formed the basis of the medieval manorial economy. But it did far more than this. As White has written of the transition from the household to the village economy:

> The standard of land distribution ceased to be the needs of a family and became the ability of a power engine to till the soil. No more fundamental modification in a man's relationship to his environment can be imagined: he ceased to be nature's child and became her exploiter.[128]

A change in attitude of precisely this kind seems to be indicated by a change in illustrated calendars which began in the early part of the ninth century. The new three-field rotation was introduced in all the estates owned by Charlemagne, and the emperor tried to rename the months of the year in terms of human activities (e.g., Ploughing, Haying, Harvest). Specifically, he tried to rename the months in accordance with the new agricultural cycle which the three-field rotation had introduced. His attempt was unsuccessful. But another change began to occur at this time which was retained throughout the Middle Ages and Renaissance period, and this was a change in calendar illustration. From Roman times until the ninth century, secular calendars were illustrated with personifications of the months, each holding her symbolic attributes. However, by the year 830 among the Franks a calendar had appeared showing active scenes of ploughing, harvesting, wood chopping, and pig slaughtering. The cycle of the seasons was thus depicted not in terms of natural or divine beneficence, but in terms of human action to make use of the natural environment.[129] White comments: 'Man and nature are two things, and man is master. Technological aggression, rather than reverent coexistence, is now man's posture towards nature.'[130]

The Carolingian court encouraged artistic, as well as technological change. It was in the Carolingian empire that Christians started to make devotional objects in the form of free-standing statues, rather than just the flat representations and reliefs which had previously been used. This made possible the construction of the Romanesque Virgin in Majesty, who has points of correspondence with Greek and Roman statues of earlier, pagan Gaul. The careful iconography of the Majesty directs the viewer's attention to the divinity of the human Christ and the incomparable honour of the mother whose flesh was assumed by the eternal Word. The devotee is confronted by the presence of the divine within the material world, rather as the earth and the elements had the sacred power of giving and withholding life. By contrast, the Gothic Virgin and Child who later supplant the Majesty figure appear to be the clever work of human hands; and although the craftsman may be imbued with quasi-divine power, the material which he works is more or less profane, as is the soil which humanity now forces to yield up its wealth.

The new agriculture which White describes provided a greater quantity and variety of food than northern Europeans had ever known before, and this led to better nutrition and consequent improvements in health.[131] The agricultural surplus also freed time and generated resources that could be put to new activities, including the expansion of the mercantile economy. And the perception of the non-human environment as an object of potentially increasing exploitation gave a new incentive to technological experiment. However, all this was gained at the cost of enormous disruption in social organization. Villages were entirely reorganized, and the improved efficiency of the new agriculture, together with the increased population generated by better nutrition, meant that the proportion of the populace engaged in agriculture began to fall and the expansion of towns became possible. From the mid-tenth century onwards, new ways of life were established in city and country alike. It is to these dramatic social changes that White attributes the anxiety which he suggests is responsible for the increasing aggression of Western European culture from the eleventh century onwards.[132]

However, we can see that a certain level of insecurity is inscribed in the very structure of the new agricultural system. The old type of economy had tried to secure basic material provisions for its members according to the principle: 'to each household according to its need'. The new system, by contrast, expressed the principle: 'to each household according to its investment'. Therefore, although the new agriculture in fact brought greater health and prosperity to those who practised it, it also introduced an element of uncertainty which had not previously existed. For although people had formerly been more overtly dependent upon unreliable natural elements, they had followed economic and legal principles which assumed that everyone had a right to a living. The communal open-field system undermined those principles by implying that the right to life's necessities was commensurate with the value of a household's contribution to the productive enterprise. There was thus no automatic social guarantee of material security, and the means for obtaining that security were inherently unreliable. It was this kind of principle which underlay the mercantile economy that was to come to dominate Western European society, notwithstanding the Calvinist good practice of the rational bourgeois business manager: indeed, it was the system's very uncertainty which made rational management a necessity.

Conclusion

It has been argued that it is in humanity's relationship with the soil that we find the initial possibility and impetus for the development of those relations of domination which became characteristic of Western civilization. There is also evidence to suggest that the relationship of humanity to the earth and other natural elements has been understood in terms of man's relationship to woman, and that in both this and other respects it has been thought to be similar to the relationship of God to creation. Since the Virgin Mary stands for creation in relation to God, the development of her cult can usefully be understood within this web of interconnected practices.

The theological distinction between Creator and creation contributed an important element to the evolution of the natural philosophy which came to be called science. It was this view of God and creation which enabled philosophers to view the universe as a single, rationally ordered entity, and the belief in a universe of this kind is a prerequisite of scientific thinking. The philosopher Errol E. Harris describes science as

> the effort to think systematically about the world as we experience it, and the results of that thinking. Apart from such systematic thinking no conception of Nature would be entertained. The idea of Nature is the concomitant of science for it is the idea of the world as a single structure of interrelated bodies and events determined by uniform and universal laws, the indispensable presupposition of scientific thinking.[133]

In the religious world-view, this unity of Nature is the creation – or part of the creation – of a God who gave it its being and crafted it into its present form. In the scientific approach to the world, Nature is the object of investigation and manipulation by the human mind, and the latter implicitly assumes itself to be outside the Nature which is the object of its study. The religious attitude leads one to stand transfixed before the sacred gaze of a Virgin in Majesty, while the scientific attitude leads one to look as an observer upon the clever craftsman's lifelike Virgin and Child.

The changing Christian sense of the relationship between Creator and creation has implied an increasingly desacralized view of the natural world. Furthermore, the image of the Creator God as a craftsman was occasionally produced in the West during the high Middle Ages,[134] whilst the doctrine of God as an essentially intellectual Creator of the universe was common to the overwhelming majority of Christian philosophers in the medieval period. This suggests that the Creator was thought of in terms which reflected the particular type of creativity of those who were picturing or describing him. It therefore seems reasonable to suppose that the desacralization of the physical universe was undergirded by the perceived separation of humanity from its natural environment. That is to say, people imagined God's relationship to creation as analogous to their own relationship to the physical world which they inhabited.

In the scientific thought and practice which superseded medieval philosophy, the desacralization of the world became intensified, and corresponded in equal measure to the effective divinization of the human mind. There are two assumptions made by modern scientific practice which indicate most clearly this new relationship between the human mind and non-human nature. The first of these is an ethical one, namely, the assumption that there are no restrictions upon the manner, and even the object, of scientific investigation; humanity is entitled to treat the natural world (including its human members) in any way it chooses if it is done in the name of scientific advancement. The religious and magical beliefs which had formerly placed limits upon the rights of humanity to intervene in natural processes could not have been incorporated into science *per se*, and it was necessary for the old customs to be overcome if science was to proceed.[135]

The second of science's anthropocentric assumptions consists in the conviction that the human mind is capable of acquiring a substantial understanding of the rational organization of the universe. It can, as it were, gain an insight into the mind of God. Scientists do not necessarily claim that the knowledge which humanity obtains will ever be complete.[136] However, the scientific approach to the world does not lay down any a priori limits to that knowledge, and the degree to which physical science is self-confident in this regard can be seen as early as the Copernican revolution. For the realization that the sun and not the earth is at the centre of our planetary system ironically implies that the human mind has powers of comprehension beyond anything assumed under the old Ptolemaic view of the universe. An astronomer who assumes that the earth is at the centre of the universe is, after all, just describing the world as he sees it. Copernicus, on the other hand, by placing the sun at the centre of his planetary scheme was asserting that the human mind could move way beyond such straightforward observation and behave *as though* it were located outside the solar system altogether and were looking down upon it. This is a world-view whose anthropocentrism outstrips any that could be deduced from a geocentric model of the universe.[137] It is a move towards placing the human intellect in the position previously occupied by the mind of God, and it thus corresponds to that replacement of divine authority by human authority which also took place in the moral sphere.

We have already seen that scientific anthropocentrism should more properly be characterized as *androcentrism*: it is not humanity, but men – or even, male scientists – who effectively hold centre-stage as the 'I' in relation to the female 'other ' of Nature. And as the 'male' intellect has become godlike, so 'female' nature has been cast as profane and suitable for subjugation. This, I suggest, is why Mary – who stands for creation in relation to God, and so corresponds to nature in relation to humanity – seems over the centuries to have lost the terrible sacred power which she once held in the Christian imagination.

Notes

1. Cited in Vladimir Lossky, *The Mystical Theology of the Eastern Church*, trans. Fellowship of St Alban and St Sergius (1957), p. 141. A brief account of Cabasilas's Mariology is given in Hilda Graef, *Mary: A History of Doctrine and Devotion* (1985), vol. I, pp. 339–42.
2. Karl Rahner, 'The Immaculate Conception' in *Theological Investigations* vol. 1, trans. Cornelius Ernst (1974), p. 203.
3. Karl Rahner, *Mary, Mother of the Lord*, trans. W. J. O'Hara (1963), p. 13.
4. Rahner, 'The Immaculate Conception', p. 203.
5. Rahner, 'The Immaculate Conception', p. 204.
6. Lossky, *The Mystical Theology of the Eastern Church*, p. 141.
7. Rahner, 'The Immaculate Conception', p. 203.
8. Lossky, *The Mystical Theology of the Eastern Church*, p. 141.
9. Edward Schillebeeckx, *Mary, Mother of the Redemption*, trans. N. D. Smith (1964), p. 54; Frederick M. Jelly, *Madonna: Mary in the Catholic Tradition* (1986), p. 116; Joseph Cardinal Ratzinger, *Daughter Zion: Meditations on the Church's Marian Belief*, trans. John H. McDermott (1983), p. 70.
10. Giovanni Miegge, *The Virgin Mary: The Roman Catholic Marian Doctrine*, trans. Waldo Smith (1955), p. 31.
11. Miegge, *The Virgin Mary: The Roman Catholic Marian Doctrine*, p. 162. The 'classical' Catholic position on this question allows that Mary exercised her free will in consenting to be Christ's mother, but holds that since the

112

RATIONALIZATION OF WESTERN CIVILIZATION

Incarnation was predestined by God, she would not in fact have refused the angel's gracious request. Mary is said to exercise *consensual* free will, but not *causal* free will. That is, she freely accepts what God has predestined, but precisely because the conception of Christ is predestined, Mary's free choice (unlike most other free choices) cannot properly be considered to be the cause of its consequence.

12. Karl Barth, *Church Dogmatics* I:2, trans. G.T. Thomson and Harold Knight (1956), p. 140.
13. Barth, *Church Dogmatics* I:2, p. 143.
14. Barth, *Church Dogmatics* I:2, p. 140.
15. See Chapter 4.
16. Michael O'Carroll, *Theotokos: A Theological Encyclopedia of the Blessed Virgin Mary* (1982), pp. 337–8.
17. Graef gives an interesting insight into the nature of this speculation in her account of an exchange between the ninth-century German theologians Paschasius Radbert and his pupil Ratrumnus (*Mary: A History of Doctrine and Devotion* vol. I, pp. 176–7). Paschasius considers that full goodness can exist only where the effects of the Fall have been completely eliminated, whereas Ratrumnus argues that all creation retains its essentially good character. Both, however, associate Mary with the goodness of God's original creation.
18. A synopsis of these, with references, is given in Mary Clayton, *The Cult of the Virgin Mary in Anglo-Saxon England* (1990), pp. 6–11. Examples are given in J. K. Elliott (ed.), *The Apocryphal New Testament* (1993), pp. 691–723.
19. *AAS* 42, II, 17 (1950, pp. 753–73).
20. This is in contrast to the iconography of the East and earlier Western art, in which the Dormition is depicted in the form of Christ receiving Mary's soul as it leaves her body.
21. The different teachings on the Assumption are presented in detail in Martin Jugie, *La Mort et l'Assomption de la Sainte Vierge: Etude historico-doctrinale* (1944).
22. Some apocryphal accounts claimed that her body remained in the tomb for three days, as Christ's had done. This remained a common belief, being taught, for example, by John Damascene ('Homilies on the Dormition' II:14; Greek text in *Homélies sur la Nativité et la Dormition*, ed. and French trans. Pierre Voulet (1961), pp. 156 and 157; English translation in *On the Dormition of Mary: Early Patristic Homilies* trans. Brian E. Daley (1998), p. 217). Peter Abelard, on the other had, taught that Mary's body was placed immediately in paradise and was resurrected from there (Graef, *Mary: A History of Doctrine and Devotion* vol. I, pp. 233–4).
23. O'Carroll, *Theotokos*, pp. 117–18.
24. Marina Warner, *Alone of All Her Sex: The Myth and the Cult of the Virgin*

Mary (1978), pp. 97–102. The modern Roman collects for the feast of the Assumption imply two reasons: one is that she was the bearer of God incarnate, and the other that she was sinless.

25. Karl Rahner, 'Le principe fondamental de la théologie Mariale', *Recherches de Science Religieuse* 42 (1954), pp. 499, 511.

26. A fuller account of the use of these texts is given in Chapter 4.

27. This may be implied in the lines of the *Exsultet*, from the liturgy of the Easter Vigil, which refer to the *necessarium Adae peccatum* ('necessary sin of Adam') and the *felix culpa* ('happy fault') which have merited our salvation. Likewise, the medieval English song '*Adam lay ybounden*' describes as 'blessed' the time when Adam took the apple, since without this action Our Lady would never have been the Queen of Heaven.

28. 'Prayer to St Mary (3)', lines 184–201, in *The Prayers and Meditations of St Anselm*, trans. Benedicta Ward (1973), pp. 120–1.

29. 'Prayer to St Mary (3)', lines 118–23, p. 118.

30. Irenaeus, *Proof of the Apostolic Preaching*, trans. Joseph P. Smith (1952), p. 68.

31. Tertullian, *Adversus Judaeos* 13, in *PL* 2:635A. Translation from Leonard W. Moss and Stephen C. Cappanari, 'In quest of the Black Virgin: she is black because she is black', in James J. Preston (ed.), *Mother Worship: Themes and Variations* (1982), p. 63.

32. Cited in O'Carroll, *Theotokos* p. 133.

33. Cited in Robert Murray, *Symbols of Church and Kingdom: A Study in Early Syriac Tradition* (1977), p. 145.

34. *Revelations* V, 12:13, in *Birgitta of Sweden: Life and Selected Revelations*, trans. Albert Ryle Kezel (1990), p. 129. Albert Ryle Kezel observes that there was a 'traditional practice of interpreting many instances of *terra*, 'earth', in the OT as mystical references to the Mother of God' (p. 262).

35. Mary of Agreda, *Mystical City of God*, trans. F. Marison [i.e., G. J. Blatter] (1914), 1, XV:219, p. 179.

36. Mary of Agreda, *The Mystical City of God* 1, XV:220, p. 179.

37. Mary of Agreda, *The Mystical City of God* 1, XV:220, p. 180.

38. Mary of Agreda, *The Mystical City of God* 1, XV:221 p. 180. The reference to Moses alludes to the belief that he was the author of the Pentateuch, the first five books of the Bible.

39. Ethelbert Stauffer, *New Testament Theology*, trans. John Marsh (1955), p. 118.

40. Miegge, *The Virgin Mary*, p. 30.

41. René Laurentin, *Court Traité sur la Vierge Marie* (1968), pp. 137–8 (my own translation).

42. Raymond Brown, *The Birth of the Messiah: A Commentary on the Infancy Narratives in Matthew and Luke* (1993), p. 298.

43. Brown, *The Birth of the Messiah*, p. 299.

44. Brown, *The Birth of the Messiah*, p. 314.
45. Brown, *The Birth of the Messiah*, p. 314.
46. From 'O Splendidissima Gemma', *Scivias* III. 13.1. The Latin text is given in Barbara Newman, *Sister of Wisdom: St Hildegard's Theology of the Feminine* (1987), p. 275. I have quoted a slightly amended version of her translation (p. 163). A freer English translation is given in Hildegard of Bingen, *Scivias*, trans. Columba Hart and Jane Bishop (1990), p. 525.
47. Rupert of Deutz, *De Glorificatione Trinitatis* IX.6, in *PL* 169:186D; trans. Newman, *St Hildegard's Theology of the Feminine*, pp. 190–1.
48. Newman, *St Hildegard's Theology of the Feminine*, p. 191, trans. from *Epistula* 47, *PL* 197:238B.
49. Lothar Heiser, *Maria in der Christus-Verkündigung des orthodoxen Kirchen-jahres* (1981), p. 119 (my own translation).
50. See, for example, Alan Watts, *Myth and Ritual in Christianity* (1954), pp. 104, 107 and 113; or the anonymously written *Meditations on the Tarot: A Journey into Christian Hermeticism* (1985), pp. 30–1.
51. E.g. Sara Maitland, *A Map of the New Country: Women and Christianity* (1983); Rosemary Radford Ruether, *Sexism and God-Talk: Towards a Feminist Theology* (1983); Helen Weinreich-Haste, 'Brother Sun, Sister Moon: does rationality overcome a dualistic world view?' in Jan Harding (ed.), *Perspectives on Gender and Science* (1986); Elaine Graham, *Making the Difference: Gender, Personhood and Theology* (1995).
52. Simone de Beauvoir, *Le Deuxième Sexe* I: *Les Faits et les Mythes* (1949), pp. 15–17. Drawing upon the work of the anthropologist Lévi-Strauss, de Beauvoir considers that the conceptual rendering of phenomena as pairs of opposites is basic to human consciousness: that the category of 'the Other' is as fundamental as consciousness itself. This view is treated critically in the present work.
53. Relevant studies of non-Christian religions include Peggy Reeves Sanday, *Female Power and Male Dominance: On the Origins of Sexual Inequality*, (1981) and S. G. F. Brandon, *Creation Legends of the Ancient Near East* (1963). Their work indicates that in creation myths in which the creator – or one of the creators – is female, she is typically immanent in the earth or water which is the natural environment of the people who tell the story. Male creators, although sometimes immanent in the immediate surroundings, are more likely to be regarded as coming from outside the group concerned – from the sky, or from some external earthly location, for example. Furthermore, this difference in the location of creators according to gender corresponds to a difference in the mode of creation that is attributed to them. Creation from goddesses is frequently through giving birth, while creation from gods can be through physical generation, speech or artistic creation.

In Christianity, since God is without limitation, he cannot be

115

adequately conceptualized in any of these ways; but it is important to understand what is signified by the ways in which Christians have attempted to represent him, and to be constantly critical of the ways in which we continue to do so.

54. G. L. Lloyd, *The Man of Reason: 'Male' and 'Female' in Western Philosophy* (1984); Ian Maclean, *The Renaissance Notion of Woman: A Study in the Fortunes of Scholasticism and Medical Science in European Intellectual Life* (1983), pp. 2–3 and 8; Mary Daly, *The Church and the Second Sex* (1968), pp. 43 and 48.

55. Maclean, *The Renaissance Notion of Woman*, pp. 22, 53–4 and 57–8; St Thomas Aquinas, *Summa Theologiae*, trans. Order of Preachers, 2a2ae Q.26. Art.10; vol. 32 (1963), p. 149. Women are sometimes said to be especially gentle or devout (e.g. Aquinas, *Summa* 2a2ae Q.82. Art.3.3; vol. 39 (1964), pp. 40–1), and this is usually regarded as praiseworthy.

56. Using both ancient and modern sources, Robert Hannaford has argued that the concept of 'person' in Western philosophy and theology is implicitly bound to notions of what it is to be masculine, so that there is always a bias towards excluding women from being considered as full persons ('Women and the human paradigm: an exploration of gender discrimination', *New Blackfriars* vol. 70, no. 827 (May 1989), pp. 226–33). Since Christians refer to God in terms which are largely personal, there is likely to be a corresponding tendency to speak of God in language which suggests masculine rather than feminine attributes.

57. Aquinas, *Summa* 1a Q.93. Art.3; vol. 13 (1963), p. 57.

58. Aquinas, *Summa* 1a Q.93. Art.5; vol. 13 (1963), p. 61. He states elsewhere that humanity's life is directed towards a more noble function than that of the lower animals, who are concerned primarily with procreation, and this nobler function is that of 'understanding things' (*intellegere*). However, within the human species itself, the female is 'directed to the work of procreation' (*femina . . . ad opus generationis ordinata*) (1a Q.92. Art.1; vol. 13 (1963), p. 37). Woman is thus implicitly accorded a place closer to the 'lower' animals than man is.

59. Aquinas, *Summa* 1a Q.15. Art.3; vol. 8 (1963), p. 71. Prime matter 'of itself is potential except in so far as it is brought to actuality by the form' (Q.14. Art.2, p. 11). See also Q.16. Art.7, p. 95; and p. 131.

60. Aquinas, *Summa* 1a Q.14. Art.11; vol. 4 (1963), p. 41. Aquinas notes here that although prime matter is 'far removed from likeness to God', the fact that it has being in any sense at all means that it retains a certain similarity to God's own existence.

61. Aquinas, *Summa* 2a2ae Q.26. Art.10; vol. 32 (1963), p. 149. The human father does not create the form of the rational soul, and to that extent he performs a task which is not analogous to God's own act of creation. But the father supplies the formative power which enables the matter of the

body to receive the soul from God, and he thus acts as God's agent in a more direct manner than the mother does.

62. Quoted in Etienne Gilson, *History of Christian Philosophy in the Middle Ages*, (1980) p. 296.

63. Gilson, *History of Christian Philosophy in the Middle Ages*, p. 298.

64. The image of God as spouse or lover of an aspect of his creation is one which occurs in the Old Testament, where the bride is Israel, in the New Testament, where the groom is Christ and the bride is the Church, and in much devotional writing, where the bride is sometimes the human soul. As a general rule, figurative motifs such as these cannot constitute a basis for dogma.

65. However, it does not tell us why God and creation should have gender attributed to them in the first place. This will be discussed in Chapter 5.

66. For a fairly recent account of the relationship between nature and grace in Christian theology, see Juan Alfaro, 'Nature: the theological concept' in K. Rahner, C. Ernst and K. Smyth (eds), *Sacramentum Mundi: An Encyclopedia of Theology* (1968–70) vol. 4, pp. 172–5.

67. Examples of such practices are given in Robert Whiting, *The Blind Devotion of the People: Popular Religion and the English Reformation* (1989).

68. On the importance of religion in the craft guilds, see Richard Mackenney, *Tradesmen and Traders: The World of the Guilds in Venice and Europe, c.1250–c.1650* (1987).

69. Caroline Walker Bynum, *Fragmentation and Redemption: Essays on Gender and The Human Body in Medieval Religion* (1991), pp. 171–5.

70. Examples of Calvinist attitudes towards related subjects are given in Phyllis Mack Crew, *Calvinist Preaching and Iconoclasm in the Netherlands: 1544–1569* (1978).

71. Examples of natural phenomena being regarded as divine omens in early modern England are given in Keith Thomas, *Religion and the Decline of Magic: Studies in Popular Beliefs in Sixteenth- and Seventeenth-Century England* (1978), pp. 103–11.

72. Thomas, *Religion and the Decline of Magic*, pp. 58–62.

73. Gary B. Deason, 'Reformation theology and the mechanistic conception of nature' in David C. Lindberg and Ronald H. Numbers (eds), *God and Nature: Historical Essays on the Encounter between Christianity and Science* (1986), p. 168.

74. Evelyn Fox Keller, 'Secrets of God, nature, and life' in *Secrets of Life, Secrets of Death: Essays on Language, Gender and Science* (1992), p. 56.

75. Keller, 'Secrets of God, nature, and life', p. 57.

76. Keller, 'Secrets of God, nature, and life', pp. 57–8. However, Keller's picture of the main lines of development in the rhetoric of seventeenth-century science needs to be qualified by considerations such as that advanced by Deason, who argues that although Newton considered

matter of itself to be entirely passive, he equally believed God to be omnipresent: 'In him are all things contained and moved' ('Reformation theology and the mechanistic conception of nature', p. 184).

77. Bynum, *Fragmentation and Redemption*, p. 151. Relevant bibliography given on p. 356.
78. Carolyn Merchant, *The Death of Nature* (1982).
79. Pliny (the Elder), *Natural History* trans. H. Rackham (1938), 2, 63 vol. I, pp. 288–95.
80. Merchant, *The Death of Nature*, pp. 30–4.
81. Merchant, *The Death of Nature*, pp. 29–41.
82. The writing of Francis Bacon is often cited in this context (e.g., Merchant, *The Death of Nature*, pp. 168–72). A more subtle consideration of Bacon's use of sexual imagery is given in Evelyn Fox Keller, *Reflections on Gender and Science* (1985), pp. 33–42.
83. Evelyn Fox Keller, *Reflections on Gender and Science* (1985), pp. 43–65.
84. Ludmilla Jordanova, 'Natural facts: a historical perspective on science and sexuality' in Carol P. MacCormack and Marilyn Strathern (eds), *Nature, Culture and Gender* (1980), p. 45.
85. Jordanova, 'Natural facts', pp. 50–63.
86. Thomas Laqueur, *Making Sex: Body and Gender from the Greeks to Freud* (1990).
87. Bynum, *Fragmentation and Redemption*, p. 221.
88. Joan Cadden, *Meanings of Sex Difference in the Middle Ages: Medicine, Science, and Culture* (1993), p. 3 and *passim*.
89. Ludmilla Jordanova, *Sexual Visions: Images of Gender in Science and Medicine between the Eighteenth and Twentieth Centuries* (1989), pp. 60–1.
90. Jordanova, *Sexual Visions*, pp. 43–58.
91. Londa Schiebinger, 'Skeletons in the closet: the first illustrations of the female skeleton in eighteenth-century anatomy' in C. Gallagher and T. Laqueur (eds), *The Making of the Modern Body: Sexuality and Society in the Nineteenth Century* (1987), p. 72.
92. Ornella Moscucci, *The Science of Woman: Gynaecology and Gender in England, 1800–1929* (1990), p. 28.
93. Moscucci, *The Science of Woman*, pp. 3–4, 36–41.
94. Brian Easlea, *Fathering the Unthinkable: Masculinity, Scientists and the Nuclear Arms Race* (1983), p. 171.
95. Easlea, *Fathering the Unthinkable*, p 172.
96. Easlea, *Fathering the Unthinkable*, p. 5 and *passim*. Evelyn Fox Keller has also examined the science of nuclear warfare in relation to gender: 'From secrets of life to secrets of death' in *Secrets of Life, Secrets of Death*, pp. 39–55.
97. See, for example, John James, *Chartres: The Masons who Built a Legend* (1982).

98. Some authors claim that it was brought in from Muslim Africa. It is also possible that the engineering advantages of the pointed arch were discovered from the crossing of arches in Romanesque buildings.

99. Lynn White, Jr, 'Cultural climates and technological advance in the Middle Ages' in *Medieval Religion and Technology: Collected Essays* (1978), pp. 230–3.

100. Jean Gimpel, *The Cathedral Builders*, trans. Teresa Waugh (1983), p. 32.

101. Jean Gimpel, *The Medieval Machine: the Industrial Revolution of the Middle Ages* (1977); Edward J. Kealey, *Harvesting the Air: Windmill Pioneers in Twelfth-Century England* (1989).

102. M.-D. Chenu, 'Nature and man: the Renaissance of the twelfth century' in *Nature, Man and Society in the Twelfth Century: Essays on New Theological Perspectives in the Latin West*, trans. and ed. Jerome Taylor and Lester K. Little (1968), p. 38.

103. D. L. D'Avray, *The Preaching of the Friars: Sermons Diffused from Paris before 1300* (1985), p. 6.

104. Chenu, 'Nature and man', p. 5.

105. Caroline Walker Bynum points out that twelfth-century critics of relics and miracles were not necessarily concerned with 'methods of research and authentication', but had in mind pious considerations of a distinctively medieval type (*Fragmentation and Redemption*, pp. 11–12). All the same, the fact that demands for more rational authentication were being made at all, whatever the motivation for such demands, does suggest that this was one of the points of the dawning of a modern materialist criticism.

106. Chenu, 'Nature and man', p. 34.

107. Chenu, 'Nature and man', pp. 10–11.

108. Chenu, 'Nature and man', p. 14.

109. Chenu, 'Nature and man', pp. 5–8.

110. See E. Rozanne Elder (ed.), *From Cloister to Classroom: Monastic and Scholastic Approaches to Truth* (1986).

111. Lynn White, 'Natural science and naturalistic art in the Middle Ages' in *Medieval Religion and Technology*, pp. 38–9.

112. White, 'Natural science and naturalistic art in the Middle Ages' pp. 31 and 23–41 *passim*. White draws heavily upon Jalabert's paper, 'La flore gothique: ses origines, son évolution du XIIe au XVe siècle', *Bulletin Monumental* XCI (1932), pp. 181–246. He also makes extensive use of Emile Mâle's *The Gothic Image: Religious Art of France in the Thirteenth Century*, trans. Dora Hussey (1972).

113. For an account of the concept of domination, see the Appendix.

114. Weber distinguished between 'instrumental rationality' (Zweckrationalität) and 'value rationality' (Wertrationalität). The former is concerned with the calculation of means for the attainment of goals, while the latter

119

is based upon concern for some value (e.g. an ethical one) for its own sake (*Economy and Society*, trans. Guenther Roth *et al.* [1968, from German ed. 1964] (1978), vol. 1, pp. 24–5). Weber uses the term 'rationalism' in a rather general manner, to refer to the application (usually frequent or habitual) of rational principles to social action, and to the practical consequences of that application. In practice, Weber's writing on rationalism is more concerned with instrumental rationality than with value rationality, so that the former often becomes rationality *tout court*.

The Frankfurt School's critique of rationalism in modern society, which influences my own analysis of the development of the cult of the Virgin Mary, could be characterized as a critique of domination by instrumental rationality, made from the standpoint of value rationality.

115. Gimpel, *The Cathedral Builders*, p. 70.
116. Max Weber, 'Science as a vocation', trans. Michael John (German original 1922), in Peter Lassman *et al.*, *Max Weber's 'Science as a Vocation'* (1989), pp. 13–14; *From Max Weber: Essays in Sociology*, trans. H. H. Gerth and C. Wright Mills (1970), pp. 350–1.
117. Wolfgang Schluchter, *Rationalism, Religion, and Domination: A Weberian Perspective*, trans. Neil Solomon (1989), p. 360.
118. Weber, 'Science as a vocation', p. 31.
119. Weber conducted a detailed study of the character of monotheistic religion and its origins in Hebrew religion, in *Ancient Judaism*, trans. H. H. Gerth and D. Martindale (1952). A more recent rendering of the material is given in Irving Zeitlin, *Ancient Judaism* (1984), pp. 1–35.
120. Lynn White, 'The Crusades and the technological thrust of the West' in *Medieval Religion and Technology*, pp. 277–96.
121. White, 'The Crusades and the technological thrust of the West', p. 294.
122. Lester K. Little, *Religious Poverty and the Profit Economy in Medieval Europe* (1978) pp. 42–9; White, 'The Crusades and the technological thrust of the West', p. 295; Jacques Le Goff, *The Birth of Purgatory* (trans. Arthur Goldhammer (1984), pp. 1–4 and *passim*.
123. White, 'The Crusades and the technological thrust of the West', p. 295.
124. R. I. Moore cites cases in which charges of witchcraft were successfully prosecuted in the tenth century. However, he also notes instances in which church authorities between the tenth and twelfth centuries were inclined to regard beliefs in witchcraft as 'superstitious' and therefore unworthy of Christians (*The Formation of a Persecuting Society: Power and Deviance in Western Europe, 950–1250* (1987), pp. 140–1). In general, Moore creates the impression that the growth of persecution during this period was aimed most strongly at Jews and heretics, although it also affected other groups, such as 'witches' and 'sodomites'.
125. White, 'The Crusades and the technological thrust of the West', p. 295.

126. Lynn White, Jr, 'The agricultural revolution of the early Middle Ages' in *Medieval Technology and Social Change* (1962), pp. 39–78. White's thesis is a revision of one previously put forward by Marc Bloch. The essay has been severely criticized for ignoring contradictory evidence in an attempt to reduce a great range of social and economic developments to a single factor (see Peter C. Perdue, 'Technological determinism in agrarian societies' in Merritt Roe Smith and Leo Marx (eds), *Does Technology Drive History? The Dilemma of Technological Determinism* (1994), pp. 169–200, esp. 174–9). However, White's later work takes account of other factors contributing to the evolution of Western European technology and wider culture, and some of these considerations are included in Chapter 5.

127. White, 'The agricultural revolution of the early Middle Ages', p. 52.

128. Lynn White, 'The life of the silent majority' in *Medieval Religion and Technology*, p. 145. In Durkheimian terms, White seems to be describing a transition from mechanical to organic solidarity.

129. White, 'The agricultural revolution of the early Middle Ages', pp. 56–7, 69; 'Cultural climates and technological advance in the Middle Ages', pp. 250–1; James Carson Webster, *The Labors of the Months in Antique and Mediaeval Art: To the End of the Twelfth Century* (1970), p. 36 and *passim*.

130. White, 'Cultural climates and technological advance in the Middle Ages', p. 251.

131. White, 'The agricultural revolution of the early Middle Ages', p. 75.

132. White, 'The Crusades and the technological thrust of the West', p. 296. White observes that the highest level of development in the new method of exploiting the soil was to be found in the area between the Channel and the Rhine, and that it was in this very region that the project of the Crusades had its origin.

133. Errol E. Harris, 'Science and nature', in George F. McLean and Hugo Meynell (eds), *Person and Nature* (1988), p. 25.

134. E.g. in the famous thirteenth-century French illumination showing God 'setting his compasses upon the face of the deep', in the National-bibliothek, Vienna; reproduced in Gimpel, *The Cathedral Builders*, facing p. 76.

135. Keith Thomas writes that in England in the early modern period, 'some species were especially venerated, for not all the world was available for uninhibited exploitation' (*Man and the Natural World: Changing Attitudes in England 1500–1800* (1984), p. 76).

136. According to the biologist Robert Haynes, 'we have good reason to be humble because our brains are so constructed that limits exist to the scientific understanding of man and of nature' ('The 'purpose' of chance in light of the physical basis of evolution' in John M. Robson (ed.), *Origin and Evolution of the Universe: Evidence for Design?* (1987), pp. 25, 31 n. 66).

137. This is contra the currently more common line of argument, which maintains that humanity's displacement from the physical centre of the universe constituted a removal from every kind of centrality. See, for example the Foreword by the physicist John Barrow to John Barrow and Frank Tipler, *The Anthropic Cosmological Principle* (1987). But as the astronomer Brandon Carter has observed, it does not follow from Copernicus' heliocentrism that humanity's position in the universe 'cannot be privileged in any sense' ('Large number coincidences and the anthropic principle in cosmology' in M. S. Longair (ed.), *Confrontation of Cosmological Theories with Observational Data* (1974), p. 291). In Chapter 2 of *The Anthropic Cosmological Principle*, Barrow and Tipler themselves draw the helpful distinction between 'world-view' and 'world-model'. My contention is that although modern science has not worked with an anthropocentric world-model, it assumes a strongly anthropocentric world-view.

Evelyn Fox Keller describes the way in which Robert Boyle gave humanity (but men in particular) a more elevated position with regard to 'nature', by denying that nature was living and active while simultaneously associating the human mind more closely with God ('Secrets of God, nature, and life', pp. 62–7).

4

⌒⌒⌒⌒⌒

From heaven restored to the devil defied: Mary's Immaculate Conception

The doctrine of Mary's Immaculate Conception is the teaching that she was conceived without original sin, and the story of the formulation and interpretation of this teaching is probably the most involved in the history of Christian dogma. Marina Warner has written: 'The ascetic strain in Catholic doctrine has struggled with its incarnational and life-affirming aspects for centuries', and when in 1854 the dogma of the Immaculate Conception was proclaimed an article of Catholic faith, 'a final blow for dualism was struck'.[1] But, leaving aside the question as to whether the 'ascetic' is really in opposition to the 'life-affirming', Warner's judgement is based on a partial reading of the evidence, which does not do justice to important defences of the doctrine or to its inherent capacity for a variety of interpretations.

In this chapter, I argue that there are certain ways in which the history of the doctrine of the Immaculate Conception follows a pattern similar to that described above in respect of Mary's motherhood. An earlier emphasis on Mary as Godbearer has given way to a focus on narrowly moral qualities. Likewise, the visual representation of Mary's conception was long ago denuded of images of physical human contact in favour of spiritual symbols. And theological interpretations of the Immaculate Conception, which were once concerned with the goodness of God and his creation, now more often present Mary as the exemplar of good, redeemed humanity in opposition to fallen nature. Yet these transformations have largely come about quite recently, and contrary understandings of the doctrine exist side by side.

Background

The story of Mary's conception is told in the so-called *Gospel of James*, or *Protevangelium*, which is thought to date from the second century.[2] It describes Mary's parents, Anne and Joachim, as righteous Jews who were distressed by the fact that they were childless. In her desolation, Anne cried out a prayer to God for the gift of a child, vowing that any child she bore in answer to this prayer would be consecrated to the Lord's service. The Lord heard her appeal, and while Joachim was tending his flocks in the fields, an angel appeared to him to announce that his wife would conceive a child. At the same time, an angel appeared to Anne in her house and delivered the same message. On hearing the news, Anne and Joachim both left their work, each running to find the other. They met at the Temple gate – which in other versions of the story is called the Golden Gate[3] – and embraced one another there. The couple then returned home, and nine months later Anne gave birth to a daughter, Mary. This story was the focus of the earliest liturgical feast in honour of Mary's conception, and scenes from it became standard features of the devotional art of the Middle Ages and Renaissance.

A celebration of St Anne's conception of the Virgin seems to have been celebrated first in the Eastern Church, at the end of the seventh century.[4] It is possible that there was a feast of Mary's Conception in eighth-century Ireland, but the earliest well-attested record of such a celebration in the West comes from England during the early eleventh century, when it was kept on 8 December, that is, nine months before Mary's birthday on 8 September.[5] After the Norman Conquest the feast of Mary's Conception was suppressed, and it was in protest against this suppression that the first thorough account of the doctrine of Mary's Immaculate Conception was expounded.

From the early centuries of Christianity it was widely believed that Mary never committed any actual sins during her life, and this became the Church's universal teaching. However, the doctrine of the Immaculate Conception states that even at the first moment of her existence, Mary was free of the condition of original sin which is the inheritance of humanity in general. Since the fifth century, the Western Church had considered the doctrine of original sin to be orthodox teaching. In most traditional accounts, original sin is the wickedness to which all humanity has been subject since Adam and Eve's fall from grace. It is a condition which affects everyone from the moment of conception, regardless of what actual sins they may or may not commit during their lifetime; but it is washed away by the waters of baptism, since baptism accomplishes the remission of all sins.

The doctrine's great champion was Augustine of Hippo (354–430), who taught that original sin was transmitted through sexual intercourse and was connected to the lust which necessarily accompanies sexual union.[6] Only Christ was free of original sin: and he, of course, was conceived without sexual intercourse. Augustine taught that human passions should always be ordered by the faculty of reason, and that reason in turn should be subordinated to the will of God. For Augustine, it is the irrational and uncontrollable nature of sexual desire which is its sinful aspect. He noticed that even in people who had been baptized, feelings of sexual lust and other inclinations towards sin remained present. From this, Augustine concluded that the general tendency to sin, known as *concupiscence*, was a vestige of original sin which baptism did not remove.

Yet Augustine's principal intention was not to denigrate the human condition but to emphasize that men and women are totally dependent upon God for their salvation. In particular, he attacked the doctrine of Pelagius, an ascetic teacher who believed that human beings could accomplish their own salvation by the living of holy lives. Against this, Augustine taught that it is only the grace of God which can bestow salvation, and that the fallen, sinful condition of humanity (apart from the limitations of created beings in general) prevents men and women from achieving for themselves the redemption which that condition requires. The doctrine of original sin makes clear humanity's inability to save itself. Pelagius pointed out that the logic of Augustine's argument was that even the Blessed Virgin must once have been in a state of sin, yet piety demands that we confess her to have been sinless. In reply to this, Augustine made the non-committal assertion: 'Where sin is concerned, I wish to have no question with regard to Mary.'[7] Thus, right at the beginning of the Western Church's discussion of original sin, the doctrine seemed to be confronted with a difficulty in the case of the Lord's mother.

Although Western Christianity was rapidly converted to belief in original sin, not everyone accepted Augustine's theory that it was transmitted in the procreative seed. Most notably, a different view was advanced by Anselm (1033–1109), the great scholar and Archbishop of

Canterbury. He taught that original sin was the absence of the original justice with which the world was created: it is a lack of justice brought about by Adam's disobedience. The main consequence of original sin is that it impedes humanity's free will, giving the will a propensity towards evil. Therefore, argued Anselm, although the potential for original sin is present in everyone from conception, it does not take effect until a child has reached the age at which it should have the possibility of exercising free will. It was Anselm's understanding of original sin which came to be used as the foundation for intellectual defences of the Immaculate Conception.

The feast of the Conception and its defence

Discussion over Mary's freedom from original sin was initiated by liturgical practice, rather than by problems of theory. In general, Christians did not celebrate the saints' birthdays, but only their death days – that is, the day on which the saint was reborn into heaven. However, there were two exceptions to this, namely, St John the Baptist and the Blessed Virgin Mary, whose birthday had been celebrated in some places since the sixth century.[8] Since Christians could not celebrate the birthdays of people who were born in a state of sin, it was argued that these two, who in any case were pre-eminent among the saints, must have been sanctified (i.e., freed from sin) before birth. In the case of John the Baptist, this sanctification would have taken place at the time of the visitation of Mary to his mother Elizabeth, when the Holy Spirit came upon her and the child leapt in her womb (Luke 1:41). However, in the case of Mary there was disagreement and doubt about the time of her sanctification, and the majority of theologians did not favour the view that she was conceived without original sin. Yet, as we have already noted, a feast of Mary's conception was being celebrated in parts of the Western Church from at least the eleventh century.

The celebration of Mary's conception met with considerable opposition, and initially, the opponents' main objection was that since a normal human conception is sinful, to celebrate Mary's conception was to celebrate a sinful event. The most famous example of such an objection is the letter which St Bernard of Clairvaux wrote to the canons of Lyons Cathedral in 1125. The cathedral had started to observe the feast of the Conception, and Bernard wrote to express his surprise and

1. *Virgin in Majesty (wood, 12th cent.), Saulzet-le-Froid (Puy-de-Dôme).*
Editions Zodiaque, La-Pierre-qui-Vire

2. *Our Lady of Lourdes (statue in grotto)*. Doucet, Lourdes

3. *Virgin and Child (wall painting, early 13th cent.), St. Mary's Church, Great Canfield, Essex. Drawing by E. W. Tristram.* Victoria and Albert Museum, London

4. *The Virgin bares her breasts to Christ on the Day of Judgement (stained glass, 14th cent.) (detail), Tewkesbury Abbey, Gloucestershire. Photo:* Catherine Oakes

5. *La Vierge à l'Oiseau (14th cent.), Church of Le Marthuret, Riom (Puy-de-Dôme).*
Photo: Editions du Lys, Clermont-Ferrand

6. *St Anne and St Joachim embrace at the Golden Gate, from Officium Beatae Mariae Virginis (Antwerp: Plantin-Moretus, 1662, p. 22).* Ushaw College, Durham

7. *The Immaculate Conception (Diego Velázquez, 1599-1660).* The National
Gallery, London

8. *The Virgin* tota pulchra, *from a Sarum Missal (Paris: Regnault, 1526). Woodcut for the feast of the Virgin's Conception (fo. iii v in section containing the Proper of Saints).* Ushaw College, Durham

9. *The Medal of the Immaculate Conception,* or the *Miraculous Medal.* Pierre Bizet, Paris

disapproval at this innovation. In this letter he asks rhetorically, 'How indeed was sin not present where lust was not absent?'[9]

This seems to have been the theological content of the Norman church's objection to the feast of the Conception in Anglo-Saxon England. Eadmer of Canterbury (1060/64–1141), a former pupil of St Anselm, wrote a treatise against the suppression of the feast. It is entitled *Tractate on the Conception of Saint Mary*,[10] and argues that it is legitimate to observe the feast of the Virgin's conception because she was conceived without original sin. Thus, the first thorough apologia for the belief that Mary's conception was immaculate (i.e., 'without stain') seems to have been written out of a desire to defend a liturgical celebration whose origin lay in devotion rather than Marian doctrine.

The structure of Eadmer's argument is important because it was followed by subsequent proponents of the teaching. It falls into three parts. Eadmer wants to show, first, that an immaculate conception is possible in principle. To do this he uses an analogy which corresponds to Anselm's understanding of original sin. He gives the example of a chestnut tree. Its seed is a thorny shell surrounded by thickest prickles. Yet the centre is a milky liquid, and the chestnut which eventually bursts out is without any thorns.[11] And this, he suggests, is the sort of thing we mean when we say that Mary is conceived without original sin: like the unharmed chestnut in its prickly covering, Mary is sinless in a world overrun with the sin of Adam.

However, the fact that an immaculate conception is possible does not demonstrate that God would ever have wanted to bring about such a thing, and hence does not show that he would have done it for Mary. So the second part of Eadmer's argument is to show that God would have wanted Mary to be preserved from original sin. Eadmer starts from the point that Mary is the Mother of God. This is the greatest gift ever bestowed upon any creature, and God's wish to give her the highest of honours is seen also in the fact that he has made her mistress of the world and empress of the universe. From this, we can know that God does not wish to withhold from her any good thing that is possible, and consequently, he must have given her the gift of freedom from original sin. Furthermore, Eadmer argues, Mary is higher than the angels, who are not tainted with sin of any kind, and in this respect God would not wish to treat her less favourably than he treats them.

Now, for God to will something is the same as for him to accomplish it. As human beings, we may will something and not have the power to realize it; or we may will something which is evil, or may change our minds. But in the classical Christian understanding of God, none of these limitations applies to him. So if God willed that Mary should be immaculately conceived, then indeed she was. Thus, Eadmer's argument follows three stages: first, it addresses the question of *how* God could cause someone to be exempt from the sin of Adam, and thus tries to show that Mary's immaculate conception is *possible*; second, the argument deals with the question of *why* Mary would have been conceived without sin, and tries to show in what way such a conception would *accord with divine providence*; and from this the argument concludes that *God did it*.

The celebration of Mary's conception spread rapidly during the later Middle Ages, gradually gaining official recognition. This led to a reversal of the earlier situation: where Eadmer had defended the feast of the Conception with an argument for the event having been sinless, later authors who wrote in support of the Immaculate Conception would sometimes appeal to the practice of keeping the feast of the Conception as evidence for the sanctity of the event which was celebrated. For example, in 1436 the Spanish Franciscan John of Segovia submitted to the ecumenical Council of Basel a series of arguments in favour of the Immaculate Conception. Amongst these, he contended that

> the Church would not institute a celebration to solemnize a work of nature, but a heavenly miracle: not a sin, but grace. It is right to understand that in the Conception there is some mystery of a singular and heavenly virtue.[12]

The liturgical observance of Mary's conception thus added weight to the belief that the conception was sinless.

The fact that the doctrine was expounded in defence of the feast, and that the feast continued to spread in the face of strong theological objections, means that popular celebration was taking precedence over technical argument.

Duns Scotus's argument for the possibility of conception without sin

The most important theological objection to the doctrine of the Immaculate Conception had been raised by the Dominican Thomas

Aquinas (1225–74). He argued from the fact that Christ alone did not need to be redeemed, while all other children of Adam stand in need of salvation. Hence, Mary too must have been saved by Christ. Thomas argued that to be redeemed meant to be 'snatched from the devil's power', like a kingdom which has fallen into enemy hands and whose king wins it back by means of battle. Therefore, Mary must at some time have been within the power of the devil, i.e., in a state of sin. Since Mary did not commit any actual sins, the only sin from which she could be saved would be that which she inherited from her forebears. So if she was not tainted even by this, then she did not need Christ's salvific work, and he is not the universal Redeemer whom Christians believe him to be. Consequently, Thomas argued, Mary cannot have been conceived without original sin.[13] St Thomas's importance as a theologian in his own religious order had the consequence that his argument on this point carried much weight amongst Dominicans for several centuries.

Yet the Immaculate Conception did not lack intellectual proponents, and the theological defences of the doctrine reveal an understanding of the human condition which gives great weight to its capacity for goodness and salvation. Aquinas's opposition was contested early on by the English Franciscan William of Ware (d. *c.* 1305), who used the analogy of debt, rather than military capture, to understand the condition of bondage to sin. Following Augustine, William argued that there are two kinds of debt: that which is contracted and must be paid, and that which is not contracted when it could have been. The sinfulness of most of humanity means that they fall into the first of these two categories, while Mary, who was always sinless, falls into the second. Nevertheless, it is only the Passion of Christ which remits Mary's debt of sin before it is incurred.[14] This type of argument was followed by William's pupil, John Duns Scotus (1266–1308), who argued that preservation from sin is better than deliverance. Consequently, to claim that Mary was preserved from contracting original sin is to say not that she did not need to be redeemed, but on the contrary, that she was the object of Christ's most perfectly redemptive action. Thus, the doctrine of the Immaculate Conception teaches that Christ's salvific power reaches to the fullest possible extent.

When Duns Scotus defended the doctrine of Mary's Immaculate Conception, there was a second major objection which he addressed. It concerned the mechanism by which original sin is transmitted, and was a more detailed version of the Augustinian type of argument which had already been raised in the twelfth century. It went as follows: Mary's procreation by her parents came about through sexual intercourse, and was therefore subject to the law of sin which affects humanity in general since the fall of Adam. This means that her body must have been formed from contaminated seed from which her soul in turn would have been contaminated when it was infused into her body.[15]

I have mentioned above that arguments in favour of the Immaculate Conception depended upon an Anselmian doctrine of original sin. This was true of Scotus's argument for how a sinless conception would be possible, and it became a standard defence of the doctrine ever afterwards. The inheritance of Anselm, in its Franciscan transformation, indicates an important aspect of the Immaculists' spiritual orientation, namely, a strong conviction that the material world has the capacity for goodness and redemption. Contrary to those who thought that original sin was transmitted in the procreative seed, Anselm argued that the seed which generates new human life is intrinsically neither sinful nor meritorious. Rather, the absence of justice affects the human will, by weakening it, but does not have an immediate effect on any other part of the person. It is the will, not the seed, which is subject to sin. And the will pertains to the rational soul, and not to the body as such.[16] Before Duns Scotus it had been more commonly believed that sin resided in human flesh from conception and that the newly created soul was tainted with this sin when it was infused into the body some weeks later. Since the sin in the flesh was a consequence of the lust experienced during sexual intercourse, anyone conceived in the normal way – including Mary – was bound to inherit original sin. Anselm's teaching that the seed and the flesh were not intrinsically sinful broke this immediate connection between procreation and original sin, and made plausible the idea that a soul might be united to a seminally conceived body but nonetheless be saved from subjection to the guilt of Adam's offspring. Nevertheless, Anselm thought that it was not wrong to speak of someone being 'conceived in sin', not least because this is a phrase found in Scripture. This means that since the Fall, one's flesh is destined from conception to become part of a human being who will lack original justice. Sin is said to be present at conception because the necessity for future sin is carried in the seed.[17]

Duns Scotus points out that when a person is baptized, original sin is removed (i.e., the guilt of not possessing original justice is forgiven), but

130

the 'contamination of the flesh' (*infectio carnis*) remains as before, without reinfecting the soul. Consequently, it cannot be the case that the contamination of the flesh necessarily gives rise to a state of sin in the soul. For this to be the case, baptism would either have to remove the contamination of the flesh, or else not remove original sin permanently from the soul. The fact that it accomplishes the sanctification of the soul but not the purification of the flesh means that the former does not depend upon the latter. Therefore, God could have sanctified Mary's soul at the first moment of her conception notwithstanding the fact that she had been engendered by her parents in the natural way.[18] Duns Scotus thus uses an example taken from sacramental teaching to support Anselm's doctrine of original sin, in which moral qualities such as evil are located in the will, not in the seed.

Anselm himself had taught that natural procreation by the children of Adam always conferred upon the offspring the necessity for future sin. He argues that all things are made, or brought about, by one or more of three 'courses', namely, by the will of God, by nature, or by the will of a creature. The generation of humanity by procreation is a work of both nature and human will.[19] Furthermore, it is in the natural and wilful propagation of humanity that men and women pass on to their offspring the evils which Adam took upon himself when he rejected the good things that he had received from God. By contrast, the virginal conception of Christ was something which occurred only by the will of God, so the lack of original justice which afflicted the rest of Adam and Eve's offspring was not passed on to him.[20] Yet in contending that the physical creation could not of itself be sinful, Anselm had opened the route by which later theologians could argue that Mary's conception was immaculate as well as being the result of sexual intercourse. If sin pertained to the will – and thus to the soul – and not to the flesh, then there was no reason why God should not have sanctified Mary's soul at the moment of its creation and infusion into her body. This is what God did for John the Baptist in his mother's womb, and what he does for anyone at baptism: he did it for Mary at the moment of her soul's creation.

By thus making a separation between the moral and physical orders John Duns makes it possible, in the first place, not to maintain that the physical conception of a child is intrinsically evil, and in the second place, to show how Mary could have been preserved from original sin. In this way, the seed of procreation and the flesh which it engenders are freed from condemnation as evil, and gain the potential to be freed from any guilt of sin even in a post-lapsarian world. Furthermore, although Anselm had claimed that in principle Adam and Eve might have begotten sinless children through sexual intercourse, he believed that because of the Fall, the only people who had in fact been created without sin were those who had come into the world by means of a miracle (i.e., the will of God), and not because of nature and the will of a creature. John Duns, on the other hand, showed that even in a fallen world, a human being conceived through sexual union could be created sinless, and he offered Mary as the example in whom this possibility had been realized.

The Immaculists' 'weak' reading of original sin

Duns Scotus's defence of the Immaculate Conception expresses an optimistic understanding of humanity's, and the physical world's, capacity for goodness and redemption. It is not surprising that such a defence should have been proposed by a Franciscan, since the Franciscan way of life had at its heart a reverence for even the humblest aspects of the created order. Over the next few centuries, proponents of the Immaculate Conception continued to be men and women who held a strong belief in the goodness of God's creatures, and Franciscans were in several respects the most important promoters of the doctrine.

St Bridget of Sweden (1303–73), a relative of the Swedish monarch, was a lay member of the Franciscan order who received a great number of revelations – or visions – of Christ, the Virgin and other sacred figures. Her revelations were generally considered to be reliable and were sometimes cited by theologians as authoritative. On one occasion, the Mother of God spoke to her, saying:

> Supposing a man wishes to fast when he feels the desire to eat, but his will resists the desire; but he has already been told by a superior, to whom he owes obedience, that out of obedience he should eat, and he – out of obedience but against his own will – does eat. That eating would be worthy of greater reward than a fast would be. The union of my parents was like this when I was conceived. And on that account it is the truth that I was conceived without original sin, and not in sin; because just as my Son and I never sinned, so no marital union would be more honourable than that from which I came forth.[21]

This text may seem humorous to some modern readers, but it illuminates a point which is important for understanding the meaning of the Immaculate Conception to the doctrine's medieval protagonists. Firstly, the doctrine was spoken about in terms which expressed a belief that the physical creation could be the bearer of goodness and grace. Duns Scotus had rescued Mary's conception from the imputation of wickedness by separating the moral condition of her soul from the 'contamination of the flesh', or necessity for later sin, which was a consequence of her parents' act of natural procreation. The theological climate in which he was arguing would not have tolerated any suggestion that Anne and Joachim's union was in itself sinless, and such an argument would have been a hostage to fortune. St Bridget, on the other hand, does not have to dispute with learned antagonists, and she not only presents Mary's passive conception in the womb as sinless, but also sees the active union of Mary's parents as meritorious. Indeed, contrary to scholastic refinements, Bridget suggests that the sinlessness of Mary's conception was in some measure caused by the honourable character of her parents' union; and in making this connection she restores the natural integrity of procreative intercourse and conception which had been betrayed in the necessary subtlety of Duns Scotus's argument. Where Augustine had argued that both sexual intercourse and conception were in some measure sinful, Duns Scotus separated the two events, retaining a weakened notion of the sinfulness transmitted in procreation but making it possible that at least in one case the conception which resulted was sinless. Bridget, however, claims both that the parents' intercourse was honourable and that the child's conception was free of original sin.

What Bridget really implies is that the sexual union of Anne and Joachim was restored to the condition which would have pertained to sexual relations had humanity not fallen from grace. For they come together not because they are driven by desire (although that is something which they feel), but out of obedience to the will of God; so their pleasure now serves God's purpose, and nature is in harmony with grace.

Bridget's account suggests that the exemption from Adam's sin which applies to Mary is partially extended to her parents, and this seems to support an anxiety about the Immaculate Conception which was expressed by some of the doctrine's later opponents, to wit, that it was the thin end of the wedge. After all, if there is even one exception to the law of original sin, then already it is not universal, and who knows how far this undermining of the doctrine of humanity's inherent wickedness might go? One Protestant commentator, Giovanni Miegge – an opponent of the Immaculate Conception – observes: 'There is evidently a sort of elective affinity between this theory [Pelagianism] that reduces the seriousness of the original fall and the doctrine of the Immaculate Conception that wants to exempt Mary from it.'[22] And indeed, there is ample evidence that the medieval defenders of the Immaculate Conception held a rather low doctrine of original sin. This is a further indicator of the Immaculists' optimism about the condition of created beings.

One may be tempted to think that belief in Mary's unique sinlessness can be sustained only to the detriment of the rest of humanity, with whom she is contrasted. That is to say, one might think that if Mary is seen as being exempt from sin, then the sin of other people will appear to be correspondingly more serious, and the difference between Mary and the rest of humanity will be strongly emphasized. Yet evidence from the doctrine's medieval protagonists suggests the very opposite to be the case. William of Ware, for instance, argued that the feast of Mary's Conception should be celebrated even if she contracted original sin, because her flesh is the 'original principle' of the body of Christ.[23] Now, if William had held a 'high' doctrine of original sin – that is, if he had placed great emphasis on its severity – then the fact of original sin would have made it improper to celebrate Mary's conception, as St Bernard and others had already argued was the case. The fact that William is willing to promote the feast regardless of whether or not Mary's conception was sinless indicates that he takes a relatively light view of original sin. Yet the argument just cited follows on immediately from arguments in favour of the Immaculate Conception.

As we have seen, original sin was often defined as the absence of 'original justice' or 'original righteousness', which was the term for the condition of grace in which Adam and Eve lived before the Fall. During the early fourteenth century, there was discussion of this topic amongst Spanish Franciscans, in which most argued that men and women have an obligation to possess original justice, so that failure to do so constitutes a *sin* in the proper sense of the word. However, one of their number, William Rubio, considered that there was no obligation to possess original justice; and consequently, original sin is not properly called 'sin', but is rather the *poena damni* or 'penalty of the condemned'.[24] This seems to be a very weak reading of the doctrine of original sin; and Rubio, its proponent, was another defender of the Immaculate Conception.

The examples given above suggest that the intention of the medieval promoters of the Immaculate Conception was not to draw attention to humanity's sinfulness: on the contrary, this was a subject which they had relatively little interest in. Rather, they were concerned with the glorification of the Virgin and of God's generosity to her.

Mary's bodily conception

Defenders of the Immaculate Conception saw humanity as inherently capable of great goodness, and Mary as the human person in whom this capability was realized. Moreover, the commemoration of Mary's sinless beginning had as its object her body as well as her soul. The Immaculists stressed that what was being celebrated on the feast of the Conception was not only Mary's spiritual sanctification but her beginning as a human being, including her flesh. The Immaculate Conception's opponents, on the other hand, argued that where the Church approved the celebration of the Feast of the Conception, then the proper object of the celebration was the sanctification of Mary's soul in her mother's womb, and not her physical origin. The Immaculists rejected this. John of Segovia pointed out that the feast of 8 December is called the Conception, not the Sanctification. As with the Assumption, this feast must be concerned with the glorification of the body, and not with the soul alone:

> Since on that day in the church's office [i.e., the prescribed prayer for the hours of the day], and even in the homily from the Fathers, mention is made of the glorification of the body, so [the feast] cannot refer only to the sanctification.[25]

St Robert Bellarmine (1542–1621), the Jesuit cardinal, likewise referred to liturgical practice when he responded to the contention that it was Mary's sanctification, not her conception, which the Church celebrated. He observed that the term 'holy Conception' is used in the divine office, and wrote, 'but it is not a conception unless [it occurs] in the first instant, when the soul is infused in the body, when in the nature of things the Virgin's whole person began its existence'.[26]

135

Bellarmine thus argues that Mary's immaculate conception is the beginning of the unity of her body and soul.

Three centuries earlier, William of Ware had laid emphasis on the importance of Mary's bodily existence. His contention that Mary's flesh is the 'original principle' of the body of Christ, and its conception a cause for celebration, shows that William held Mary's physical conception in high esteem. When the eternal Word of God was 'made flesh', it was Mary's flesh that he took, and hence, her conception is the beginning of the flesh that will be united to God in the Incarnation. William's interest is in the physical connection between Mary's conception and the Incarnation of Christ.

The continuity between the Virgin's body and Christ's went on being alluded to in later defences of the Immaculate Conception. In one of the *Revelations* of St Bridget, God the Father tells her that Mary had been conceived without sin in order that the Son should be born without sin.[27] Elsewhere, the Blessed Virgin says to Bridget: '[The Son of God in me] came with honour, since all sin of Adam was separated from me. Whence the most honourable Son of God took on most honourable flesh.'[28]

An association between the Immaculate Conception and the Incarnation is expressed also in a poem on the Immaculate Conception by the English Jesuit Robert Southwell (1560–95). In 'The Conception of Our Ladie' he writes, 'Earth breedes a heaven for God's new dwelling-place.'

A similar association seems to underlie the vow taken by the Jesuit scholastic John Berchmans in 1621. He died in August of that year and was later canonized. The seventeenth century saw a great movement for the promotion of the Immaculate Conception to the status of official Catholic teaching, and it was not uncommon for the doctrine's protagonists to make dramatic gestures in support of their cause. After John Berchmans' death, a piece of paper was found on which he had written the following words:

> I, John Berchmans most unworthy son of the Society of Jesus, do declare before you and before your Son, whom I believe and confess to be here present in the most glorious sacrament of the Eucharist, that always and everywhere, in so far as a decision of the Church does not oppose it, I will profess and defend your Immaculate Conception. As testimony to this, I have signed in my own blood, and traced below, the sign of the Society of Jesus. The year 1621. John Berchmans, IHS.[29]

St John's vow points to the integrity of the various elements of his faith, and especially to the link between Mary's conception and the Incarnation. Mary's conception is the beginning of the soul who will freely accept Christ into the world for the world's salvation. And her conception is equally the beginning of the flesh which is eventually to be united with the eternal Word of God in Christ. It is this flesh of Christ which is again made real in the host on the altar, in whose presence St John wrote his profession of faith. Moreover, the letters IHS are the first three letters of Jesus' name in Greek, so that the sign of the Society of Jesus at the end of John Berchmans' declaration enhances the connection between Mary's conception and the Incarnation. The conception of the Virgin, the eucharistic host and the name of the incarnate Lord are all constituent parts of a single mystery whose unity can be traced to the conception of the Virgin: Christ's first earthly dwelling place, whose flesh and blood he took for his own.

It must be acknowledged that it is not always clear what kind of anthropology underlies the Immaculists' insistence that the feast of Mary's Conception refers to her body as well as her soul. Duns Scotus's demonstration of how an immaculate conception would be possible refers back to Anselm's teaching that sin resides in the will rather than the seed, and it may be that for some authors, this understanding was itself sufficient to legitimate the celebration of a bodily conception. But even for Anselm, the body of someone conceived through nature and human will carried a propensity for the flowering of sin in the soul to which it would be united; and the fact that some of the Immaculists, such as St Bridget, imply that there is a causal link between Mary's immaculate conception and the flesh from which the body of Christ is made, may suggest that some of the defenders of the doctrine believed that not only Mary's soul but also her body was sanctified. Certainly, some later authors, such as Jean-Jacques Olier (1608–57), believed both that original sin was transmitted in the flesh and that Mary was immaculately conceived.[30]

However, there is a defence of the Immaculate Conception which would be consistent with Duns Scotus's understanding and which would also explain why the doctrine's protagonists might have insisted that the immaculacy of Mary's conception included both body and soul. This argument holds that since the flesh of the incarnate Word was taken from the flesh of the Virgin, it is inconceivable that the Virgin's flesh would ever have been united to a soul contaminated by sin.[31] This might suppose an action which is the reverse of that described in the Augustinian view: it is not that the soul is contaminated by the flesh, but that the flesh may in some way be adversely affected by the soul. It seems probable that what underlies the argument is a notion of ritual pollution; that is to say, when something which is ritually clean comes into contact with something which is unclean, then that which is clean becomes contaminated. Since everything about Christ must be as holy (and therefore as clean) as possible, the flesh from which he is made must never have been bound to anything impure. It is true that the idea that the body of Christ might in principle be subject to pollution is one which has rarely been given house-room in Catholic theology; but Christian sentiment is not always congruent with academic argument.

In any event, what seems clear is that in the hands of its medieval and Renaissance promoters, the doctrine of the Immaculate Conception was concerned with the sanctification of Mary's whole humanity, including her flesh – flesh which in turn would be united to the Word of God in Christ.

Mary's predestination to divine motherhood

The Immaculists' optimistic understanding of the human condition can be seen in the further connection which they made between the Immaculate Conception and Mary's predestination to be Mother of God. In Chapter 1 we saw two ways of understanding the relationship of the Incarnation to human salvation. The first of these held that the world's salvation was accomplished in the Crucifixion and Resurrection of Christ, and that this was effective because he was both divine and human. The Incarnation was the necessary condition for the work of redemption. The second view did not deny the first, but added to it, stating that God was already redeeming the world in the act of taking flesh in Mary's womb. The Incarnation is not only a preparation for salvation but is itself salvific. Duns Scotus went beyond both these views, claiming that the Incarnation would have taken place even if Adam had never sinned – which is to say that although the Incarnation did indeed bring about the world's salvation, this was not the primary purpose for which it was ordained.

Duns Scotus taught that before the sin of Adam was foreseen, God intended that the Word should become flesh in Christ in order that human nature should be glorified.[32] Later Scotists argued that if God willed from eternity that the Word should take human flesh, then the woman from whom that flesh was to be taken must likewise have been predestined from eternity to be the Mother of God. Mary therefore shares in the predestination of Christ. Since Mary was predestined to her sacred office prior to Adam's fall, it was argued that her humanity was ordered in the first instance to her divine motherhood; so if the existence of original sin meant that there would be some tension between Mary's descent from Adam and her office as Mother of God, then – provided it was possible – the former must be subordinated to the latter.

I have described this Scotist understanding as 'optimistic' because it sees the Immaculate Conception as deriving in the first instance from God's intention to glorify human nature, and because it is tied to an anthropology which holds that the predestination to glory is prior to any human wickedness.

Holy Wisdom in the liturgy of the Conception

The association between Mary's predestination and her conception may have been influenced by the liturgy, which in most rites employed a Wisdom text as the lection, or first reading, for the Mass of the feast.

The Wisdom of God is portrayed in the Hebrew Scriptures as a female figure who is responsible for the right natural and moral order of the world (e.g., Proverbs 8). She calls men and women to live in accordance with God's Law; but she is also the one through whom God created the world from the beginning. It is through her that God accomplishes the right ordering of creation, and if men and women attend to her teachings then their own lives will likewise be properly ordered and in harmony even with the foundations of the universe. Similar texts occur in the Apocrypha – the Greek Old Testament books which are included in the Catholic canon of the Bible

In the New Testament and early Christian writings, Jesus Christ is identified with Wisdom (e.g. 1 Cor 1:24; 8:6), and in liturgy, Wisdom texts came to be used for the feasts of virgin saints, to suggest that they were 'wise virgins' who had kept their lamps burning for Christ the bridegroom.[33] Alcuin of York (d. 804), the great liturgist at the court of Charlemagne, seems to have been the first to introduce a Wisdom text into a liturgy for the Blessed Virgin Mary. He wrote two votive masses in the Virgin's honour, and in one of these he employed the text: 'From the beginning and before the ages I was created, and until the age to come I shall not cease to be' (Ecclesiasticus 24:14) (v.9 in Hebrew and English Bibles). It is not known why Alcuin used these words in a Marian mass. He seems to have had a great devotion to holy Wisdom and used Wisdom texts in a number of liturgies.[34] But whatever Alcuin's reason for this introduction, the innovation spread rapidly and widely. As early as 853, Haymon, Bishop of Halberstadt, preached on Ecclesiasticus 24:14 as applied to Mary. His homily explains that the Wisdom of God took flesh of the Virgin, but that it is not unsuitable to apply this text to the Mother of God herself, since the Wisdom of God was created from her, 'that through her the Son of God might be created without human concupiscence, to ransom human nature'.[35]

Ecclesiasticus 24:14–16 (9–12) came to be commonly used as the lection for the vigil mass of the Assumption, with other Wisdom texts being used in the liturgy and divine office for this and other Marian feast days. Of particular note is the inclusion of Proverbs 8:22–31 as the lection for the mass of the Virgin's Conception and that of her Birthday. In this passage, Wisdom speaks of having been present with God from before the creation of the world. It begins: 'The Lord possessed me at the beginning of his ways.' In verse 24, the RSV translation gives: 'When there were no depths I was brought forth.' But the Latin Vulgate version, which was used universally in the Latin rites of the Catholic Church, translates the Hebrew slightly differently, thus: 'When there were no depths, already was I conceived.' The choice of the word 'conceived' (concepta) made this text especially applicable to the feast of Mary's Conception, and after the Council of Trent (1545–63) it was the standard lection for both the Conception and Nativity of the Virgin. The Gospel for the same feasts was usually the genealogy of Christ from Matthew Chapter 1. In these readings there is scarcely any mention of sin. They give the impression of God's goodness being present in creation from the beginning, and of his plan being fulfilled in Christ through Mary

The iconography of Mary's Conception: changing interpretation

The motif of Mary's predestination was also taken up in the iconography of the Immaculate Conception. In this case, however, it eventually signified the undermining, more than the enhancing, of the sanctity of the flesh, although ambiguities of meaning can be detected throughout.

The medieval understanding of Mary's immaculate conception as a physical, and not purely a spiritual, event was expressed in the art as well as the theology of the period. The most common representation of the Virgin's conception showed her parents, Anne and Joachim, embracing at the Golden Gate (Plate 6). This did not necessarily indicate a conception without sin, and was acceptable to both the supporters and the opponents of the Immaculate Conception. Images which were expressly concerned with the conception's sinlessness included representations of St Anne with the Virgin visibly present in her womb; although here again, the image was sometimes used by those who believed that Mary was sanctified by the Holy Spirit after conception, rather than that she was conceived immaculately.

In the modern period, by contrast, and especially from the seventeenth century, the images of parental embrace and infant presence in the mother's womb have been supplanted by a type of image which is intended to represent a simply spiritual aspect of the Virgin's conception. This type of image shows the Virgin as a young girl standing alone, sometimes at prayer, sometimes treading on a serpent, sometimes standing on the moon, sometimes crowned with stars – but not in physical contact with another human being, although having some limited association with those aspects of the physical creation which appear alongside her (Plate 7). This iconography signifies that Mary was conceived in the mind of God before the foundation of the world, and associates her with the figure of Wisdom. The association of Mary with Wisdom shows that thoughts of the Mother of God permeated the Christian understanding of creation and redemption. But the image which alludes to Proverbs 8 bears many other connotations as well. Some of these carry an open reference to warfare within creation and associate Mary with the victorious side in its defeat of evil.

The representations of the Immaculate Conception by such artists as Diego Velázquez (1599–1660) and Bartolomé Esteban Murillo (1617/18–82) draw on older iconography. When Adam and Eve are expelled from Eden, God says to the serpent, 'I will put enmity between you and the woman, and between your seed and her seed; he shall bruise your head, and you shall bruise his heel' (Gen. 3:15). In Christian exegesis,

141

the woman and her seed had long been understood as the Virgin and Christ, crushing the devil in the person of the serpent.[36] In the Latin Vulgate, however, the second half of the prophecy was rendered: 'She will crush your head, and you will lie in wait for her heel.' Thus, in the usual Catholic reading it was the woman, rather than her seed, who would be at war with the serpent. So the verse was read as a prophecy principally concerning Mary: Mary is the second Eve, and by her the devil will be destroyed. In both art and theology, the motif of the woman trampling the serpent underfoot was applied to Mary's immaculate conception, since her freedom from sin was a sign of the devil's total defeat.

During the Counter-Reformation period, Catholic scholars addressed the question of the Latin Bible's mistranslation of the Hebrew, and argued that although the primary meaning of the text was that Christ, i.e., the woman's seed, would crush the serpent, nevertheless, since Christ imbues his saints – and pre-eminently his mother – with the grace to share in this work of destroying evil, it is right to apply the text to Mary as well.[37]

In art, the image of the woman crushing the serpent was sometimes combined with the image of the woman in the Book of the Apocalypse (or Revelation) 12:1–6. The latter is described as 'clothed with the sun, with the moon under her feet, and on her head a crown of twelve stars'. The passage continues:

> And the dragon stood before the woman who was about to bear a child, that he might devour her child when she brought it forth; she brought forth a male child, one who is to rule all the nations with a rod of iron, but her child was caught up to God … and the woman fled into the wilderness, where she has a place prepared by God.

Then there is war in heaven, with the archangel Michael fighting against the dragon. The dragon is defeated: 'And the great dragon was thrown down, that ancient serpent, who is called the Devil and Satan' (12:9).

Over the centuries, there has been general agreement that the woman in this passage at least partly signifies the Church, or the righteous people of Israel. However, exegesis from at least the fourth century down to the present day has frequently maintained that she is also Mary, the mother of Christ, who is herself the Church's principal type.[38] The battle which is described here is the final battle of God's angels against the devil, and the defeat of the dragon can thus be read as the fulfilment of the prophecy of Genesis 3:15, since the woman's offspring crushes the serpent. The perfect redemption of Mary in the Immaculate Conception is the first fruit of Michael's triumph over the serpent, who is the devil, as it is recounted in the Book of the Apocalypse.

The art historian Maurice Vloberg considers that the earliest certain representation of the Virgin of the Immaculate Conception trampling underfoot the head of the serpent is a wooden statue which was ordered for the church of St Mary of Cremona in 1407. The statue was to be 'crowned with twelve stars and with the ancient serpent under her feet', thus drawing together the imagery of Genesis 3:15 and the Apocalypse 12:1.[39] From the end of the fourteenth century onwards, there are also representations from Germany and the Low Countries in which the Virgin and Child are shown standing on the moon, as is the woman of the Apocalypse.[40] An English missal of the same period shows the Virgin clothed with the sun and standing on the moon, with the Blessed Trinity above her.[41]

A further contribution to the iconography of the Immaculate Conception was made by the *tota pulchra* image (Plate 8). This probably had its source in German representations of Mary as she lived in the Temple as a young girl, the *Ährenkleidjungfrau* – so called because she was shown with ears of wheat on her dress.[42] The basic image was taken up and used to illustrate a text from the Song of Songs: 'You are all fair, my beloved, and there is no stain in you [Latin: *macula non est in te*]' (Song 4:7). Christians had always interpreted the Song as a love song between Christ, who is the groom, and the Church, who is the bride. In the high Middle Ages it became customary to accord Mary the part of the bride, or the beloved. So, for example, the 'sealed fountain' and 'garden enclosed' (4:12) became figures for her unbroken virginity, and sometimes for her freedom from sin, which found no place by which to enter her. Not surprisingly, then, the quotation, 'there is no stain in you', seemed to invite an immaculist interpretation. Commenting on the many fifteenth- and sixteenth-century book engravings which represent the Beloved of the Song, the art historian Suzanne Stratton writes:

> The presence of God the Father above the banderole that reads 'Tota pulchra es . . .' in the engravings emphasizes the creation of the Virgin in the mind of God, before all things, reflecting the new theological emphasis on the Immaculacy of her spiritual rather than physical conception.[43]

Compared with the embrace at the Golden Gate, or the infant in her mother's womb, the image of the pure young girl was indeed a long way from the physical details discussed by medieval theologians of the doctrine. Yet this was only one image of the Immaculate Conception, and when taken with the others it contributed to a richness of iconography which enhanced the variety of meanings that were to be found in liturgy, theology and devotion. However, during the sixteenth and seventeenth centuries, Spanish painters who were promoting the doctrine formulated an iconography which drew upon certain of the earlier types of image but excluded others. The iconography which they developed has remained the standard representation of the Immaculate Conception down to the present day, so its character is of more than historical interest.

Francisco Pacheco, in his influential *Art of Painting* (1649), rejected the embrace at the Golden Gate as a representation of Mary's conception, on the grounds that many people misinterpreted the image to mean that Mary was conceived miraculously at the time of her parents' embrace, rather than through sexual intercourse. This is a very reasonable objection: but it is not one which could apply to an image of the unborn Mary in her mother's womb, yet this image also failed to find favour with the great Spanish painters and fell out of use. Vloberg expresses the following opinion: 'The art of the fifteenth century pushed the narrative style much too far, with a realistic image that strikes us today as in very bad taste: the infant visible in the womb of St Anne.'[44] This comment is reminiscent of some which I quoted in Chapter 2, revealing a difference in attitude to bodily processes which distinguishes modern sensibilities from those of the Middle Ages. The demise of the image of St Anne with the intra-uterine Virgin Mary might indicate that such sensibilities were already arising in the seventeenth century.[45] This suspicion is reinforced by the fact that it was at this time that the image of the Virgin and Child was also removed from the iconography of the Immaculate Conception. Commenting on an image which shows the Virgin without Christ, Vloberg says: 'The Blessed Virgin appears alone, without her Son, as befits her who is not yet the Mother of God, but has been prepared for that unique dignity by the unique privilege of exemption from original sin.'[46] Yet this line of reasoning scarcely constitutes a watertight argument. For it is the divine motherhood which provides the starting point for every medieval argument that Mary was immaculately conceived, and it is in virtue of her Son's merits that the grace of sinlessness is bestowed upon her. Accordingly, it could be argued that any symbolic depiction of the Immaculate Conception should incorporate a representation of Christ. But Spanish artists opted instead for the *tota pulchra* image of the young girl standing alone, leaving the iconography of the Immaculate Conception bereft of any maternal symbol.

Pacheco, drawing on the visions of Blessed Beatrice de Silva (d. 1490), foundress of the Conceptionist order of nuns, judged that the Virgin of the Immaculate Conception should be shown crowned with twelve stars, clothed with the sun, and standing on the moon. He also wrote: 'This lady should be shown in the flower of age, as twelve or thirteen years old, as a very beautiful *niña*.'[47] All these directions were followed by later painters, and most of them by sculptors as well. The insistence on extreme youth may derive from a Hispanic belief in childhood goodness and innocence,[48] but the international popularity of the iconography requires some other explanation.

It is noteworthy that theological writing of the early seventeenth century bears witness to a corresponding change of attitude towards Mary's physical motherhood. We have seen above (Chapter 2) that Francisco Suárez, writing in the 1580s, identified three ways in which the Blessed Virgin assisted in the world's salvation, and that the third of these is 'by conceiving Christ, the author of our salvation'.[49] In 1618, Hernando Chirino de Salazar published a work which included a quite different account of Mary's co-operation in the work of redemption. We have already seen that he rejected Suárez's argument, since the act of engendering was of itself 'a work of nature, and consequently neither free nor meritorious'.[50] Instead, Salazar proposed that Mary contributed to the work of salvation by willingly offering her Son as sacrifice at the Crucifixion, which is to say, her contribution is one principally of the will, rather than the flesh. Now, we have seen that some medieval interpreters of the Immaculate Conception considered Mary's moral purity to pertain in some way to her body as well as her soul. We have also seen that when Duns Scotus had used the argument that moral qualities did not pertain to the flesh as such, but only to the will, he was liberating the flesh from its Augustinian burden of sin and evil, and showing how it was possible for someone to be conceived in a state of grace. But in the thought of Salazar, a similar theoretical consideration – that is, that freedom and merit are not attributes of physical nature – becomes the ground for asserting that a natural action, even when freely

145

undertaken by a moral agent, never has a moral status. That is to say, it is morally worthless. Small wonder, then that the childbearing of Mary and Anne were losing interest for Christian iconographers.[51]

The Immaculate Conception in the nineteenth and twentieth centuries

The new image of the Immaculate Conception was used as a battle standard in the campaign to have the doctrine defined as part of the Catholic Church's official teaching. It spread throughout the Hispanic world and is found, for example, in the images of Our Lady of Guadalupe – patroness of Mexico and the Americas – and Nossa Señora Aparecida, the patroness of Brazil. But it did not become dominant in the devotion of Western Europe until the nineteenth century.

In 1830, Catherine Labouré, a novice in the Daughters of Charity, had a series of visions of the Virgin in the chapel of the sisters' convent in the rue du Bac in Paris. In one of these, Mary asked Sister Catherine to have a medal struck (Plate 9). On the obverse side is an image of the Virgin with her arms outstretched and rays of light emanating from her hands. She is standing on a globe, but this is not understood to be the moon. Rather, it is the whole world, receiving the graces which are signified by the rays of light. The image usually includes a snake which the Virgin is treading underfoot. The tableau is placed against an oval background around whose edge are inscribed the words: 'O Mary conceived without sin, pray for us who have recourse to thee.' The reverse of the medal shows the hearts of Jesus and Mary, surmounted by a Cross intertwined with a letter M, surrounded by twelve stars. The medal was first distributed in 1832 and was called the Medal of the Immaculate Conception. It was immediately popular, and the large number of miracles attributed to it led to its being known unofficially as the Miraculous Medal – the title by which Catholics throughout the world know it today.[52]

In 1854, Pope Pius IX issued the Bull *Ineffabilis Deus* which declared the doctrine of Mary's Immaculate Conception to be the faith of the Church. Less than four years later, in 1858, Bernadette Soubirous of Lourdes received visions of a lady who said that she was the Immaculate Conception. The lady's appearance was very similar to that of the Virgin on the Miraculous Medal, the most notable difference being that in Bernadette's vision Mary held her hands together in prayer and that the cosmic symbols of globe and stars were missing (Plate 2). Through thousands of copies, the statue of Our Lady of Lourdes, derived from Bernadette's vision, is now familiar to people across the world.

Subsequent apparitions of Mary have often manifested her in a similar form. The most famous of these is probably that which was seen by three children at Fatima in Portugal in 1917. The principal seer, Lucia dos Santos, later said that she had had visions in which Christ and the Virgin requested devotions to her Immaculate Heart,[53] and consecration to the Immaculate Heart forms an important aspect of the cult of Our Lady of Fatima.

It was noted in Chapter 1 that the new Virgin of the Immaculate Conception has displaced the regal Virgin and Child as the dominant focus for Catholic Marian devotion. Physical motherhood has given way to moral purity and authority has been displaced by humility. But it is also the case that in the modern period, the iconography of the Immaculate Conception has itself changed from one of physical contact to one of solitude.

Yet notwithstanding the fact that the less authoritative and less maternal image of Mary enjoyed increasing popularity during the eighteenth and nineteenth centuries, much that was written about the Immaculate Conception during this period continued to follow the medieval pattern of argument, associating the Virgin's sinless conception with her divine motherhood. For example, Alphonsus Liguori's popular work *The Glories of Mary*, first published in 1750, gives as the principal reason for the Immaculate Conception that Mary was predestined to be the Mother of God.[54] Likewise, Pope Pius IX's Bull *Ineffabilis Deus* begins with an account of God electing Mary from before all time to be mother of the incarnate Word. Her immaculate conception is then related back to this.[55] But in the nineteenth and twentieth centuries, the divine motherhood has been reinterpreted in ways which have led to its definitive position being undermined.

The most interesting example of this shift is seen in the writing of Karl Rahner and recent authors who have been influenced by him. In his important essay 'The Immaculate Conception', Rahner ties the doctrine to an anthropological position which holds that God's love for humanity is more fundamental and important than the consequences of human sin, and he thus echoes the medieval approach to the doctrine's interpretation.[56] Rahner also follows a Scotist line in arguing that the distinctiveness of Mary's sanctification follows from her predestination to be Mother of God. He acknowledges that both the physical and the moral aspects of the divine motherhood are necessary, but he parts company with his medieval predecessors in the particular emphasis which he places upon her assent. It is because of her exceptional state of grace that Mary is able to consent fully and freely to a vocation which demands the participation of her whole person, and it is in this respect that Rahner understands Mary's Immaculate Conception to have a direct bearing on her motherhood.

However, more recent mariological authors have almost abandoned references to Mary's motherhood in their own accounts of the Immaculate Conception. The Spanish theologian Joseph Paredes, in a work which describes itself as 'a synthesis of Mariology', gives four reasons why the Church teaches that Mary was immaculately conceived. Two of the reasons make no reference to her motherhood, although one of these is concerned with her '*fiat*' – her acceptance of God's will. The argument seems to be influenced by Rahner, claiming that Mary's consent would have embraced her whole life and must therefore have its roots deeply laid in her. But where Rahner speaks of Mary's active choice, Paredes says that she was 'utterly open and docile to God'.[57] Both here and throughout the book, Mary's motherhood is subordinated to a notion of her vocation as something which is principally concerned with spiritual attitude, to the point at which her physical maternity becomes more or less incidental. Thus, it is not the divine motherhood, but 'Mary's personal act of faith and the believing attitude she maintained all her life [which] was the cause of salvation for the whole human race'.[58] Of the reasons Paredes gives for the Immaculate Conception, the two which do allude to Mary's motherhood describe her not as mother of God, but as 'the Holy Mother of Jesus', and as mother of 'the "new Humanity"'.[59] The fact that it is only because of the divine motherhood that Mary's faith has such salvific consequences seems to have been forgotten.

Another recent work, Kathleen Coyle's *Mary in the Christian Tradition*, makes no attempt to account for why the Immaculate Conception is necessary or 'fitting'. So notwithstanding references to Eadmer and Duns Scotus,[60] the divine motherhood is not mentioned. Coyle presents Mary's sinlessness as the realization of that holiness to which all Christians are called and to which the Church is destined. But no explanation is given as to why Mary should be the one in whom this perfection is already accomplished.[61]

148

The loss of the motif of physical motherhood in iconography, and its replacement by a more narrowly spiritual image, have been followed by a similar development in mariological writing. At the same time, the most recent changes to the mass of the Immaculate Conception in the Roman rite encourage a different reading of the doctrine from that which had been promoted in the liturgy for the previous eight hundred years. For the reading from Proverbs 8 has now been removed and replaced by Genesis 3:9–15 and 20, which includes the prophecy of the woman's seed crushing the head of the serpent and Eve being designated 'Mother of All the Living'. So a reading which invited the hearer to see the Immaculate Conception in the light of God's entire work of creation has been supplanted by one which sets the doctrine within a strongly anthropo-centric perspective. The new reading tends also to draw attention to the contrast between sin and redemption, and to the division of the world between good and evil – or at least, to the difference between the lesser figure of Eve and the greater figure of Mary – rather than to the grace of God which upholds the cosmos from its foundations.

Yet the major changes to the interpretation of the Immaculate Conception, apart from those of visual representation, seem to have occurred only recently, in the twentieth century. This may be because the doctrine contains an inherent antagonism to the sorts of development which have occurred in the Virgin's cult more widely, so that the doctrine's reinterpretation has been retarded.

Evidence that the doctrine is still interpreted in terms of God's care for the material world is provided by Andrea Dahlberg's anthro-pological study of three English pilgrimages to Lourdes, conducted in the 1980s. The shrine at Lourdes centres upon its healing spring and is particularly associated with prayer for the sick. Dahlberg examined the way in which bodily suffering is interpreted by sick and healthy pilgrims, and by staff at the shrine. The focus of devotion at Lourdes is care for those who are suffering illness or injury, and prayer for physical healing, but Dahlberg found that the healthy human body became a metaphor for other kinds of wholeness. For example, one pilgrim said that she was not sick but she had 'come to pray for "healing for all and especially for the sick"'.[62] Thus, 'healing' was sought even for those who did not suffer physical ailments. Conversely, the moral perfection which is realized in Mary's sinlessness is seen as a source of physical health. Dahlberg argues that the pilgrims' behaviour revealed two distinct understandings of bodily suffering. The first of these she calls the 'Miracle discourse', and the second the 'Sacrificial discourse'. Both discourses make an association between sin and physical suffering, but they deal with them differently.

The attitudes of most ordinary pilgrims towards bodily suffering constitute the 'Miracle discourse', which focuses upon the image of Our Lady of Lourdes. Pilgrims say that she is 'beautiful' – a whole body without imperfection of any kind. The aim of the Miracle discourse is to obtain miraculous healing,

> to eliminate sin in the body and so effect a cure. It is chiefly identified with Mary as Our Lady of Lourdes; Mary herself exemplifies the human being without sin by her perfect body and is also the source of the power the people hope to contact and thereby perfect themselves. The Miracle discourse is oriented to life in this world and in this body; it is premised upon the hope that the divine will intervene positively in the life of a person as God intervened in the life of Mary from the moment of her conception.[63]

So an image whose ostensible meaning is one of specifically spiritual perfection becomes simultaneously a symbol of hope for physical health. Perhaps this is not surprising, since the cult of a healing spring is founded upon the belief that divine power may work through material things, and since the Virgin of the Immaculate Conception is associated with Holy Wisdom, who directs both the natural and moral orders of the world.

By contrast, the 'Sacrificial discourse' sanctifies bodily suffering itself by construing it as a participation in the suffering of Christ:

> As a means of expiation, atonement and of achieving personal sanctity bodily suffering is valued. This discourse draws its power from the sacrifice of Christ. It is Christ in the passion, an image of death and of the shattering of the unity of His two natures which provides an image for it. This discourse emphasises the redemptive power of the suffering of the innocent. It is oriented to the other-world where the sacrificial victim is rewarded and in relation to which bodily suffering is meaningful and valuable. This discourse teaches transcendence; this world is passed through and authentic existence is realised in the next.[64]

The Sacrificial discourse is that which is promoted by the clergy and lay officials at the shrine, who try to avoid talk of miracles, and who focus their attention on Christ at the expense of Mary.

It is tempting to characterize the Sacrificial discourse as 'pie in the sky when you die', and the Miracle discourse as 'the opium of the people, the sigh of the oppressed', who know that what they need is change in the here-and-now, but being unable to see any practical means of obtaining it, have recourse to the hope of divine intervention. Yet it may be that the vision of physical and moral perfection which is associated with Our Lady of Lourdes could be made a vision of a world transformed, and so become an inspiration for social, economic and personal change. It may also be the case that suffering in the present is a necessary step on the path towards a future in which the world is healed of its ailments and finally redeemed from evil.

Notes

1. Marina Warner, *Alone of All Her Sex: The Myth and the Cult of the Virgin Mary* (1978) p. 236.
2. *The Protevangelium of James* in J. K. Elliott (ed.), *The Apocryphal New Testament* (1993), pp. 48–67.
3. 'The Gospel of Pseudo-Matthew' in Elliott, *The Apocryphal New Testament*, p. 88.
4. Michael O'Carroll, *Theotokos: A Theological Encyclopedia of the Blessed Virgin Mary* (1982), p. 180.
5. Mary Clayton, *The Cult of the Virgin Mary in Anglo-Saxon England* (1990), pp. 40–43.
6. An account of and references for Augustine's understanding of the transmission of original sin are given in Jaroslav Pelikan, *The Christian Tradition: A History of the Development of Doctrine* 1. *The Emergence of the Catholic Tradition (100–600)* (1971), pp. 299–301.
7. *De Natura et Gratia* 36:42 in *PL* 44:267. The Pelagian Julian of Eclanum also took issue with Augustine over the question of Mary's sinlessness: *Opus Imperfectum contra Julianum* 4:CXXII, in *PL* 45:1417–18.
8. Christopher O'Donnell, *At Worship with Mary: A Pastoral and Theological Study* (1988), p. 158.
9. Bernard of Clairvaux, Letter 174 (*PL* 182: 335C), cited in Carlo Balić, 'The medieval controversy over the Immaculate Conception up to the death of Scotus' in Edward Dennis O'Connor (ed.), *The Dogma of the Immaculate Conception: History and Significance* (1958), p. 173, n. 60. A full translation is given in *The Letters of St Bernard of Clairvaux*, trans. Bruno Scott James (1998 [1953]), Letter 215.
10. *Eadmeri Monachi Cantuariensis Tractatus de Conceptione S. Mariae*, ed. H. Thurston and T. Slater (1904).
11. Eadmer, *Tractatus de conceptione S. Mariae* 10, pp. 10–11.

12. Ioannis de Segovia, *Allegationes et Avisamenta pro Immaculata Conceptione Beatissime Virginis* (1965 edn), p. 23.
13. C. Balić, 'The medieval controversy over the Immaculate Conception', pp. 192–6.
14. C. Balić, 'The medieval controversy over the Immaculate Conception', p. 203.
15. John Duns Scotus, *Opus Oxoniense* III.3.1, in Ioannis Scoti *Theologiae Marianae Elementa*, ed. P. Carolus Balić (1933), pp. 21–22. An account of Duns Scotus's defence of the Immaculate Conception is given in Allan B. Wolter and Blane O'Neill, *John Duns Scotus: Mary's Architect* (1993), pp. 54–84.
16. Anselm, 'De conceptu virginali et de originali peccato' 7, in *S. Anselmi Opera Omnia*, ed. F. S. Schmitt (1946), vol. 2, pp. 147–9.
17. Anselm, 'De conceptu virginali et de originali peccato' 7–8, pp. 148–9.
18. Duns Scotus, *Op. Oxon.* III.3.1, pp. 27–8.
19. Anselm, 'De conceptu virginali et de originali peccato' 11, pp. 153–4.
20. Anselm, 'De conceptu virginali et de originali peccato' 12, pp. 154–5.
21. St Bridget of Sweden, *Revelations* 6, 49 (my own translation) in *Revelationes Caelestes Seraphicae Matris S. Birgittae Suecae* (1680), p. 507.
22. Giovanni Miegge, *The Virgin Mary: The Roman Catholic Marian Doctrine*, trans. Waldo Smith (1955), p. 111.
23. C. Balić, 'The medieval controversy over the Immaculate Conception', p. 203, n. 205.
24. Wenceslaus Sebastian, 'The controversy over the Immaculate Conception from after Duns Scotus to the end of the eighteenth century' in O'Connor (ed.), *The Dogma of the Immaculate Conception*, p. 219.
25. Ioannis de Segovia, *Allegationes et Avisamenta pro Immaculata Conceptione*, p. 21.
26. 'Sententia Roberti Bellarmini pro Immaculata Conceptione Sanctissimae Virginis Mariae' in James Brodrick, *The Life and Work of Blessed Robert Francis Cardinal Bellarmine, SJ*, vol. 1 (1928), p. 513. Although St Robert supported the doctrine, he argues elsewhere that, since the Church allows either opinion on the Immaculate Conception, there is at least a doubt as to whether it is right to celebrate the feast of the Conception ('De Ecclesia Triumphante' 3:16 in *De Controversiis Christianae Fidei* vol. 2: *De Conciliis, et Ecclesia* (1721), p. 514.
27. St Bridget of Sweden, *Revelations* 5, Interrog. 16 in *Revelationes Caelestes S. Birgittae*, p. 440.
28. St Bridget of Sweden, *Revelations* 6, 12 in *Revelationes Caelestes S. Birgittae*, p. 456.
29. Quoted in E. Villaret, 'Marie et la Compagnie de Jésus', in Hubert du Manoir, *Maria: Etudes sur la sainte Vierge* tom. II (1952), pp. 948–9.
30. M. Olier, *Vie Intérieure de la Très-Sainte Vierge* [collected from Olier's writings] (1866) tom. I, pp. 88–9.

31. This argument is given in Gabriel M. Roschini, *Mariologia* (1948), tom. II, pars II, p. 82.
32. Wolter and O'Neill, *John Duns Scotus: Mary's Architect*, pp. 49–54.
33. Etienne Catta, 'Sedes Sapientiae' in Hubert du Manoir (ed.), *Maria: Etudes sur la Sainte Vierge* tom. VI (1961), p. 694.
34. Ruth A. Meyers, 'The Wisdom of God and the Word of God: Alcuin's mass "of Wisdom"' in Martin Dudley (ed.), *Like a Two-Edged Sword: The Word of God in Liturgy and History* (1995), pp. 39–59.
35. Haymon Bishop of Halberstadt, *Homilia V. In Solemnitate Perpetuae Virginis Mariae*, PL 118:765D.
36. E.g. Gregory of Nyssa (*c.* 335–95), '*Homily on the Annunciation*', PG 62:765–6. English translation in Costante Berselli and Giorgio Gharib (eds), *In Praise of Mary: Hymns from the First Millennium of the Eastern and Western Churches*, trans. Phil Jenkins (1981), pp. 24–6, 100.
37. This is the argument of Peter Canisius; see James Brodrick, *Saint Peter Canisius, SJ* (1963), p. 646.
38. O'Carroll, *Theotokos*, pp. 375–7.
39. Maurice Vloberg, 'The iconography of the Immaculate Conception' in O'Connor (ed.), *The Dogma of the Immaculate Conception*, p. 471.
40. A synopsis of some of the art historical research is given in Sophie Guillot de Suduiraut, *La Vierge à l'Enfant d'Issenheim: Un chef d'oeuvre bâlois de la fin du Moyen Age* (1998), pp. 11–13.
41. Margaret Rickert, *The Reconstructed Carmelite Missal: An English Manuscript of the Late XIV Century in the British Museum (Additional 29704-05)* (1952), pp. 46–7 and Plate D. The illumination is for the votive mass of the Holy Trinity, not the feast of the Immaculate Conception.
42. Suzanne L. Stratton, *The Immaculate Conception in Spanish Art* (1994), p. 40.
43. Stratton, *The Immaculate Conception in Spanish Art*, p. 43.
44. Vloberg, 'The iconography of the Immaculate Conception', p. 465.
45. Amongst the Sevillian painters who developed the new iconography, it is improbable that there was any intention to repudiate the flesh as a vehicle for that which is sacred. The cult of statues used in Andalusian street processions placed great emphasis on the carnal experience of Christ and the saints, and Pacheco was a painter of such statues. Flesh was the locus of both sin and redemption (Jason Preater, '"Not wood but flesh": confraternity statues in post-Tridentine Andalusia', forthcoming in *Maria: A Journal of Marian Studies*). However, my concern here is with the significance which the image of the Immaculate Conception acquired when it was taken out of its culture of origin and became internationally popular. The context of its first painting in sixteenth-century Spain nevertheless points to the kind of ambiguity which nearly always attends Marian doctrine and devotion.

46. Vloberg, 'The iconography of the Immaculate Conception', p. 471.

47. Cited by Vloberg, 'The iconography of the Immaculate Conception', p. 493.

48. See William A. Christian Jr, *Apparitions in Late Medieval and Renaissance Spain* (1981), pp. 215–22. St Teresa of Avila imagined the Blessed Virgin 'with the grace of a young girl, *niña*' (see Vloberg, p. 493), and according to legend, Juan Diego, the visionary of Our Lady of Guadalupe, saw the Virgin as a young girl of 'about fourteen years old' (sources cited in Michael Carroll, *The Cult of the Virgin Mary: Psychological Origins* (1986), p. 182).

49. Francisco Suárez, *De Mysteriis Vitae Christi: Commentarii et Disputationes in Tertiam Partem D. Thomae* (1860 edn), Disp. XXIII, Sec. I:4, p. 331.

50. René Laurentin, *Marie, l'Eglise et le Sacerdoce: 1. Essai sur le Développement d'une Idée Religieuse* (1952), p. 244. Quotation from Hernando Chirino de Salazar, *In Proverbiis* 1618 (edn Paris 1619), vol. 1, VIII,206–7, p. 621.

51. The shift away from a focus on Mary's childbearing is seen also in changing ideas about the kind of union which exists between Mary and Christ. For Suárez, as for many earlier authors, what is important is the physical union of shared flesh; but for most subsequent authors, the union is a moral one – a union of wills or hearts.

52. René Laurentin, *The Life of Catherine Labouré, 1806–1876*, trans. Paul Inwood (1983); Joseph I. Dirvin, *Saint Catherine Labouré of the Miraculous Medal* (1984 [1958]).

53. Sandra Zimdars-Swartz, *Encountering Mary: Visions of Mary from La Salette to Medjugorje* (1991), p. 69.

54. Alphonsus de' Liguori, *The Glories of Mary* vol. II, trans. Anon. (1937), p. 19.

55. Latin text given in Cardinal Gousset, *La Croyance Générale et Constante de l'Eglise Touchant l'Immaculée Conception de la Bienheureuse Vierge Marie* (1855), pp. 761–75; English translation, *Apostolic Constitution of Pius IX Defining the Dogma of the Immaculate Conception*. The understanding of Mary's predestination which the Bull presents is not the Scotist one outlined earlier in this chapter. Rather, it holds that the Incarnation and divine motherhood were predestined because Adam's sin was foreseen from eternity.

56. Karl Rahner, 'The Immaculate Conception' in *Theological Investigations* vol. 1, trans. Cornelius Ernst (1961), pp. 201–13.

57. Joseph Paredes, *Mary and the Kingdom of God: A Synthesis of Mariology*, trans. Joseph Davies and Josefina Martinez (1991), p. 228.

58. Joseph Paredes, *Mary and the Kingdom of God*, p. 151.

59. Joseph Paredes, *Mary and the Kingdom of God*, p. 228

60. Kathleen Coyle, *Mary in the Christian Tradition from a Contemporary Perspective* (1996), pp. 37–8.

61. Kathleen Coyle, *Mary in the Christian Tradition*, pp. 35–44.

62. Andrea Dahlberg, 'The body as a principle of holism: three pilgrimages to Lourdes' in John Eade and Michael J. Sallnow (eds), *Contesting the Sacred: The Anthropology of Christian Pilgrimage* (1991), p. 45.

63. Andrea Dahlberg, *'Transcendence of Bodily Suffering: An anthropological study of English Catholics at Lourdes'* (London School of Economic and Political Science, PhD thesis, 1987), p. 286.

64. Dahlberg, *'Transcendence of Bodily Suffering'*, p. 286.

5

Domination and repression: psychological aspects of changes in Marian devotion

Large-scale transformations of society have been accompanied by changes in moral values, and developments which have occurred in the cult of the Virgin Mary can be understood more fully with reference to psychological, as well as sociological, factors. This chapter will supplement the theoretical considerations of Chapter 3 in an attempt to give a more thorough account of the dynamics of change in Marian devotion: change from a devotion which attended to the unity of spirit and matter to one whose concern is more narrowly spiritual, and from a reverence for a paradoxical majesty to the veneration of barely compromised humility. But we have seen that there are ambiguities or contradictions in the political significance of Marian images and texts, and if changes in theology and devotion are sometimes symptomatic of changes in social psychology, then these ambiguities in turn rest in part upon the psychic or emotional matrix which underlies the attractiveness of the Virgin's cult.

The merit of labour and self-control

The new surplus production in medieval agriculture made possible the growth of a new merchant class and the expansion of towns which were the centre of their trade. The expansion and internal development of the capitalist economy of Western Europe, together with the associated rationalization of many aspects of the society's culture, depended, amongst other things, upon a positive evaluation of manual labour. The application of rational principles to physical work can advance to the level of sophisticated technology only when there is an overlap between those members of society who are trained to carry out intellectual work and those members who have practical skills, since a rigid separation of these two groups will prevent the academic abilities of the one from being brought to bear upon the labouring tasks of the other. Technological development thus demands that those who are academically educated should hold physical work in sufficiently high regard to be willing to devote time and interest to consideration of its execution: or, conversely, that labourers and craftsmen who already hold their work in high esteem should have the resources and inclination for intellectual reflection upon their own technical procedures.

Lynn White Jr has argued that Western enthusiasm for technology is partly rooted in the ethos of the monasteries of the early Middle Ages.[1] Christianity had inherited from Judaism a respect for manual labour which made it an important aspect of monastic life,[2] so that monks both studied and worked.[3] This was more or less true of monasteries in both the East and the West, and yet it was only in the West that there arose the passion for technology which became so central a feature of the development of Western society as a whole. The reason for this discrepancy probably lay in the different social conditions in which the monks of the two halves of Christendom found themselves. In the East there were deeply ingrained cultures of non-Christian learning, in well-established societies which typically had a class of lay literati who would manage economic and political affairs. The learning of the Greek monasteries was therefore purely sacred in character. In the West, by contrast, Latin monks would often deal with all aspects of their surrounding culture, since they were sometimes the only people with sufficient education and organizational skills to manage an enterprise of any size.[4]

In addition to this, the Christian emphasis on compassion led monks to encourage the development and use of technology in order to save the pains of the worker.[5] The high evaluation of human labour combined with a concern for human dignity to reduce some of the labourer's more arduous and time-consuming tasks.

157

Yet this attempt to alleviate the time and effort devoted to work was a project which could succeed only in so far as there was a clear limit to the increase in productivity which was expected of the labourer. For if expectations remain constant, then new machinery can indeed reduce working hours; but if the machine is used primarily with the intention of increasing productivity, then the labourer's hours of toiling at the machine can be just as long as those which were worked before the machine was invented. Moreover, the surplus produce will accrue in the first instance to the owner of the machine, who will not necessarily be the same as the labourer.[6] By the time of the early modern period, technological development was undergirded less by the motive of compassion than by that of increasing productivity, with the latter's accompanying profit for a new, economically powerful class.

From the time of the high Middle Ages, Europe saw a significant growth in the size and influence of the urban middle class – and especially of the merchant class – for whom labour and technology had a different range of significance from that which it held for the monks who were perhaps initially responsible for the moral elevation of these activities. Rather than being concerned with the exercise of compassion, or with a remedy for 'physical weakness',[7] this was a class of people whose whole livelihood depended upon the properties of materials and the ways in which humanity could make use of those properties.[8] The bourgeoisie did not work the land, and neither did it exact taxes or tithes: it lived by buying, selling and manufacturing raw materials and artefacts. Investigative science and the application of technology, therefore, always had the potential to become central to its own well-being, and this indeed occurred. Furthermore, with the growth of a capitalist economy which required ever-increasing productivity to maintain capital accumulation, work came to take on a greater aura of moral worthiness than it had done previously. Indeed, it became necessary for people to believe that work was good in itself, and idleness sinful, and to be willing to work beyond the time that would ensure the remuneration that would merely maintain their existing standard of living. According to Weber, this change in attitude was one of the most distinctive achievements of the Protestant ethic in the formation of modern Western economies. Protestantism's affirmative attitude towards labour, industry and the pursuit of profit, contributed a vital ingredient to that radical change in world-view which freed capitalism from the constraints of medieval Catholicism and opened the way to eventual economic and corresponding technological expansion on the greatest scale that the world has ever known.[9]

Lynn White has argued that one manifestation of the ascendancy of the middle class was change in educated people's attitude towards the virtue of temperance, a change which occurred during the thirteenth and fourteenth centuries. In official Catholic teaching, it has always been charity which is regarded as the greatest of the cardinal virtues, and White argues that in common practice and perception it was treated as such during the early Middle Ages. However, during the thirteenth and fourteenth centuries, it was temperance which came to be esteemed most highly, and this development was especially associated with the evolution of the mechanical arts.[10] In particular, White highlights the importance of the clock in the ideology which supported the moral supremacy of temperance. For just as a clock should be well regulated and properly balanced, so, according to this interpretation of the value of *Temperantia*, the human body should likewise be governed.[11] By the end of the fourteenth century, the seeds had been sown of the culture of reification which Georg Lukács was to describe six hundred years later, for 'the mechanism [had] become the icon of the Christian life'.[12] Moreover, by the beginning of the fifteenth century, increasingly accurate clocks were being built, no longer corrected according to the change in the length of the hours of day and night which varied with the seasons; rather, the cycle of day and night became conceived as twenty-four hours of equal length. Thus, human life began to be regulated not by natural or experiential time, but by abstract mechanical time.[13] The new machine was created to serve the convenience of humanity, but it was not very long before human activities would be controlled by the demands of the clock; and indeed, such a development was already presaged in the notion of the human person as an object suitable for moral regulation.

During the sixteenth century the personified Temperance was expressly associated with punctuality, verbal discretion and industriousness; and in visual representations her symbols, in contrast to those of the other virtues, were modern inventions such as mechanical mills.[14] Temperance became elevated in importance, and was associated with labour, technology and self-control. An orientation of this kind was fundamental to the philosophy and practice of rationalization, and it was taken up wholeheartedly by many of the Protestant reformers. R. H. Tawney observed that 'it was the mastery of man over his environment which heralded the dawn of the new age, and it was in the stress of expanding economic energies that this mastery was proved and won'.[15] But that victory could be accomplished only by means of the kind of self-mastery that channelled human energy into austere economic and technological enterprises. This meant that mastery of the self was a prerequisite for mastery of the environment; and a powerful religious impetus to self-restraint and industriousness was provided by Calvinist theology with its 'insistence on personal responsibility, discipline, and asceticism'.[16] An emphasis upon the duty to labour and the evil of idleness pervaded dominant strands of Reformed theology and social teaching, and was strongly associated with the ideal of self-discipline.[17]

The domination of woman and nature

Authors of the Frankfurt School tried to tease out the connections between the domination of nature, domination by social class and by gender, and the self-mastery of each person. Their work drew heavily upon Marxism, but revised it in a manner which included the extensive use of Freudian psychoanalytical writing. This enabled the theorists to present a picture of social domination in terms of the development of both economic and psychological factors, and of the interaction between the two. The legitimation of domination was thereby presented as part and parcel of a larger cultural complex, rather than as the unmediated imposition of an ideology by one social group upon another. With hindsight, we can see that this mode of analysis has also made possible an understanding of the provenance of the social and psychological dualism that has been identified by feminist theorists, and has simultaneously contained the insight that the domination of women by men is central to relations of domination in general. It is partly because the Virgin Mary is a woman that she can be a key indicator of such relations.

Adorno, Horkheimer and Marcuse understood the domination of women by men to be closely tied to humanity's domination of the natural world – the term 'natural' referring here to both the external, non-human environment and also to the sensuous and other physical aspects of the human person. In his *Minima Moralia* (1945) Adorno wrote a piece on the 'feminine character' (*'der weibliche Charakter'*) in

160

which he stated: 'The feminine character is the negative imprint of domination ... Whatever is in the context of bourgeois delusion called nature, is merely the scar of social mutilation.'[18] And of Nietzsche he writes:

> He fell for the fraud of saying 'the feminine' when talking of women. Hence the perfidious advice not to forget the whip: femininity is itself already the effect of the whip. The liberation of nature would be to abolish its self-fabrication.[19]

Horkheimer and Adorno's *Dialectic of Enlightenment* articulates more thoroughly the relationship between the domination of women and that of nature. The first two essays of the *Dialectic* take humanity's experience of its position in non-human nature as their starting point, and then present a story of the growth of several different modes of domination, using a psychological account of the construction of the male bourgeois personality to supply the link between the domination of humanity and that of nature in general.[20] It is an account which resonates with the historical evidence given in Chapter 3.

Adorno and Horkheimer describe a particular path of development in the evolution of human consciousness. It is a path which leads from an initial state in which human beings feel themselves to be at one with their natural surroundings – or at least experience only temporary and limited separation from them – to the bourgeois state, in which the adult male personality is obsessed with maintaining his distinction from, and mastery over, his non-human environment and also his fellow men and women.

In the most ancient, magical perception of the world, human beings frequently experience themselves as being continuous with the elements of their environment – as participating in them. In contrast to Freud, who claimed that the most primitive human experience is one in which the environment is regarded as an extension of oneself, the *Dialectic* claims that this primitive experience is one in which the human consciousness understands itself to be an extension, or component part, of the various natural phenomena with which it engages.[21] That is to say, the primitive human mind gives priority to its surroundings, and is subsumed by them. But gradually, the experience of interaction with the non-human world leads humanity to realize that it is able to predict the consequences of certain of its own actions upon that world, and hence, that a certain amount of change to the non-human world can be instigated by human choice. This indicates that there is some sense in which human consciousness is separate from, and has priority over, its non-human surroundings.[22]

This experience of increasing separation takes the form of humanity's growing awareness both of the unity of its surroundings, and also of the unity of its own consciousness. In the older, magical view of the world, everything is diverse and various: each tree or river or animal manifests a different spirit; and magical activity consists in a mystical entry into and participation in the life of the particular phenomenon which is being venerated. The magician thus takes on the identity of the object whose powers he or she is invoking, and hence the magician can be seen as lacking the kind of discreet and continuous identity which characterizes the bourgeois individual. The increase in the sense of distance from one's surroundings, which I have mentioned above, comes about through the realization that there is a coherence, a consistency, and a unity to a world which has previously appeared to be characterized principally by its diversity. People learn that there are similarities or analogies between different objects and events, and that the identification of such similarities can help to inform human action in respect of those objects. Systems of classification thus begin, which means the beginning of the train of events by which all physical phenomena are reduced to their lowest common denominators. Classification, such as the categorization of plants into poisonous and non-poisonous varieties, arises as a result of human interactions with surrounding phenomena, and the classifications in turn inform human action. Humanity thereby understands itself to have a certain distinctiveness from the objects which it classifies – that is, the objects become 'other' than the consciousness which perceives them – while the objects themselves are increasingly perceived in terms of principles of unification. This process thus initiates the first stage in the formation of a dualistic world-view which is radically constituted in terms of 'self' and 'other'. This is a mode of being a self in which the self acquires its identity through being *not* 'other'.

Ironically, this self-awareness is gained at the cost of self-estrangement. The self of which consciousness becomes aware is an attenuated self: it is a consciousness which does not acknowledge its own fullness. This arises out of the fact that the domination of the external world requires the man who would dominate it to gain mastery not only over external phenomena, but also over himself at the most profound level.

The hunter or warrior must overcome his immediate fear of death and injury, for the sake of survival in the longer term. And the farmer or herdsman must regularly forgo his immediate physical comfort in order to tend his crops or his herds in inclement weather, or when having to compensate for inadequate soil or pasture. His control over his environment is thus partly dependent upon the mastery of his own desires and even his fundamental needs. In psychoanalytical terms, this control requires the repression of pleasure-orientated instinct, and the consequent formation of the ego, with its orientation towards the reality principle. The body's immediate demands, which focus on sexual desires, are denied in favour of longer-term goals.

Now, the actor in this series of events undergoes the experience of repressing his own emotional preferences in order to overcome certain aspects of the external world, and when he is successful, he also experiences the simultaneous accomplishment of those two ends. It seems reasonable to suppose that this experience might generate in the actor an association between the two sets of objects of control – between, on the one hand, external phenomena as they present themselves to his consciousness, and on the other, the features of his own emotional life which have also to be subdued. But the analogy between these two groups of phenomena does not consist only in their both being obstacles which have to be overcome. It goes beyond this, because the act of identifying certain features of his own emotional life as objects for control means that they must in some sense be viewed as 'other' than the actor who is doing the controlling. These aspects of self must be comprehended as 'not-self'. The 'I' which constitutes the actor's identity must see the desires which have to be repressed as being separate from itself if it is to accomplish the act of repression successfully. The actor thus perceives (or tries to perceive) certain of his own feelings as falling into the same category as that of the external world, that is, into the category of 'other' or 'not self'. His view of the world centres on an 'I' who acts, and who is distinct from and has to overcome the 'not I' or 'other'. And this latter category includes elements both of the external environment and of the actor's own person. So feelings of desire for physical comfort are conflated with the external environment, as the analogous objects of attempted mastery come to participate in a common category of experience, and hence to have overlapping identities. The domination of *external* nature becomes interwoven with the domination of *internal* nature.

It is the attempted identification of certain aspects of the self as 'other' which forms the link that connects the domination of the non-human environment to subsequent modes of domination amongst purely human actors. The repression of self, it has been argued, is instigated by external factors. Subsequent relations of domination, in common with this initial pair, operate within the psychological structure of 'self and other'. The self's repressed emotions are denied, but do not disappear completely, and they find expression in transference onto subsequent relations of domination. But because the roots of the relationship lie in the attempted mastery of external nature, it is this relationship which provides, as it were, the language in which these other relationships of domination are articulated.

The relationship between domination of self and domination of others is brought out in the *Dialectic* by way of a commentary upon that part of Book XII of the *Odyssey*[23] in which Odysseus encounters the Sirens.[24] Homer's account is treated as an allegory of social and economic domination, in which a central element is the formation of Odysseus as 'a prototype of the bourgeois individual' through a process of self-denial, which is a central aspect of self-domination. When Odysseus hears the Sirens' singing, his desire is to stay with them. They start to lure him back with a force which would threaten to bring an end to his whole voyage, such is the enchanting seductiveness of the song's beauty. But Odysseus is determined to continue the course of his journey; and so, to avoid the Sirens' charm, he has himself tied ever more securely to the mast, and the ears of his crew stopped up as they row away from the source of temptation. Odysseus thus maintains control of his ship by constraining himself in order to refuse his desire. These acts of self-constraint and self-denial make it possible for him to continue to be a commander of men. But perhaps the sailors would not feel that they have the same interest in self-denial as their commander does, and hence would find the lure of the Sirens' song more appealing than the prospect of continuing with their harsh and dangerous voyage. For the means by which Odysseus ensures that his commands will be obeyed is the denial to his subordinates of any exposure to the temptation by which he himself has been assailed. Thus, the relationship of domination between master and subordinate is maintained by self-denial on the part of the master, and the denial of desire amongst his subordinates.

From this example, it is possible to see how it is that relationships of domination between human groups come to share in the structure of

164

the relationship of domination which has already been established by humanity over certain features of its natural environment. The domination of the human other, like the mastery of the non-human world, is dependent upon the domination of self, that is, of physical desire; and since this kind of domination is itself derived from the attempt to overcome the natural environment, there are elements of this original form of domination which, via the medium of self-denial and self-control, become translated into the form of domination amongst humanity.

The fact that Odysseus has men who are his subordinates, whom he must command and control, indicates that he already relates to some of his fellow human beings in a manner which is structurally similar to the way in which a self relates to its other: the sailors in relation to their commander are like the natural environment in relation to humanity, and like alienated physical desire in relation to the 'I' who wishes to subdue it. The sailors are members of the category 'other', in respect of which Odysseus is the commanding self. For Odysseus, any failure on the part of the crew to obey the orders of their captain would be analogous to his own failure to control his own desires. The similarity between Odysseus's command of his men and that of his own emotions is intensified by the role which the actual suppression of desire plays in the maintenance of Odysseus' control over the feelings and actions of his crew. He and they are vulnerable to the same kind of desire, and he takes measures to ensure that they do not have that desire aroused in them. His command of the sailors depends upon his denying to them the desire which he experiences himself, and in that sense, his command depends upon the control of emotions at one remove. Yet in addition to this, Odysseus' domination of the sailors entails his constraining his own body as well as theirs, because his body is the locus of the same desire as that which he denies to them, so that without constraint he, like them, would be overwhelmed by this emotion. If this were to occur, Odysseus would be incapable of remaining as commander. He must be master of himself if he is to be master of others. In this way, the relationship between the domination of self and the domination of other people is parallel to that which has already been described as existing between the domination of self and the domination of the non-human environment: that is, not only do the objects of domination in the two cases occupy the same category of experience, but in each case, the domination of self is a prerequisite for the successful domination of the other.

Now, it has already been contended that the domination of self, or internal nature, is founded upon the domination of external nature, and shares some of its characteristics. It has also been suggested that in the case of the domination of human subordinates by a commander, the domination of physical desire is essential both in the commander and the subordinates. Since the domination of physical desire is already interwoven with the domination of the natural world, and since it is this external world which has initially provided a basic category within which potential objects of domination are to be comprehended, it is reasonable at this stage to suppose that the commander's domination of his subordinates will likewise be structured, both psychologically and practically, in a manner similar to humanity's domination of the external environment.

The connections between the domination of nature, domination of self, and domination of others is shown most clearly in Adorno and Horkheimer's analysis of Book X of the *Odyssey*,[25] which is concerned with Odysseus' encounter with Circe[26] (on whose advice Odysseus will subsequently protect himself and his crew against the Sirens). In this case, the domination of others refers specifically to the domination of women by men.

According to the analysis found in the *Dialectic*, Circe represents nature. She is daughter of the Sun, and grand-daughter of the Ocean, which signifies that she represents the primal state of undifferentiation, when human consciousness has not yet categorized the phenomena which are present to it. When Odysseus' party encounter her, she is surrounded by animals such as wolves and lions, whom one would normally expect to be ferocious but who in this case are tame and friendly towards Odysseus' sailors. However, Homer's account does not treat this as a lost 'Golden Age' in which animals and humans lived harmoniously together, nor is it viewed as an ideal towards which the world might be striving; rather, it is seen as the consequence of an enchantress's spells. Indeed, it turns out that Circe turns men into animals: Eurylochus' party are turned into swine by partaking of the food which the goddess offers them. This myth signifies a return to an earlier stage of consciousness, in which the distinction between the realms of the human and the non-human was much less clearly defined than it was at the stage which Eurylochus' party have reached before they encounter Circe. Yet the transformation into an animal that was once sacred does not constitute the recovery of a state of harmony

166

between gods, humans and animals. Rather, since the sailors-turned-swine 'have already been men, the civilised epic cannot represent what has happened to them as anything other than unseemly degradation'. To human consciousness which is already separated from nature and wishes to subdue it, Circe is nothing other than a threat. Odysseus, however, is able to resist the enchantress's charms, and is therefore the hero of the story. For Odysseus has taken a drug which is an antidote to the substance with which Circe turns men into animals. He then defends himself against her by drawing his sword. She suggests that they learn to trust one another by going to bed together, but Odysseus refuses to sleep with her unless she promises not to use her powers 'against' him again. Circe accedes to this request, and a relationship of mutual mistrust is thus established between them. After they have slept together, Circe agrees to restore the sailors to their human form, indicating that power over men has been wrested from Circe and now lies with Odysseus.

Although Odysseus is the winning partner in his deal with the goddess, Adorno and Horkheimer present him as being also a loser, since his bargain with Circe is accomplished through self-renunciation. That is to say, Odysseus' own nature – his desire – would have led him to surrender to Circe's wishes. But he pits his powers of renunciation against the goddess's magic, and ends by denying both her and his own nature, and by preventing the possibility of their ever experiencing a relationship of mutual trust. In this respect, Circe is even more representative of woman than she is of nature. Woman evokes in man the desire for sexual contact and for emotional comfort which, as we have already seen, must be subdued if he is to accomplish the domination of the natural world and of other people. The man who seeks this kind of mastery seeks to subjugate women because they represent to him the feelings of desire which they evoke in him. The desire for self-domination which is a primary requirement for the domination of nature, gives rise to the desire to dominate women. The domination of women thus emerges concomitantly with the domination of nature, and forges a perception of identity between the two. Man wishes to dominate woman because he wishes to govern his own emotions; but the domination of self is once again a necessary precondition for the domination of others, because the man cannot secure the relationship with the woman on his own terms unless he is prepared to postpone the fulfilment of his desire, and even to forgo it altogether.

In its construction of the world in terms of 'self and other', the evolving masculine (and to some extent generally human) consciousness identifies woman as 'other'. But this is not simply the same kind of identification as that which takes place in relation to male subordinates, because in addition to being located in the category of 'other', woman is perceived as having an especially strong affinity with the non-human world. Male self-consciousness is constructed in the first instance in distinction from nature, and also in distinction from woman. This will be discussed again when we consider the psychological construction of the relation between mother and child, and its connection with domination; but for the present, we can note that the specifically sexual element in men's relationships with women makes an important contribution to men's identification of woman with nature. Sexual ecstasy, particularly in intercourse, tends to obliterate the distinction between self and other, in two respects: first, because it is a state in which emotions which are normally suppressed and rendered 'other' are again dominant and refuse to be disowned; and second, because the distinction between the two partners, between man and woman, is partially overcome. Sexual activity is therefore inclined to recall the primal condition of unity with the natural world, and to undermine the consciousness in separation which the man in particular has developed. The woman with whom he loses his sense of separation and difference is therefore in the same relationship to him as the natural environment would be if he were to abandon his self-consciousness in relation to it. The common association made between sexual intercourse, or orgasm, and death, can be interpreted as a recognition that the cultural self which has been constructed in distinction from nature, dies when the self is again ascendant in sexual ecstasy. And since sexual activity is one of the areas of life in which women have the potential to exercise the greatest power over men, it is in this domain that men seek to establish the most thoroughgoing control over women.

Where nature is seen as an omnipotent and all-enveloping divine force, then the emergence of human consciousness through labour to ensure survival, and its subsequent development through labour to create culture beyond mere survival, must be construed as a wrestling and negotiating with unreliable powers of great magnitude. The human mind can imagine that the world could be different from the way it is; and in his attempt to realize his peculiarly human projects, the Homeric hero must try to separate himself from nature, and then reduce its power over him, since it maintains and even constitutes the status quo. Yet he is himself a part of that same nature, and thus denies himself in the very actions by which he most strives to realize himself.

In Western Christianity, the Virgin Mary has stood (amongst other things) for the 'other' which is 'nature', 'woman', or forbidden desire. She has stood for this 'other' in its ideal relationship to the dominating 'I', and for this reason her cult acts as an index of social relations of domination, manifesting very different characteristics amongst different social groups at different times and places. The regal mother of the medieval Virgin in Majesty points to a natural world filled with sacred power, before which humanity kneels in awe. By contrast, the humble maiden who stands alone at prayer speaks of a natural world which is subdued by human skill. She stands also for the human person in whom self-mastery has been not so much perfected as found redundant: all that the art of domination seeks to suppress had never been present in her. But just as 'woman' and 'nature' can still remind man that there are other, less oppressive ways of living, so Mary has the potential to evoke a vision of future liberation.

Mary in the maintenance of dualism

The dualistic construction of the cultural world into the dyad comprised, on the one hand, of male/self/master/culture/intellect, and, on the other hand, of female/other/subordinate/nature/feeling, has had a bearing on the Christian understanding of God and the Virgin Mary. I have argued that the Christian view of the relationship between God and creation frequently renders it analogous to the relationship between humanity and nature, so that God's creativity is seen to be similar to humanity's own creative activity. Furthermore, God has sometimes been presented implicitly as male and creation as female, while humanity's relationship with nature has become increasingly one of domination and has, in turn, been characterized in the language of man *vis-à-vis* woman. In this understanding, God has in effect been slotted into the dominant half and creation into the subordinate half of Western civilization's ever-encroaching dualism. Mary as representative of creation has come to take on the characteristics of the subordinate group in the dyad. As I have already suggested, there may be points at which Mary can threaten to disrupt the dualism altogether, but it is

169

helpful first to clarify some of the respects in which Marian devotion expresses or enhances existing states of unfreedom.

Although Mary signifies creation in its relationship with the Creator, and hence acts as an index of human domination of several aspects of the natural world, I have suggested that her significance is more precise than this, since typically she represents creation specifically in what is considered to be its right and undistorted relationship to God. What counts as 'right' and 'undistorted' may contain contradictions, but under social conditions of domination she frequently signifies the object of domination when it is in the condition of accomplished subordination (whatever that may be at a given time and place), and not when it is in a state of rebellion. It is for this reason that Mary can be used as a tool of the dominator against the oppressed: in theology and devotion, Mary can be presented as creation which is good and is therefore in opposition to that which is evil, while in political terms she is the subordinate who accepts her lot, and not the one who resists. In this way, Mary can be brought into play in the drama of dualistic domination, on the side of the powerful rather than the subordinate. A number of examples can indicate this use of the figure of Mary in the practice of Christian teaching.

We have already seen that Mary has been contrasted with Eve since the early centuries of the Christian Church, and that this can be understood as a sign that Mary shares essentially the same human condition as her forebear. However, at least in recent centuries, emphasis has usually been placed upon the contrast, rather than the similarity, between the two women: Eve's disobedience of the Lord is compared unfavourably to Mary's acceptance of his will. Now in general, the purpose of this contrast is to use Eve as a foil to the glorification of Mary. That is to say, the intention is not so much to besmirch the former as to praise the latter. Yet the comparison articulated as oppositional states that Mary is righteous where Eve is wicked; and the message which is conveyed here need not necessarily be that Mary reveals the inherent capacity of all creation for redemption but, rather, can seem to say that whereas Mary represents that which is specifically good within creation, Eve represents that which is wicked. Christians are typically enjoined to imitate Mary and to shun the wrongdoing of Eve, and in this way, under social conditions which incline people to construct the world in terms of the dualism of 'self' and 'other', Mary is easily subsumed into the camp of the dominating 'self', and set against the 'other' which is to be subdued.

The precise identity of the self's antagonist in this drama has varied according to time and place. Modern Western observers of the cult of the Virgin may think that it is sexuality which is the main opponent of the virtues which Mary represents. Wilhelm Reich, for example, when arguing that the social psychology of fascism was founded upon sexual repression and distortion, quoted a Catholic pamphlet entitled *Veneration of the Virgin Mary and the Young Man*[27] to indicate the manner in which the cult of the Virgin was employed by Christians in their own attempt to impose restrictions upon the experience and expression of sexual desire. The gist of the pamphlet is that if a young man thinks appropriately of the 'purity' of the Virgin Mary, then he will lose any desire to 'deprive a woman of her chastity'.[28]

Another supposedly 'evil' opponent of Mary's goodness in the modern period has been communism. As in the case of Eve, communists, together with other groups campaigning for social change, have been associated in Catholic propaganda with the devil, and thus with that which is most wicked in creation, whilst Mary has been portrayed as the Christian's sinless and most reliable ally in combating this particular force for evil.[29]

However, the figures who have most consistently been presented as opponents of Christian orthodoxy have for centuries been the Jews. Eamon Duffy, writing about the England of the late Middle Ages, states: 'The classic medieval representative of culpable unbelief, the ultimate outsider, is of course the Jew.'[30] He points out that Jewish unbelief is seen to reside most particularly in refusal to acknowledge the truth of the Incarnation; accordingly, Jewish characters are strongly associated with stories about eucharistic miracles, in which the miracle typically leads to the Christian conversion of the Jew concerned.[31] But it is not only the Eucharist which is associated with the doctrine of the Incarnation: Mary also is intimately bound to this teaching. Moreover, it has often been claimed that a right understanding of Mary's role at the Incarnation is the touchstone of Christian orthodoxy, and for this, as well as other, political, reasons, she has been lauded as the Victrix over heresies.[32] Consequently, it is no surprise to find that Jews play a not insignificant role in the miracles of the Virgin, just as they do in the miracles of the Eucharist.

One of the most popular medieval collections of miracles of the Virgin was that of Johannes Herolt, which was published in the mid-fifteenth century and widely circulated in northern Europe for the next hundred years.[33] One of Herolt's miracles (number 66) recounts a story which is typical of those involving Jews:

> In a church where it was the rule that the responsory 'Rejoice, Mary', with the verse 'Gabriel' in which there is 'Let the Jew take shame', should be sung daily, a certain scholar, because of the sweetness of his voice, was ordered to sing it.

As the responsory was being sung, some Jews were passing the church, and when they heard it, they were driven by shame to kidnap the scholar and kill him. However, the 'Glorious Virgin Mary' revived the unfortunate boy and told him 'to sing her praise with confidence'. The Jews were amazed to find the boy alive again, and so they questioned him. The scholar told them that it was Mary who had rescued him, and in consequence of this, no small number of Jews 'were converted to the glory of the Glorious Virgin Mary'.[34]

Collections of substantial numbers of Marian miracle stories began to be written down in the West during the twelfth century. However, another of the stories involving Jewish characters is one which, according to Richard Southern, 'was widely current in both East and West long before the end of the eleventh century'.[35] This story concerns a Jewish boy who received Christian communion (or was actually converted to Christianity) and in punishment for this, the boy's father threw him into a furnace. The Virgin rescued the boy from the flames, and this miracle led to the conversion of the father, as well as his son. This story was immensely popular throughout Northern Europe for the remainder of the Middle Ages.[36]

If we recall that it was Jews who were the victims of indiscriminate massacres on the part of Christians, then when we read Christian stories which concern the murder of Christian children by Jews, it is hard not to conclude that a considerable amount of psychological projection is involved in the construction of these narratives. According to Susan Griffin's analysis of pornography, it is in a cycle of denial and projection that the pornographer expresses his hopeless quest for victory over his own materiality, and it is that same hopeless quest which is articulated in certain aspects of anti-Semitism.[37] In the medieval miracle stories, then, Mary is rallied to the support of Christians who imagine that their eternal and spiritual truths are under attack from physically murderous infidels.

Yet in the stories cited so far, Mary's own role is not essentially vindictive or especially anti-Jewish: she rescues her children from death.

However, in another story which was widely popular, the Virgin seems herself to be the author of harm. This anecdote is told, amongst many other places, in John Damascene's second homily on the Dormition, in which he makes a diversion from his main narrative in order to tell it. The anecdote relates that amongst those who were present at the procession of the Virgin's body to the tomb, there were Jews 'from among those who hadn't lost all right judgement'. Amongst their number, there was a Hebrew man who was a 'slave to sin and bound by a pact with error'; indeed, he had become an instrument of the devil.[38] This man made to attack the bier on which the Virgin's body was placed, but as soon as he reached it, his hands were mutilated. At this very moment, he yielded to faith and repented, and his hands were then healed.[39]

This story was told again in the ever-popular *Golden Legend*[40] and in miracle plays such as those performed in Brussels in the later fifteenth and earlier sixteenth centuries.[41] In the Brussels play, two attempts are made 'to prevent the Virgin's glorification'. The first is made by 'the Devils *in propriis personis*', and the second by the Jews. The devil's party is successfully opposed by St Michael. Lucy de Bruyn describes the sequel to this:

> The Jews, Michael resumes, hate her as the Devils do, because they do not believe that she is the Mother of God. They are in league with hell. And indeed, the Devils having failed to obtain the Virgin's soul, now incite the Jews to get the mastery of her body after death, but the Jews meet with the same defeat as the Devils.[42]

This example provides a helpful indicator of the nature of Mary's position within Christian dualism. In the story of the attack on Mary's body, the Jew or Jews are associated explicitly with the devil. In one example, the Jew is said to be under the influence of the devil, and in another, a group of Jews who are 'in league with hell' have the same intention as a group of devils who carry out an identical action. Mary, however, is able to ward off the attack – a fact which reflects one of the perennial characteristics of her cult, namely, that she is the devil's most formidable opponent, and therefore the most powerful defender of the righteous. Mary is said to be the most perfect of God's creatures, and as such, she is the strongest adversary of the most wicked of the world's beings. For this reason, a confrontation between Mary and the devil has been a popular form for the articulation of Christian dualism.

Genesis 3:15, which speaks of the woman's seed crushing the serpent's head, has frequently been said to be a prophecy of Mary's defeat of the ultimate spiritual enemy. The Bull of the Immaculate Conception, *Ineffabilis Deus*, alludes to this verse, suggesting that Mary's sinlessness constitutes 'a decisive triumph' over the 'poisonous serpent'.[43] In 1884, Pope Leo XIII likewise associated Mary's immaculate conception with her triumph over the forces of evil, in an encyclical against secret societies: 'The faithful were to invoke Mary, "so that she, who from the moment of her conception overcame Satan, may show her power over these evil sects, in which is revived the contumacious spirit of the demon".'[44]

Marina Warner observes that the overcoming of the serpent is related to the contrast between Mary and Eve. For where Eve had been obedient to the word of the devil in the guise of the serpent, Mary was obedient to the word of the Lord when it was delivered to her by his messenger. And this is the essential difference between 'good' creation and 'bad' creation in Christian dualism: the one is attentive to the will of God in heaven, whilst the other is seduced by deceit which comes from the creation itself. Where Mary says 'yes' to God, the wicked say 'no'.

The psychology of domination

For relations of domination to be legitimated, it is necessary that the majority of those involved in such relations give their assent to them, so there are always psychological processes undergirding social relationships. Adorno and Horkheimer were trying to unravel these in their essays on the *Odyssey*, and it was in order to understand more fully the mechanics of the ideology of domination – that is, the process by which men and women both learn to desire the domination of others and also become willing to accept their own domination – that the Frankfurt theorists turned to the work of Sigmund Freud. The introduction of psychoanalytical theory into social theory has enabled the construction of an understanding of some of the interconnections between the different modes of domination which continue to characterize modern societies.

In common with Engels and others, Freud believed that human societies had probably once been matriarchal.[45] In Freud's case, the theory of social origins was derived from his understanding of the psychology of the individual person and was analogous to that psychology.[46] It is this central psychoanalytic understanding of man (*sic*) which is significant for the theories under discussion here.

According to Freud, the root of human oppression lies in the Oedipal drama that the infant boy enacts with his mother.[47] He begins his life in a state of blissful union with her: initially in her womb, and then sucking at her breast. She is the centre of his universe. The boy wishes to continue to live in this state of pleasurable union with her, and his wish takes the form of sexual desire, since it is sexual relations between mother and son which can most nearly fulfil the conditions the son is seeking. However, the son recognizes that his father is a rival to his mother's affections, and fears that his father will punish his (the son's) incest by castrating him. The son therefore wishes to eliminate his rival: he desires to kill his father. But this desire incurs feelings of guilt, and he therefore represses the desire into his unconscious. Nevertheless, the fear of the father's punishment is still effective, and so the son must censure his desire for sexual union with his mother. He therefore represses not only the desire to kill his father, but also the incestuous desire which his mother arouses in him. Thus, the fear of the father's punishment is superficially deprived of its substantive content. But the boy's fear has not been destroyed: it has only been repressed; and it comes to be expressed in the form of a generalized fear of authority. The boy also projects all these primary, repressed fears and desires on to people and events that he encounters in later life. And ultimately, in Freudian psychoanalytical theory, all human domination can be traced back to some re-enactment of the son's fear of the father, and to transference or projection deriving from the primary Oedipal complex.

Thus, Freud argues that the transition from mother-orientation to father-orientation is simultaneously a movement away from a world of comfort and delight, and towards a world of fear and obedience: it is the transition from the enjoyment of pleasure to its repression. And that psychological repression is the dynamic which is expressed socially in relationships of domination.[48]

Several members of the Frankfurt School incorporated this psycho-analytical model into their work[49] and, like Freud, they considered that the separation of the boy from his mother corresponded to the child's growing awareness of his distinctiveness from his environment in general. The desire to control and master his surroundings, both human and non-human, is thus an expression of a man's neurotic fear of

175

'returning' to that state of union which he most desires, but which will lead to disaster for his own person. Men dominate women, other men and nature, because these groups are all 'other' to the Oedipal self who seeks to maintain separation from his mother and from all who symbolize her, that is, anything or anyone for whom he experiences attraction which might lead to self-abandonment. Surrender to these deepest desires would lead to the death of the self which has been formed in opposition to the object of those desires. According to this understanding, the dualistic construction of the world as 'self and other' is rooted in the infant's earliest experiences with his mother. At the same time, the continuing fear of the father's punishment not only ensures the need to dominate others (for fear of committing the forbidden act of union), but also indicates a willingness to be oneself an object of domination, since the sense of guilt occasioned by the desire for primal union makes punishment by a superior force seem inevitable, or at least, justly deserved.

The key difference between Freud's own understanding of social domination and that of the Frankfurt School is that Freud regarded repression and domination as more or less inevitable consequences of the Oedipal drama and as components of civilization, whilst the Frankfurt theorists saw repression and domination as constituent parts of historically specific conditions which in principle could be replaced by conditions of mutual respect and freedom.[50] Social liberation would therefore be undergirded by an end to psychological repression and by a morally successful resolution of the Oedipal conflict in the members of a free society. The dualism which characterized a mind or a culture founded upon repression would have no reason for existing, and the deepest cause of false perceptions and mistaken relationships would have been removed.

Adorno, Horkheimer and Marcuse consider that social relations of domination have changed according to a pattern which is similar to the psychological development of the individual man, and that the typical psychological structure of each man and woman corresponds in turn to the current state of social relationships. On this principle, the developments which I have described in the cult of the Virgin signify a society that has moved from having a strong maternal focus - one in which men and women experience themselves as continuous with a powerful natural world, and dependent upon it - to being orientated instead towards the father,[51] so that society's members are trying to break free from the bond with the mother by gaining mastery over everything which signifies her presence. In the cult of the Virgin, physical maternity and universal authority have been replaced by ethereal and docile girlhood.

The Frankfurt theorists followed Freud in giving priority to the experience of the male: the boy or the man. They are interested in the 'subject', but in bourgeois culture 'subjectivity' is defined by reference to male, not female, experience. More recent psychoanalytical theorists have paid greater attention to gender differences, and a critical reading of the work of Robert Stoller and Nancy Chodorow[52] helps to explicate more fully the connections between gender, motherhood and domination, and so shows how the major changes in Western culture which I argue are manifested in the cult of the Virgin constitute an intensification of male dominance.

Chodorow has argued that the dyad of 'self' and 'other' – which, I have suggested, is fundamental to the construction of domination – is a mode of perception and of relationship to which men have a greater predisposition than do women. Drawing upon a Freudian under-standing of the psychological construction of gender, Stoller and Chodorow argue that key differences in male and female identity are a consequence of the fact that both sexes gain their earliest experience of their own gender in relation to mothers, who are female. Thus, it is through interaction with a member of her own sex that a girl learns to recognize her gender, while a boy learns about his gender through interaction with someone who is not of the same, but of the opposite sex to himself. Chodorow pays great attention to the social dynamics of a specific type of family structure, but nonetheless sees biological gender as one of the determining factors in the formation of the individual ego. Because a girl learns about her identity in relation to a body which is fundamentally similar to her own, and in relation to an adult who is also aware of this similarity, the girl is likely to develop an understanding of herself as someone who is, as it were, continuous with her surroundings and connected to other people. A boy, by contrast, learns about his own body as something which is markedly different from that of his mother. He therefore bases his gender-identity on a negative experience – that is, the experience of being not-mother, or not-like-mother – and he thinks of himself as someone who exists in separation from others, rather than in continuity with them. Male identity is therefore constructed at an early stage according to the dualistic pattern of 'self and other'.[53] Moreover, this basic male identity is not simply a construction formed in terms of self and other, but in so far as the element of separation and difference is regarded as important to it in later life, male identity is inherently very fragile. Because it is constituted in the negative terms of 'not-mother', it is weakly based and is continually threatened with the possibility of being lost as a clear identity altogether. It is therefore constantly trying to assert itself, and does this by setting itself against a world on to which it projects the imaginary 'mother'.

This analysis implies that a man's fear of being engulfed and thereby losing his masculine identity makes him peculiarly susceptible not only to a dualistic world-view, but also to a tendency towards the domination of others, and of women in particular. However, whether or not this susceptibility is realized in practice depends upon the social environment in which the man has been raised. Men and women are both capable of sympathizing and identifying themselves with others, and are both capable of recognizing their personal distinctiveness and possibilities for exercising power over their surroundings. It follows that a culture which emphasizes the interconnections amongst its human members, and between humanity and its non-human environment, will not be one which creates an isolated 'self' and its 'other', and then encourages a sense of estrangement between the two; conversely, a culture which constructs human identity and, in particular, masculinity in such sharply dyadic terms will probably tap the deep source of potential insecurity, and generate patterns of aggression and domination in many areas of men's behaviour. Hence, a socio-economic system which demands combat or competition for its continuation will, if it is successful, create for itself a culture of insecure manliness which will fulfil those requirements. A society based upon co-operation would be unlikely to generate this neurotic masculinity to the same extent.[54]

As it stands, this theory provides a description of the human psyche in its present condition as male and female, but does not look to the possibility that that condition might be transformed – that men and women might struggle out of the infantile transferences which social relations of domination depend upon, and look at one another directly, rather than in the mirror of childhood relationships. Yet this kind of liberation should be the goal of psychoanalysis, and it is an aim which is incorporated also into the project of Critical Theory.

Bearing in mind the hope for fundamental liberation, I argue that since the high Middle Ages, much of Western European culture has been marked by just this kind of dualistic domination, and that the cult of the Virgin bears witness to it in a variety of ways. In part, Mary has been celebrated as a signifier of successful domination, and although this seems to be more especially the case in the modern period, in certain ways it is true even of the examples which I have given of the august Marian devotion of the twelfth century. For although Mary was once widely honoured in her physical maternity, and although she was once revered in association with the whole of the material and spiritual creation, these facts did not prevent the cultural construction of a nature which was seen as a proper object of domination: on the contrary, Mary's cult was subsequently adapted to suit these new conditions. The numinous Marian poetry of the first Christian millennium, and the majestic Romanesque Madonnas, seem with hindsight to express a world which had not yet been subject to intense human domination, rather than one which was positively refusing such domination in the interests of something more free and compassionate. Moreover, the powerful, awe-inspiring, regal mother of the earlier Middle Ages is herself a sign of the domination of humanity by natural forces of many kinds. She speaks of a world in which men and women were not so much living harmoniously with their surroundings as bowing in abject submission to them. In psychoanalytical terms, she represents a less masculized view of the world than that which was to come with rationalization, since she indicates a state of mind in which people still felt at one with their mother, and had not experienced the 'masculine' realization of separation to the extent that was to come at a later period of history. The 'mother' here is the earth and other elements and their inhabitants, and the Virgin in Majesty signifies her devotees' unfreedom in the face of these overwhelming natural forces.

When the Reformers of the sixteenth century objected to Christ being represented as a child dependent on his mother, they were also giving veiled expression to human aspirations to greater autonomy in political, social and economic life; they were indicating the increasingly realizable desire for mature separation from an all-supportive parent. But in practice, this 'separation' was accomplished too much as a destructive hatred of that which was identified as 'mother', and as an infantile identification with a supposedly omnipotent father.

In fact, human beings are entirely immersed in, continuous with, and dependent upon most of what is called 'nature'. Yet we human beings are also able to transcend our immediate circumstances, by imagining a world in which things are different from the way they are now, and by acting within our natural limitations to effect those changes which we judge to be desirable. The project of liberation is one which is concerned both to accept our limitations and to realize our capacity for autonomy.

The vision of freedom

There is something Marcuse said of art which may also be true of religion: that it can evoke in us the memory of infant closeness to the mother, and in doing so may provide a comfortable refuge from an unjust world and thus allow injustice to continue; but it may on the other hand provide belief in the possibility of a world which is good and harmonious, in such a way as to inspire political action directed towards the realization of that goodness and harmony.[55] If the Virgin Mary has been the most common focus for maternal transference in Christianity, then it is not surprising if both these responses are present in her cult.

It is common for revolutionaries to look back to some imagined Golden Age and to present their vision of the future as the restoration of something that has been lost. Radical English Puritans in the seventeenth century looked back to England before the Norman Conquest, and modern feminists have sometimes looked back to supposedly matriarchal cultures of antiquity. But perhaps all this looking back refers at one level to the personal history of each man and woman, and perhaps this personal experience is touched both immediately and indirectly by the multiple manifestations of Mary.

The doctrine that Mary is Mother of God encompasses both the limitations of the human condition and its capacity for glory. It is in the flesh that we suffer and die, and according to much Christian teaching, it is the weakness of the flesh which causes us to sin. Yet it is Mary's flesh which is united to the Word of God in Christ, 'in order that he might bless the beginning of our existence', as Cyril of Alexandria writes in defence of the title *Theotokos*. Because Mary is the Mother of God, we know that God has been united to humanity from its foundations and seeks the glorification of even those parts of us which are most transient.

If we ask what exactly is the 'blessing' which Cyril speaks of, then the answer must be that we cannot properly know this until it is fully realized. Like the kingdom of God, and as an integral part of it, perfected humanity is beyond our immediate grasp, as the perfect society cannot be adequately imagined from within the one we now inhabit. Yet from our present experience of beauty and truth and fruitful relationships, and perhaps especially from our earliest experience of union with our mothers, we gain sufficient inkling of this future perfection so that present imperfections can be judged in its light. The Immaculate Conception and the Assumption say that perfect humanity, holy and glorified, has already been accomplished and so is possible. We cannot fully imagine what such a condition is like, but we know by comparison that the world as it is is tarnished and in need of healing. In this way, we can feel our way towards a world in which all dualism is ended. As the infinite Creator was united to mortal flesh in the tiny space of Mary's womb – as virginity and motherhood were incomprehensibly united in her conception of Christ – so the lesser divisions inscribed in domination and psychic repression can surely be overcome.

Yet this does not mean that liberation or perfection is indistinguishable from unsocialized infancy. The ending of repression is not the abandonment of maturity, but its fulfilment. Marcuse makes this clear in the difference he describes between repression and sublimation, arguing that whereas repression is a removal of something from consciousness and the denial of that which is removed, sublimation is the constructive, and even conscious, directing of desire into other channels.[56] Thus, the memory of infantile union with the mother may be expressed in devotion to the Virgin as an image of perfected humanity who inspires profound works of art or political action for justice.

Furthermore, this reasoning must not be mistaken for a reduction of religious faith to social and psychic activity. On the contrary, it is only faith in God which can finally keep open the hope which is rooted in our flesh. It is easy for the constant critique of the present to degenerate into the decadent attitude which holds that in the end there is no truth, only points of view or 'discourses', none of which has any greater intrinsic merit than any other. This leaves no ground on which to form a critique of injustice or to take seriously bodily suffering. Faith in the God who is beyond human knowing, yet whose presence is everywhere, is the only guarantee of a final end and guiding point for all critique.

Yet it is at least as easy, and far more common, for perpetual critique to be abandoned in favour of some thoroughly articulated ideal which is petrified and set up as an idol, forbidding anyone to look beneath or beyond it. Here again, it is only faith in God which prevents this happening, because only God throws all idols into their true perspective as limited beings.

But perhaps even this is not enough, for we need also a point of connection between ourselves as we are now and the God in whose promise we trust. It is in the Word made flesh together with the Godbearer who gave him that flesh that is established the supreme meeting of Deity with creation. Indeed, that it is mortal flesh which is bound to the eternal Word reveals the cosmic nature of the Incarnation, because physical being is what humanity holds in common with the whole material world, subject as it is to change and decay; and the Word's becoming flesh in Mary promises the glorification of the whole created order, which, like humanity, by this act may already become blessed. The divine intention to sanctify all creation stands as condemnation of abuses of both human and other nature. Social processes of rationalization, with their benefits and injuries, must stand judged in the light of this, as must the corresponding psychological tendencies both to divide the world into a righteous 'self' and its wicked 'other', and to seek liberation from domination.

Notes

1. Lynn White Jr, 'Cultural climates and technological advance in the Middle Ages' in *Medieval Religion and Technology: Collected Essays* (1978), pp. 237–49.
2. This was especially true of the Benedictine reform, which spread through the Latin monasteries during the latter part of the first millennium. The Rule of St Benedict places great emphasis on manual labour as part of the monk's daily routine (Timothy Fry, *et al.* (eds), *The Rule of St Benedict: In Latin and English with Notes* (1981), ch. 48, pp. 249–54).
3. White, 'Cultural climates and technological advance', p. 241.
4. White, 'Cultural climates and technological advance', p. 243.
5. White, 'Cultural climates and technological advance', pp. 237, 245.
6. According to Jean Gimpel, the day labourers who worked on the construction of the Augustinian convent in Paris do not seem to have worked more than four or five days a week (*The Cathedral Builders*, trans. Teresa Waugh (1983), p. 37).

7. White, 'Cultural climates and technological advance', p. 248. The idea that work is a remedy for weakness is found in the writings of Hugh of St Victor and Richard of St Victor.

8. Lynn White Jr, 'Natural science and naturalistic art in the Middle Ages' in *Medieval Religion and Technology*, p. 26.

9. Max Weber, *The Protestant Ethic and the Spirit of Capitalism*, trans. Talcott Parsons (1985), pp. 158–64 and *passim*.

10. Lynn White Jr, 'The iconography of *Temperantia* and the virtuousness of technology' in *Medieval Religion and Technology*, pp. 181–204.

11. White, 'The iconography of *Temperantia*', pp. 193–7.

12. White, 'The iconography of *Temperantia*', p. 197.

13. White, 'The iconography of *Temperantia*', pp. 197–8.

14. White, 'The iconography of *Temperantia*', pp. 199–200.

15. R. H. Tawney, *Religion and the Rise of Capitalism* (1975), p. 77.

16. Tawney, *Religion and the Rise of Capitalism*, p. 121.

17. This theme runs throughout Weber's *Protestant Ethic*, in which he makes special mention of the works of Richard Baxter (pp. 156–8 and 260–1). The same concern is recurrent in Tawney's *Religion and the Rise of Capitalism*.

18. Theodor W. Adorno, *Minima Moralia: Reflections from Damaged Life*, trans. E. F. N. Jephcott (1974), p. 95. 'Der weibliche Charakter ist ein Abdruck des Positivs der Herrschaft ... Was überhaupt im burgerlichen Verblendungs-zusammenhang Natur heisst, ist bloss das Wundmal gesellschaftlicher Verstümmelung' (in *Gesammelte Schriften* Band 4 (1980), p. 105).

19. Adorno, *Minima Moralia*, p. 96. 'Er verfiel dem Schwindel, »das Weib« zu sagen, wenn er von Frauen spricht. Daher allein der perfide Rat, die Peitsche nicht zu vergessen: das Weib selber ist bereits der Effeckt der Peitsche. Befreiung der Natur wäre es, ihre Selbstetzung abzuschaffen' (in *Gesammelte Schriften* Band 4, p. 106).

20. Max Horkheimer and Theodor W. Adorno, *Dialectic of Enlightenment*, trans. John Cumming (1979), pp. 3–80; original German, *Dialektik der Aufklärung: Philosophische Fragmente* (1988 [1944]), pp. 9–87.

21. Horkheimer and Adorno, *Dialectic of Enlightenment*, pp. 9–11.

22. Horkheimer and Adorno, *Dialectic of Enlightenment*, p. 13.

23. Horkheimer and Adorno, *Dialectic of Enlightenment*, pp. 32–6.

24. Homer, *Odyssey* XII, 154–200 in *Odyssey Books I–XII*, i.e. *Homeri Opera*, ed. T. W. Allen (1917), tomus III; for an English translation see Homer, *The Odyssey*, trans. E. V. Rieu (1946), pp. 193–4.

25. Horkheimer and Adorno, *Dialectic of Enlightenment*, pp. 69–74.

26. Homer, *Odyssey*, X, 133–400; English trans, in *The Odyssey*, pp. 155–70.

27. Pamphlet by Gerhard Kremer, *Katholisches Kirchenblatt* no.18, 3 May 1931; discussed in Wilhelm Reich, *The Mass Psychology of Fascism*, trans. Vincent R. Carfagno (1972), pp. 164–6. Uta Ranke-Heinemann also cites from

Nazi Germany a publication which praises virginity, and which makes a favourable association between Mary, chastity and racial purity (Father E. Breit, *On Being a Virgin* [Kevelaer, 1936; with *Imprimatur*], quoted in *Eunuchs for the Kingdom of Heaven: The Catholic Church and Sexuality* (1990), p. 331).

28. Reich, *The Mass Psychology of Fascism*, p. 165.
29. The Blue Army was established in the United States after the Second World War. It is a Marian organization which was established for the purpose of opposing the Red Army of the Soviet Union. Among the Marian devotional works which include references to Mary's opposition to Communism are Francis Johnston, *Fatima: The Great Sign* (1980); and Albert Joseph Herbert, *The Tears of Mary and Fatima: Why?* (1992).
30. Eamon Duffy, *The Stripping of the Altars: Traditional Religion in England 1400–1580* (1992), p. 105.
31. Duffy, *The Stripping of the Altars*, pp. 105–7.
32. Nicholas Perry and Loreto Echeverría write, 'Louis XIII … laid the foundation stone of Notre-Dame des Victoires in thanksgiving for the triumph over heresy' (*Under the Heel of Mary*, 1988, p. 46).
33. Johannes Herolt, *Miracles of the Virgin Mary*, trans. C. C. Swinton Bland (1928).
34. Herolt, *Miracles of the Virgin Mary*, pp. 92–3.
35. R. W. Southern, 'The English origins of the 'Miracles of the Virgin'', *Medieval and Renaissance Studies* 4 (1958), p. 192. Southern's source is E. Wolter, *Der Judenknabe* (Halle, 1879).
36. For example, from the twelfth century, Nigel of Canterbury, *Miracles of the Virgin Mary, in verse: Miracula Sancte Dei Genitricis Virginis Marie, Versificie*, ed. Jan Ziolkowski (1986), pp. 62–4; from the fourteenth century, Hans-Georg Richert (ed.), *Marienlegenden aus dem Alten Passional* (1965), pp. 187–205; and from the fifteenth century, the wall-paintings in the Lady Chapel of Winchester Cathedral. A version also appears in Jacobus de Voragine's *Golden Legend: Readings on the Saints*, trans. William Granger Ryan (1993), vol. II, pp. 87–8.
37. Susan Griffin, *Pornography and Silence: Culture's Revenge against Nature* (1981), pp. 156–99. This connection is observed by other feminist writers, e.g. Carol Adams, *The Sexual Politics of Meat* (1990), pp. 44–5 and 150–5, and Susanne Kappeler, *The Pornography of Representation* (1986), pp. 92 and 153–4. Adorno and Horkheimer similarly recognized the identification of the Jew as the 'Other' in Nazi anti-Semitism (*Dialectic of Enlightenment*, pp. 168–208).
38. Jean Damascene, 'Homilies on the Dormition' II, in *Homélies sur la Nativité et la Dormition*, Greek text with French trans. Pierre Voulet (1961), pp. 154–5; *On the Dormition of Mary: Early Patristic Homilies*, trans. Brian E. Daley (1998), pp. 216–7.

39. Jean Damascene, *Homélies sur la Nativité et la Dormition*, p. 156–7; *On the Dormition of Mary*, p. 217.

40. Jacobus de Voragine, *The Golden Legend* vol. II, p. 81.

41. Lucy de Bruyn, *Woman and the Devil in Sixteenth-Century Literature* (1979), p. 31.

42. De Bruyn, *Woman and the Devil in Sixteenth-Century Literature*, p. 32.

43. The day after the proclamation of the dogma, Pope Pius IX held up the doctrine of the Immaculate Conception as a means of refuting rationalism, since it expresses the world's dependence upon God, not human skill (quoted in Barbara Corrado Pope, 'Immaculate and powerful: the Marian revival in the nineteenth century', in Clarissa Atkinson *et al.*, *Immaculate and Powerful: The Female in Sacred Image and Social Reality* (1985), pp. 181–2).

44. Perry and Echeverría, *Under the Heel of Mary* (1988), p. 146. Quotation from *Humanum genus*, 20 April 1884.

45. Freud did not, however, believe that matriarchy was humanity's earliest condition. Rather, it had arisen out of the overthrow of an original patriarchy (*Totem and Taboo*, trans. James Strachey (1950), p. 144; *Moses and Monotheism*, trans. James Strachey (1974), p. 82).

46. Freud, *Moses and Monotheism*, p. 130. However, he also states, 'It is not easy for us to carry over the concepts of individual psychology into group psychology,' so that 'we will make shift with the use of analogies' (p. 132).

47. Accounts of the Oedipus complex are given in Sigmund Freud, *The Complete Introductory Lectures on Psychoanalysis*, trans. James Strachey (1971), pp. 328–38; and *The Interpretation of Dreams*, trans. James Strachey (1976), pp. 356–68.

48. Sigmund Freud, *Civilization and its Discontents*, trans. Joan Rivière (1963), pp. 60–70 and *passim*. Freud describes the social significance of the Oedipus complex as it is expressed in explicitly religious practice in *Totem and Taboo*, pp. 140–61.

49. David Held, *Introduction to Critical Theory: Horkheimer to Habermas* (1980), pp. 110–47; Rolf Wiggershaus, *The Frankfurt School*, trans. Michael Robertson (1994), pp. 265–73 and refs. throughout.

50. Herbert Marcuse, *Eros and Civilisation* (1987 [1956]) pp. 11–20.

51. In the iconography of the Holy Kinship in the sixteenth and seventeenth centuries, St Anne was replaced by St Joseph as the principal figure alongside Christ and the Virgin.

52. Nancy Chodorow, *The Reproduction of Mothering: Psychoanalysis and the Sociology of Gender* (1978). The part of Chodorow's work which is relevant for the present argument is drawn almost entirely from Robert Stoller, *Sex and Gender* vol. 1 *The Development of Masculinity and Femininity* (1984 [1974]); *Presentations of Gender* (1985); *Perversion: The Erotic Form of Hatred* (1986 [1975]).

53. Chodorow, *The Reproduction of Mothering*, pp. 92–129 and 166–70.

54. Authors concerned with domination (most notably, Karl Marx) often draw on Hegel's famous passage concerning the relationship between master and slave (G. W. F. Hegel, *Phenomenology of Spirit*, trans. A. V. Miller (1977), pp. 111–19). The dyad which Hegel considers to have some sort of ontological priority over other types of relationship might well be considered a striking example of the fantasy which Chodorow describes as emerging out of a characteristically masculine infancy. This of course does not invalidate Hegel's description of domination as a phenomenological account. A feminist critique of Hegel is given in Patricia Jagentowicz Mills, *Woman, Nature and Psyche* (1987), pp. 3–49.

55. Marcuse, *Eros and Civilisation*, pp. 144–5, 184–5.

56. Marcuse, *One-Dimensional Man* (1986 [1964]), pp. 73–6.

6

୧୬ଏ୬ଏ୬ଏ୬

Virginity and sorrow in Mary's childbearing

The belief that Mary gave birth to Christ 'without loss of her physical virginity' seems to be one of the most difficult for Northern Europeans of the twentieth century to accept. Yet for hundreds of years this teaching was barely controversial. It was not disputed, for example, by the major Protestant Reformers.[1] This chapter will not examine arguments for and against the doctrine, but will critically consider aspects of its interpretation and will set these alongside a similar consideration of devotion to Mary at the Cross, arguing that there are social and psychological factors at work in these devotions which reveal not only constraint by present circumstances but also hope for the future.

Background

In the apocryphal *Gospel of James*, or *Protevangelium*, the midwife who comes to assist Mary in her delivery discovers 'a new sight', that is, that 'a virgin has brought forth, a thing which her condition does not allow'. The midwife tells this to Salome, who, like doubting Thomas, will not believe the truth of this unless she places her finger inside Mary's body to test her condition. When she does this, her hand is withered by fire in judgement for her unbelief, but is restored again when she repents and, on the instruction of an angel, touches the child.[2] Salome concludes from this that 'a great king has been born to Israel', and this comment reveals what was probably the main point of the doctrine of Mary's virginity in childbirth, namely, that it showed the divinity of Christ. This seems to be the purpose that it serves in the *Tome* of Pope Leo which was received by the Council of Chalcedon in 451. He writes:

> The same eternal, only-begotten of the eternal begetter was born of the holy Spirit and the virgin Mary. His birth in time in no way subtracts from or adds to that divine and eternal birth of his: but its whole purpose is to restore humanity ... so that it might defeat death .... [He whom death could not hold down took up our nature and made it his own.] He was conceived by the holy Spirit inside the womb of the virgin mother. Her virginity was as untouched in giving him birth as it was in conceiving him.[3]

This miraculous childbirth would of its nature exclude the pain which was the distinctive penalty imposed upon Eve at the expulsion from Eden, and many authors considered the virginal childbirth to be a reversal of the Fall – as befitted the birth of him who in this act of Incarnation began to redeem men and women from the sin of their first parents.[4]

The idea of Mary as the most excellent 'sacred vessel' (Chapter 1, pp. 30–1) may also have contributed to belief in the virginal childbearing, since such a holy thing as Mary's body would be preserved by God from any injury or corruption. The common analogy between physical and moral corruption (a word originally denoting something physical but now carrying predominantly moral connotations) may also have encouraged the view that the woman who was sinless would not have suffered bodily rupture in giving birth to him who was to remove corruption of a spiritual kind.[5]

Virginity has popularly been seen as the state of greatest fertility, and this assumption underlies Nicholas of Cusa's very interesting rationale for Mary's virginal parturition. The idea that virginity is fullness of fertility seems to derive from the idea that fertility is something whose quantity is reduced each time it is in any way sapped by fruitful generation. Virgin earth is the most fecund soil, and the virginal person is likewise the most fertile. Mary's unaltered virginity therefore signifies that her childbearing left her fertility undiminished. Nicholas's presentation assumes this correspondence between fertility and virginity, and it also assumes a degree of understanding of the concept of *infinity* – a concept which he himself may have been the first to properly articulate. Infinity is not a number bigger than anyone can count, but is qualitatively different from number of any kind. If I have fourteen buttons and take six away, then I have eight buttons left; or if I have 563 buttons and take six away, then I have 557 buttons left. But if I have an infinite number of buttons and take six away, then I still have an infinite number of buttons remaining. For Nicholas, anything which is perfect must be infinite, since any number is by definition limited, and he discusses at some length the implications of the infinity of God.[6] Christ, who has perfect human nature, is the Son of God, and to give birth to this exceptional son, Mary's fertility would have to be correspondingly the greatest possible, which is to say, infinite, and this is seen in her incorrupt virginity:

> Had she not remained a virgin after this birth, she would, beforehand, have furnished to this most excellent birth a center of maternal fertility not in her supreme perfection of brightness but in a divided and diminished way, not proper to so unique and supreme a son. Therefore, if this most holy virgin offered her whole self to God, for whom she fully participated the complete nature of her fertility through the work of the Holy Spirit, then before, during and after the birth virginity remained in her, immaculate and uncorrupted, beyond all natural ordinary procreation.[7]

Virginity corresponds to fertility, and if Mary's virginity were ever diminished, then her fertility would not be as excellent as possible, and she would not have given it to the work of Christ's birth with the fullness which that birth required.

Nicholas's understanding offers an image which shows Christ and the Virgin to be far removed from the mundane, fallen condition in which Adam's descendants normally live, so that on the one hand it is an image of a man and woman who seem disconnected from the world in which they dwell, but on the other hand offers a vision of humanity perfected and glorified even in the midst of this world, so that it inspires hope for the possibility of a world transformed beyond anything we can now imagine.

So the doctrine of the *in partu* virginity has resonated in the Christian imagination in a variety of ways. Yet recent writing on Mary, including work by devout and orthodox Catholics, has found the idea difficult to deal with. Hilda Graef expresses a common suspicion when she says that the doctrine of the virginal childbirth was influenced by Platonic scorn for matter and the body.[8] This may or may not be true, but what can be said with some confidence is that medieval and Renaissance religious writers who favour the doctrine of the *in partu* virginity take bodily processes very seriously, believing that they may reveal something about their Creator; and these authors accordingly address many questions concerning the physical details of childbirth which are passed over by contemporary theologians, be they 'conservatives' or 'liberals'.

Karl Rahner on the Virginitas in Partu

In Chapter 1 I described differences between Suárez's and Rahner's approach to Mary's childbearing, pointing out that whereas Suárez gives an intimately physical account of the process, Rahner's main interest is in her spiritual attitude to the event. Rahner is in part trying to provide a corrective to a type of theological anthropology which was so concerned with biological functions that it lost sight of both their theological meaning and the integrity of the human person, so that it was in danger of reducing the human being to something more or less mechanical. But the interpretation which Rahner suggests as an alternative does not make things much better, for he places such enormous emphasis on the spiritual and psychological aspects of childbearing that he fails to take account of the reality of bodily suffering. The spiritual and the physical are still not integrated with one another.

Rahner acknowledges that there is a problem about pain in childbirth, but he thinks that the problem resides in people's dispositions, or spiritual attitudes. What is 'wrong' is not the physiology of the thing: rather, it is our *appropriation* of that physiology. As a general view, this has much to commend it, since there are circumstances in which such an approach to physical pain may be very liberating. But I question whether this reading of pain and suffering holds true in the case of childbirth.

I start my questioning with the observation that the degree of suffering involved in childbearing can be extremely great. In Europe before the advent of modern medicine, and in most of the world still today, childbirth quite frequently not only involves pain, but can lead to serious illness, permanent disability or death for the mother. Women die in order that the next generation can have life. That state of affairs is shocking, and, as I shall go on to illustrate, Christians for centuries have found it so. It is not for nothing that the author of Genesis 3 thinks that women's pains in labour are the consequence of a curse. Under these circumstances, to claim that the pangs of childbirth are principally the result of a wrong attitude on the mother's part merely adds insult to injury. So Rahner's view of the *in partu* virginity is not very plausible unless we first impose the condition that Mary's labour was fairly quick and without medical complications – which is to say that the doctrine must after all include some specification of physiological details.

However, for the sake of argument, let us move on from this reflection to suppose that the ideal Rahnerian mother nevertheless exists: she experiences labour without experiencing the sensations as painful; perhaps she undergoes serious illness and is able to greet that with equanimity and to accept it; perhaps she dies in childbirth and can face even death without fear. We can imagine such a noble and heroic being. Yet it still leaves the difficulty that the mother is not the only person to be affected by all this. It is not infrequently that a father says he feels shock and guilt that he is responsible for the suffering which the mother has undergone in giving birth to their child. And can the child of a woman who died as a consequence of giving birth to him or her ever be fully reconciled to that state of affairs? Indeed, *ought* they to be? It is not their *fault* that their mother died, but all the same, the woman who gave them their life has by that very act lost her own.

Guilt at maternal suffering has made an important contribution to Marian doctrine and devotion, and that is the subject of the greater part of this chapter.

The Virgin Birth as a sign of hope to women in labour

In about the year 1270, shortly after embarking upon a life of religious asceticism, the Italian poet Jacopone da Todi wrote the following autobiographical lines:

> When I was in the belly of my mother, I had already contracted to die; I cannot describe how I lived in that place, all closed in and locked up. I came forth and there was great pain and grief at my presence. I came in a sack and this was the coat I had on. When the sack in which I lay was opened, I was a wretched little thing, all dirty. Then I began to cry for the first time, and this was my first song as I entered the world.
>
> Those who were there took pity on me and picked me up. My mother

was in a very bad way because of the birth from her womb, which was very painful. (*Lauda* XXIV, lines 3–18)[9]

Later in the same poem he wrote:

If mother should come and tell the trouble she had in feeding me! She had to get up at night and give me the breast, suffering with cold and standing at her service, and I was crying. I had no reason to cry. She, thinking that I was sick and might die, trembled all over; she had to light a light to see me, and then she examined me and found no reason for my crying – why it should have been.

O my mother, here is the reward which you earned in one night! To carry me nine months in your belly with such strong and frequent spasms of great pain, to have a painful delivery, to have trouble in feeding – you paid a bad price for that reward. (Lines 27–44)[10]

A century later, St Bridget of Sweden wrote an account of the birth of Christ, which she had been privileged to witness in a revelation:

... the Virgin knelt with great reverence, putting herself at prayer; and she kept ... her face lifted to heaven toward the east. And so, with raised hands and with her eyes intent on heaven, she was as if suspended in an ecstasy of contemplation, inebriated with divine sweetness. And while she was thus in prayer, I saw the One lying in her womb then move; and then and there, in a moment and the twinkling of an eye, she gave birth to a Son, from whom there went out such great and ineffable light and splendor that the sun could not be compared to it ... And so sudden and momentary was that manner of giving birth that I was unable to notice or discern how or in what member she was giving birth. But yet, at once, I saw that glorious infant lying on the earth, naked and glowing in the greatest of neatness. His flesh was most clean of all filth and uncleanness. I saw also the afterbirth, lying wrapped very neatly beside him ... And the Virgin's womb, which before the birth had been very swollen, at once retracted; and her body then looked wonderfully beautiful and delicate.

... the Virgin ... at once ... with great dignity and reverence ... adored the boy and said to him: 'Welcome, my God, my Lord, and my Son!' And then the boy, crying and ... trembling from the cold ... rolled a little and extended his limbs, seeking to find refreshment and his Mother's favor. Then his Mother took him in her hands and pressed him to her breast, and with cheek and breast she warmed him with great joy and tender maternal compassion. Then, sitting on the earth, she put her son in her lap and deftly caught his umbilical cord with her finger. At once it was cut off, and from it no liquid or blood went out. And at once she began to wrap him carefully ... [Joseph] adored him on bended knee

192

and wept for joy. Not even at the birth was that Virgin changed in color or by infirmity. Nor was there in her any such failure of bodily strength as usually happens in other women giving birth ... Then ... she and Joseph put him in the manger, and on bended knee they continued to adore him with gladness and immense joy.[11]

These two accounts of childbearing could scarcely be more different from one another: where Jacopone's birth caused pain and illness to his mother, the birth of Jesus was quick and effortless; where Jacopone was enclosed in a caul and was dirty when it was opened, Jesus was clean and had his afterbirth wrapped neatly beside him; where Jacopone's mother had difficulty in feeding him, Jesus's mother experienced great joy when she pressed him to her breast; where Jacopone's birth is a cause of grief, Jesus' birth brings gladness and adoration. The list of contrasts could continue. Perhaps the only thing which the two accounts have in common is the motif of pity and compassion towards the tiny, dependent baby.

Yet each author would have entirely understood the other's description. Jacopone wrote of the nativity of Christ:

O unheard of birth – the son comes out of the belly of a sealed mother! The beautiful son is born without breaking the seal, leaving his castle with the gate locked. (*Lauda* II, lines 42–5)
O Mary, how could you stand it when you saw him? How is it you did not die smothered by love? How is it you were not consumed when you looked at him, when you contemplated God veiled in flesh? When he sucked you, how could you bear the love, its immensity being nursed by you? When he called you and named you mother, how is it you were not consumed to be called the mother of God? (Lines 48–55)[12]

Conversely, St Bridget was the mother of eight children, and undoubtedly had a very difficult labour during at least one of her deliveries. I suggest that the long-lived and widespread belief in Mary's miraculous parturition has in several respects gained its popularity from the fact that under normal circumstances, childbearing is accompanied by pain and danger. If a woman in labour is suffering torment and feels her life to be at risk, then what supernatural figure could be of greater assistance to her than a compassionate and powerful woman who has herself given birth safely and painlessly? For much of Christian history, this has surely been a central attraction of the doctrine of Mary's virginity *in partu*: it has offered hope to women who are themselves to become mothers.

The first biographers of St Bridget, who had known her well, reported that the Virgin Mary had appeared in person to help Bridget during one of her confinements, and the biographers made a connection between the assistance given to Bridget, and Mary's own painless childbearing.

> Now at one time Lady Birgitta was imperiled during childbirth, and her life was despaired of. That night, the women who were present to watch over her were awake; and as they looked, a person dressed in white silk was seen to enter and stand before the bed and handle each one of Lady Birgitta's members as she lay there – to the fear of all the women who were present. When, however, that person had gone out, Lady Birgitta gave birth so easily that it was a thing of wonder and not to be doubted that the Blessed Virgin, who gave birth without pain, was that person who mitigated the labors, the pains, and the peril of her handmaid, just as that same Virgin afterwards told her in a vision when she spoke this revelation:
> ... 'When you,' she said, 'had difficulty in childbirth, I, Mary, entered unto you. For that reason, you are an ingrate if you do not love me. Labor, therefore, that your children may also be my children.' (*The Life of Blessed Birgitta* by Prior Peter and Master Peter, 20–1)[13]

There are other examples of the Virgin's intercession being especially associated with the safe delivery of women in childbirth. In the medieval English ritual of churching, or purification of women after childbirth, the dominant element in the liturgy was that of thanksgiving for the safe deliverance of the mother. Duffy writes: 'It was the custom after childbirth for women, when they came to be churched, to present themselves and their babies before the principal image or altar of Our Lady, and to offer a candle in thanksgiving for their safe delivery.'[14] At the village of Ranworth, in Norfolk, the Lady altar has behind it paintings of three women saints with their children. These saints are Mary Salome, Mary Cleophas, and the Blessed Virgin, all of whom were safely delivered of their sons. In addition, there is a painting of St Margaret, who was traditionally associated with safe delivery in childbirth.[15]

In her study of the social history of Iceland, Kirsten Hastrup writes: 'Until the Reformation, the Virgin Mary had a tremendously important position in popular religious practice, and during the purification rite after childbirth, the women would salute Mary in their local church.'[16] It is possible that this ritual was a thanksgiving for the gift of fertility, rather than for the preservation of the mother's life, but comparison with the English examples would suggest the latter, and in any case, the two functions are often jointly attributed to Mary as the guardian of all things to do with female fecundity.[17]

Even in the British Isles in the twentieth century, Mary has been invoked as protectress of women in labour, as Marian McNeill explains:

> A charm still used in the Hebrides is the *Airne Mhoire* (literally, the Kidney of Mary), or the Virgin's Nut, on which the mark of a cross is faintly discernible. These seeds are carried across the Atlantic by the Gulf stream and are occasionally cast up on the shore. Being rare, they are highly prized. In the Roman Catholic islands they are often blest by the priest. The charm is used by women in childbed, the midwife placing it in the hand of the expectant mother, who clasps it tight in the belief that it will ease her pain and ensure a safe delivery.[18]

> A friend of the present writer's, a Roman Catholic, who lives in the Hebrides, has in her possession a Virgin's Nut on which a small silver cross has been mounted, and which has been blessed by a former bishop of the diocese. Late one evening, in 1936, a young man arrived breathless at her door and begged her to lend him the nut. His wife was expecting a first child and was already in labour; a friend of his had lost his wife in similar circumstances and he was resolved to take no risks. The nut was safely returned with the news that all had gone well.[19]

McNeill also reports that the saint who is known in Ireland as Brigid and in Britain as Bride, is called in Western Scotland 'Bride of the Isles' and is said to have been midwife to the Virgin Mary. Bride of the Isles was formerly invoked by women in childbirth,[20] which again suggests a connection between beliefs about Mary's own childbearing and the hope for a safe delivery for other women and their infants.

These examples indicate that Mary has been quite widely associated with the protection of women in labour, and several of the examples imply that belief about Mary's power of protection is intertwined with the belief that Mary's own labour was painless. The story of the miraculous birth of Christ has thus been not only a piece of academic theology, but also a sign of hope to women – and to children and men – in their particular circumstances of danger and suffering.

Several commentators on the cult of the Virgin have failed to observe that Mary's painless childbearing has the potential to be viewed in the manner just described, and instead, have seen Mary's freedom from birth-pangs only as an assertion of the vast distance which separates the

Virgin from more ordinary women. Mary's painless delivery thus becomes a measure which other women are bound to fall short of, contributing to the construction of her as an 'impossible model' for other women to attempt to imitate.[21] The rigid separation of Mary's graces from the imperfections of other women maintains a dualism of that which is heavenly and perfect on the one hand, and that which is earthly and flawed on the other. Mary occupies the superior category of this dyad, and other women are relegated to the inferior one. Within this structure, there are few points at which the opposite poles of the dyad are reconciled to one another, and the glories which are attributed to Mary offer little hope for the women who find themselves in the wrong half of the duality. Thus, the mythic image does not speak of the possibility of a world transformed – of the realization of heaven on earth – but asserts only the inevitability of the status quo. In Marcuse's terms, this is one-dimensional thinking. But it is equally one-dimensional to claim that since most women suffer pain, sickness, and even death during labour, we should believe that Mary likewise endured the pangs of childbirth; for this teaching is just as rigid as its opponent in its refusal to grant a utopian aspect to the mythic image, and in its failure to allow a vision of hope to a humanity which is naturally subject to sorrow and death.

Mary's painless childbirth as consolation for infant guilt

Apart from the hope which it has afforded women in childbirth, the belief that Mary's labour was painless seems also to have performed an important function for people of both sexes who are, quite simply, the children of ordinary mothers.

Marcuse wrote of the guilt incurred during the oedipal drama:

> The overthrow of the king-father is a crime, but so is his restoration – and both are necessary for the progress of civilization. The crime against the reality principle is redeemed by the crime against the pleasure principle: redemption thus cancels itself ... There is guilt over a deed that has not been accomplished: liberation ... Freud spoke of a pre-existing sense of guilt, which seems to be 'lurking' in the individual, ready and waiting to 'assimilate' an accusation made against him [ ]. This notion seems to correspond to the idea of a 'floating anxiety' which has subterranean roots even beneath the *individual* unconscious.[22]

Although there is probably truth in Marcuse's assertion that people feel guilt over their failure to accomplish their own liberation, there is surely a more radical cause of the 'lurking' guilt to which Freud refers, and it is this particular source of guilt which Jacopone da Todi describes with such vividness. For prior to any conflict with other members of its family, the infant gains its very existence at the expense of the health, and even the life, of its mother. It is this, I suggest, which is the most fundamental ground of human guilt; and it is this agony of knowing that one's life depends upon the suffering of another which has inspired many occasions of remorse and asceticism amongst Christians through the ages. Hence, the teaching that Mary gave birth without pain, and even without loss of her virginity, provides devotees with a mother whom they have never wounded, and who therefore does not seem to have cause to reproach them simply for being alive in the world.

The notion that Christians have been horrified by the suffering of mothers, and especially by the pains of parturition itself, is one which receives ample support from the history of Christian writings. St Jerome, writing to a daughter to persuade her to return to live with her mother, said:

> She carried you long, and she nursed you for many months; her gentle love bore with the peevish ways of your infancy. She washed your soiled napkins and often dirtied her hands with their nastiness. She sat by your bed when you were ill and was patient with your sickness, even as she had before endured the sickness of maternity which you caused.[23]

Centuries later, Rupert of Deutz considered that 'the more fertile a woman is, the more wretched she is'. And when she does not suffer in childbirth, she suffers 'the pain of menstruation'.[24] Another twelfth-century writer, Arnold of Bonneval, wrote: 'When the chains of nature are ruptured from within, the afterbirth comes forth as the infant wails, the trembling hands of the midwives meet the clinging babe – truly, it is a miserable business!'[25]

One of the most widely read works of the Middle Ages was Pope Innocent III's *De miseria conditionis humanae*, which was written at the end of the twelfth century,[26] and popularly known as *De contemptu mundi*. Amongst the many griefs pertaining to the human condition, the author states: 'There is no pain like that of a woman in labour: thus Rachel died from the excessive pain of childbirth and, dying, called her son's name Benoni, that is, son of pain.'[27] He says that woman 'conceives with uncleanness and stench, gives birth with sorrow and pain, feeds with difficulty and labor, and protects with constancy and fear.'[28] Innocent III was also a great devotee of the Virgin Mary, and preached notable sermons on mariological themes.[29]

Another Marian devotee was Jacopone da Todi. Significantly, it was apparently the death of his wife which set him on the course of penitence and poverty.[30] According to his biographer, Jacopone's wife Vanna was a very devout woman who would have chosen to live a simple life; but in order to please her husband, who was a lawyer, she dressed in fine clothes and mixed in fashionable circles. In 1268, when they had been married for only a year, she went to a party which he was unable to attend, and while the party-goers were dancing, the balcony on which they were situated collapsed. Fortunately, no more than one person was killed in this accident, but that one person was Jaco's wife, Vanna. When they removed her clothing after her death, she was found to be wearing a hair shirt beneath her finery. This act of asceticism was something that her husband had never suspected, but it revealed to him that she was a deeply devout woman who only pretended to enjoy her life of worldliness.[31]

Jacopone's modern biographer, George Peck, writes, 'It seems likely that right from the beginning Jacopone saw the death of his wife as a retribution for his sins - a clear warning from God.' Peck suggests that the lawyer realized that his wife would not have gone to the party of her own volition, and asks, 'Did he ... feel that he was the cause of his beloved Vanna's death? That he was guilty?'[32] At any rate, this seems to have been the event that instigated Jacopone's life of penitence. Thus, the man who was soon to be lamenting the suffering which his birth had caused his mother, was driven to his sorrowful austerity by the death of the woman who in adulthood was closest to him, perhaps feeling that this was a death for which he bore some responsibility.

Against this background, it is easy to see how Mary's miraculous parturition could provide a sign of hope that the world did not have to be bound by such suffering and guilt. St Hildegard, whose medical concerns included the collecting of herbs and prayers for assisting women in labour,[33] was an enthusiast for the doctrine of Mary's virginity *in partu*. Barbara Newman writes:

> While this teaching may appear to proclaim a grace that denies rather than perfecting nature, for Hildegard it was quite the opposite: the so-called 'law of nature' is really the false law of death imposed on Eve by the serpent. Mary, on the other hand, gives birth to Christ in a way that

both restores and surpasses the law of Paradise, which would have obtained before the fall.[34]

I suggest that this vision of Paradise has been a source of moral support not only for women in labour, but also for the children of their suffering.

The Mother of Sorrows

To suffer pain has frequently been viewed as something which is redemptive.[35] Indeed, one of Christianity's central claims is that the world has been saved from sin by the suffering and death of Christ on the cross. Moreover, one of the most common similes used to express the fruitfulness of suffering is that of the woman in labour, who suffers agony, but is immeasurably rewarded by the new life which she has borne.[36] In the 'Farewell Discourse', which John's Gospel reports Jesus as having given at the Last Supper, Jesus says,

'You will be sorrowful, but your sorrow will turn into joy. When a woman is in travail she has sorrow, because her hour has come; but when she is delivered of the child, she no longer remembers the anguish, for joy that a human being is born into the world.' (John 16:20–1).

This is a prophecy of the Crucifixion and its consequences, and the maternal imagery is subsequently reinforced by the account of the mother of Jesus being present near the cross (John 19:25–7), and by the report that Nicodemus, who had previously asked the question: 'Can a man enter a second time into his mother's womb and be born?' (John 3:4), brought spices to embalm the Lord's body after death (John 19:39). In medieval writing and illumination, the two motifs of the Crucifixion and the woman in labour were sometimes drawn into a single thought or picture. Thus, the fourteenth-century nun, Marguerite of Oingt, wrote:

My sweet Lord ... are you not my mother and more than my mother? ... For when the hour of your delivery came you were placed on the hard bed of the cross ... and your nerves and all your veins were broken. And truly it is no surprise that your veins burst when in one day you gave birth to the whole world.[37]

The Old English *Dream of the Rood* had compared the exaltation of the cross, from which eternal life is sprung, to the exaltation of Christ's mother Mary.[38] More commonly than this, however, Mary is herself described as being a mother at the Crucifixion. Rupert of Deutz, who expressed great sorrow at women's suffering in childbirth, considered that Mary had become truly the mother of Christians when she suffered 'birth-pangs' during her Son's Passion.[39] This theme has been reiterated quite frequently during the history of Marian devotion. The fourteenth-century English poem 'Stond well Moder under rode', expresses a very similar orientation to that articulated by Rupert. At the Crucifixion, the dialogue between Christ and Mary includes the following lines:

> 'Moder, now thou might well leren
> What sorewe haveth that children beren,
> What sorewe it is with childe gon.'

> 'Sorewe, iwis, I con thee tell!
> Bote it be the pine of helle,
> More sorewe wot I non.'

> 'Moder, rew of moder care,
> For now thou wost of moder fare,
> Thou[gh] thou be clene maiden-mon.'[40]

In the period since the Counter-Reformation, a popular mariological theme has become the mystical union of Mary with her Son, and this is a motif which is especially common in meditations on the Sorrowful Mother at the foot of the Cross. Even in 'mainstream' Catholic devotion of the period since Vatican II, this union has been expressed as an act of childbearing which is accomplished by Christ on the cross, and shared by his mother. During Lent 1988, James Hickey, the Cardinal Archbishop of Washington, gave a retreat to Pope John Paul II and the papal household, and the theme which he chose for this retreat was 'Mary at the Foot of the Cross'. During one of his meditations, he quoted from the work of the spiritual teacher Columba Marmion (1858–1923) on the subject of Mary's participation in the Passion and death of Christ:

Christ Jesus willed to make his Mother enter into this mystery by so special a title and Mary united herself so fully to the will of her Son, our Redeemer, that, while keeping her rank of simple creature, she truly shares with him the glory of having at that moment brought us forth to the life of grace.[41]

Hans Urs von Balthasar expressed a similar view, although his orientation is more ecclesiological than Marmion's, and he keeps Mary's own motherhood at one remove from the birth-giving which is accomplished at the Crucifixion. Writing about the moment of Jesus' death, Balthasar says:

> At the heart of this turning point lies the Church's hour of birth; the Body of God's Word ... can now be distributed eucharistically, and from the pierced Heart there run out the water and blood of the sacraments. In the midst of this great event, this Body cannot forget its origins and its connection with its Mother's body. And the body of Jesus' Mother could bear this fruit only because she had consented in advance to Jesus' whole mission; this is why Mary is present under the cross at the moment when God's incarnation is consummated and the Church is born. She suffers along with her Son; in her spirit she experiences his death ...[42]

Infant guilt and social change in devotion to Mary

Now, although the act of parturition culminates in a joy which can make the memory of its attendant agony pale into insignificance, there is an inherent ambivalence about Christian devotion to the cross, and I suggest that this ambivalence is inextricably bound up with the association between the Crucifixion and childbirth. For on the one hand, the Christian knows that the Crucifixion was an act of atonement for sin, which culminated in the victory of the Resurrection, and which washes away all guilt; but on the other hand, the Christian also knows that his or her own eternal life is dependent upon the horrible suffering and death of another person, and may thus feel an unappeasable sense of guilt and unworthiness that he or she should have received such grace. The latter of these experiences evokes the sense of appalling responsibility which the child feels towards the sufferings of its mother; and the use of the imagery of childbirth to describe the giving of life through the Passion and death of Christ both expresses and reinforces the sense of guilt which worshippers associate with their own births.

Since the time of the high Middle Ages, the image of the crucifix and the cult of the Cross and Passion have been tied to the demand for repentance and to a culture of perpetual penitence. Within Catholicism, the cult of the Passion has also included devotion to Mary as the Mother of Sorrows. We have already seen several examples of this devotion, which was immensely popular in the late Middle Ages. It received expression in many different ways: in the visual image which art historians call the *Pietà*, in which the weeping Mary holds across her lap the body of her dead Son; or in the poetry and music of the *Stabat Mater* and other lamentations of the Virgin.

It has often been observed that the representation of Our Lady of Pity holding her dead Son forms a visual analogy to the enthroned Madonna and Child, since they both show Mary seated with Christ upon her lap. One of these images signifies birth, and the other, death – although that death is itself a preparation for new life. This comparison is not purely a modern one, since medieval imagery and poetry itself sometimes implies a connection between the two. Thus, on the church at Walpole St Peter in Norfolk, the South door is flanked on one side by a small relief carving of Our Lady of Pity, and on the other, by a parallel figure of the Virgin in Majesty. They date from the fifteenth century and are obviously intended to form a pair.

In medieval Italy, one of the most widely performed dramas was Jacopone da Todi's *Donna del Paradiso*,[43] which is a lament of the Virgin at the Cross. It gained popularity immediately, and subsequently influenced later representations of the same drama.[44] It naturally emphasizes the closeness of mother and son, and, like the *Pietà*, it seems to recall Mary's relationship with the infant Jesus, since she cries out, 'O my little son [*figliolo*] taken from me. O my son, my tender son, who has killed you? They would have done better to cut my heart out than for me to see you stretched on the cross' (lines 39–42).[45] The Crucifixion is thus made to recall the Nativity.

Leo Steinberg, the art historian, has made a study of what is probably the most famous of Michelangelo's *Pietà*s, the so-called 'Rome' *Pietà*, which is housed in St Peter's. Steinberg draws attention to the youthfulness of Mary's face in this statue, and observes that contemporaries of Michelangelo were rather surprised by the figure, and commented that the mother of the adult Christ was portrayed as being 'too young'.[46] Steinberg himself argues that the principal reason for Mary's youthful appearance is that Michangelo intended the symbolism of the image to be sexual; that death signifies the union which in life is suggested by sexual intercourse, and presumably represents the desire for return to the maternal womb. Steinberg suggests that the shock which was expressed by the first viewers of this statue was due to their intuitive perception of its real, sexual meaning.

Now, it is quite possible that the reception which greeted the *Pietà* was indeed guided by an unease at the sexuality which was implied in a lifelike image of Christ being held in the arms of a beautiful young woman. It is also the case that Mary as representative of the Church does indeed become the bride of Christ in much Christian symbolism. However, I suggest that, given the other parallels which have been drawn between the *Pietà* and the Virgin with Child, and between the Crucifixion and the birth of the Church or the world, it is most likely that the primary significance of Mary's youthfulness in this statue is that she is the mother who has given birth to salvation.

The recalling of the Nativity at the Crucifixion expresses entirely orthodox theology, since the Incarnation and death of Christ are inseparable. The former is the necessary condition for the latter. But the uniting of these motifs in the context of the Passion also adds weight to the idea that the suffering of Christ, and the compassion of Mary, were indeed perceived as an act of parturition.

Moreover, the cult of the Sorrowful Mother has been almost universally associated with penitence. In Italy in the thirteenth century, there arose bands of *disciplinati*, who were similar to flagellants; they went about singing hymns and psalms of praise, and performing acts of penance. Peck observes that the 'hymnbooks of the *disciplinati* all over Italy contain only two major themes: that of penitence and that of the worship of the Virgin'.[47] The *disciplinati* went from town to town, singing such hymns as the *Stabat Mater* and preaching the gospel of repentance. They spread themselves throughout much of Europe, and would have extended their movement even further had it not been for the fact that the state authorities in some countries prevented their entry.[48]

In Spain in the fifteenth century, the increasingly popular penitential cults frequently included strong Marian elements,[49] and in England, a widespread devotion to the Passion and the Wounds of Christ were especially associated with penitence and delivery at death.[50] At the same time, devotion to the Sorrows of Mary was, in Duffy's words, 'the most distinctive manifestation of Marian piety' in this country.[51]

All authors seem to agree that the Black Death of the fourteenth century, and other waves of plague, were an important provocation to the intense penitential cults of the Passion which swept across Western

Europe in the late Middle Ages.[52] But this explanation does not account for the particular forms that the devotion took, and in particular, it does not explain why it is that imagery which was specifically related to motherhood was so important to the penitents.

Michael Carroll has argued that the widespread association of penitence with Marian devotion has its origins in the Oedipus complex. That is to say, the male devotee transfers his desire for his own mother on to Mary, and then undergoes the remorse and punishment which he feels he deserves for harbouring such a forbidden longing.[53] However, quite apart from any internal weaknesses in Carroll's argument, the evidence which I have cited above indicates that the motif of pain in childbirth is an important aspect of penitential devotion to the Mother of Sorrows, and Carroll's theory has the defect that it does not take any account of this. Therefore, in contrast to Carroll's emphasis on the Oedipus complex, I argue that the fundamental psychological mechanism involved in penitential devotion to Mary is the worshippers' sense of guilt that their own lives are dependent upon maternal suffering. The deeply rooted nature of this awareness accounts for the fact that when the culture of medieval Christianity was assaulted by plague and warfare, the horror which people felt in response to such upheavals expressed itself very easily through the drama of the life-giving Crucifixion and the Sorrowful Mother. (It should be remembered here that according to a number of authors, it is specifically Mary's suffering at the cross which makes her the Mother of all Christians.)

In addition to these considerations, we can detect a relationship between the development of the cult of the Passion, and changes in economic conditions. It has already been noted that the twelfth century witnessed changes in Western Christianity which suggest that there was a growing mentality of fear and dissatisfaction. Lynn White has related these changes to the social transformations which followed upon the revolution in humanity's relationship to the earth and to other natural powers or resources. I have also argued that the perception of Mary in Western Christianity, and especially of her motherhood, reflects humanity's relationship to its natural environment. Therefore, it is reasonable to suppose that the growth during the Middle Ages in devotion to the Mother of Sorrows was partly generated by Christians' unease at their changed and changing relationship to the non-human nature which sustained them. Specifically, I suggest that the apparently increased separation of humanity from its natural surroundings, and humanity's increased capacity to dominate natural forces, were experienced as a child might experience growth away from its mother, so that the radical alterations which people imposed upon their physical environment, and which they experienced as a changed relationship with a powerful source of sustenance and deprivation, evoked the guilt of the child who believes it is responsible for harming its mother. Mary signifies that mother, and sorrow at her suffering became a dominant element within Christian piety. At the same time, devotees attempted to restore a state of harmonious union with the earth and with their own mothers by the vicarious means of praising and seeking help from a Virgin Mother who is endlessly merciful.

Devotion to the Passion and to the Mother of Sorrows in fact began to increase in Western Europe two centuries or more before the Black Death, concomitantly with some of the other changes in Christian culture which have been mentioned above. In the early Middle Ages, for example, a common representation of Christ on the cross showed him reigning in glory, fully clothed, with an erect, rather than a contorted body. This image signified the Triumph of the Cross and Resurrection over sin and death. By the twelfth century, however, Christ was frequently depicted as dead or suffering, and was sometimes flanked by representations of Mary and John in a state of grief.[54] Verbal devotions underwent a similar transformation. Duffy describes the changes which occurred to the form and wording of the prayer *Adoro te, Domine Jesu Christe*, from the time of its appearance in the ninth century *Book of Cerne* to its incorporation in the Books of Hours which were used by the bourgeoisie in the late Middle Ages. The changes which were made to the prayer included separating the invocations concerning Christ's Passion from their original context, which had included the whole history of creation and redemption, in order to use the Passion texts as an independent devotion. This isolation was made in the Anglo-Saxon period for liturgical use. However, the prayer was also used for private worship; and when it appeared in the Hour books, changes were made which placed an emphasis upon Christ's painful suffering, where such an emphasis had not been present in the earlier version. Thus, for example, the late medieval prayer books said that Christ passively 'hung' on the cross, where the Anglo-Saxon text had said that he 'ascended' the cross.[55]

Devotion to the Mother of Sorrows gained in popularity during the same period. Reflections of Mary's agony at the foot of the cross had occurred as early as the fifth century in the work of the Syrian poet Jacob of Sarug,[56] but it received only intermittent attention by Greek and – to a much lesser extent – Latin authors during the remainder of the first millennium. One Byzantine writer of the tenth century, Simeon Metaphrastes, wrote a *Lament of the Blessed Virgin* in which Mary recalls her Son's childhood as she holds his dead body in her arms.[57] The lament observes that 'he who is even now reviving the bodies of the dead in hades is killing his own mother with sorrow'.[58] Simeon's *Lament* is a precursor of the medieval *Laments* of the Latin West.

In the year 1011, an oratory at Herford, Paderborn, was dedicated to 'Mary at the Cross',[59] and in subsequent centuries, this devotion was spread by the mendicant orders, and especially by the Franciscans.[60] In the twelfth century, Arnold of Bonneval, who apparently pitied the lot of women in childbirth, emphasized the union of Mary with Christ on the cross, and her participation in the work of redemption.[61] Contemporary with Arnold's writing were some of the German *Laments*, or *Marienklagen*, which present Mary as distraught with grief at her Son's death, and which continued to be popular for the next two centuries.[62] Rupert of Deutz, also writing in the twelfth century, was the first commentator to interpret John 19:25–7 to mean that Christ on the cross gave Mary to be the Mother of Christians.[63]

It may be significant for the present argument that in Italy, the bands of *disciplinati* which arose in the thirteenth century were located overwhelmingly in the North, where a new mercantile economy was developing, and occurred scarcely at all in the more conservative South.[64] It may also be significant that the early Franciscans, who preached penitence and sang the praises of the Virgin, orientated much of their spiritual life towards the celebration of God's creation – including plants, animals and the elements – and immediately gained an enormous following in all aspects of their mission.

I suggest, therefore, that a central underlying motive for the popularity of devotion to the Mother of Sorrows was an anxiety which was generated in Christians ultimately by their changed relationship to their natural environment.

Oedipal accounts of Marian devotion

I have argued that the character of popular devotional images of Mary has changed in accordance with the rationalization of Western society, in line with corresponding changes in the cultural construction of gender. These developments have also affected people's perception of the Mother of Sorrows. In a strongly patrifocal culture, a relationship between mother and child which does not include the father poses a threat to the father's overriding authority. And in a rationalized society, in which human intimacy is frequently interpreted only in terms of genital sexuality, it can be hard to understand passionate desire and bereavement without referring to the relationship in question as a sexual one. Yet I have argued that Mary's virginity in childbirth and her grief at the Crucifixion have gained much of their popular support from the fact of human distress at maternal suffering, and that this is a distress which, at its most fundamental level, is concerned only with the relationship between mother and infant, and does not derive from a sexual motive. The assumption that all human relationships are fundamentally patriarchal and sexual has prevented many commentators from perceiving this motif within Marian devotion, and has led them to interpret both Mary's virginity and her grief at the Passion in terms of the Oedipal complex.

Oedipal interpretations are fairly frequent amongst works which consider the psychology of Marian devotion. Steinberg and Carroll both use an Oedipal model for understanding phenomena which I have suggested should be understood at least partially as a cultural response to the pains of childbirth. Of particular significance, however, are Peck's comments upon *Lauda* XXIV by Jacopone da Todi. When Jacopone has described the pain and unhappiness surrounding his own birth, Peck comments: 'Jacopone continues in the same vein of horror at his guilt in relation to his mother and of pity and love for her at the same time – the theme classically illustrated by Oedipus in his relations with Jocasta.'[65] After quoting Jacopone's account of his mother's distress over her difficulties in feeding him, Peck refers to 'Jacopone's Oedipus complex'.[66] But in fact, Jacopone makes no reference to love which is sexual or forbidden, he expresses no fear that his father might disapprove of any aspect of his relationship with his mother, and Jacopone's sorrow arises not because of the threat of punishment, but because of his belief that he has caused great pain to the very person who gave him his life. Nonetheless, Peck is able to miss this point, and in doing so, he illustrates the fact that in a society which has deprived motherhood of authority and of public importance, it is easy to overlook the heartfelt concern of even the passionate Jacopone.

This failure to address the anguish which a child can experience at hurting its mother can be understood not only as a consequence of changes in the ideology of the family, but also as an expression of the corresponding intensification in humanity's domination of human and non-human nature. Where people perceive their own condition to be that of a self which must continually try to separate itself from its natural origins and to subdue and control them, then a sympathetic concern for the consequences of human action upon the natural environment will threaten to undermine that project of self-establishment. If this development takes place within a culture which mediates it through the symbolism of a child's growth away from its mother, then a failure to attend to the child's sorrow in respect of its human mother takes on the additional significance of refusal to acknowledge the meaning which the domination of 'nature' holds for the human 'self' and for the object which it wishes to master. In its efforts to accomplish the domination of non-human nature and of fellow human beings, the masculine bourgeois self must attain mastery over its own emotions. At the most fundamental level, these emotions consist not only of sexual desire, but also of a creaturely fellowship which derives from the original unity between mother and child and from the continuing dependence of the human person upon its own physical constitution and environment. Hence, the suppression or denial of bodily feeling entails a rejection of emotions which include not only those which are narrowly sexual, but also the guilt and the desire for amendment which accompany the belief that one has harmed the very source of one's existence. It is this latter anxiety which is expressed and partially alleviated in those aspects of Marian devotion which have been the subject of the present chapter.

Notes

1. Martin Luther wrote, 'Christ, we believe, came forth from a womb left perfectly intact', and 'It is an article of faith that Mary is Mother of the Lord and still a virgin.' (Quoted from WA 6, 510 and WA 11, 319–320,

in Michael O'Carroll, *Theotokos: A theological Encyclopedia of the Blessed Virgin Mary* (1982), p. 227.

2. J. K. Elliott (ed.), *The Apocryphal New Testament* (1993), pp. 64–5.
3. *DEC*, p. 77.
4. The quotation in Chapter 1 above (p. 28) from Cyril of Alexandria's Third Letter to Nestorius seems to make this connection. See also the reference to Hildegard of Bingen, above, pp. 198–9.
5. Gabriel Roschini writes, 'It was fitting that he who came to take away corruption, should not corrupt his mother's unimpaired virginity', (*Mariologia* vol. III, 1948, p. 259).
6. Nicholas of Cusa, *On Learned Ignorance* in *Nicholas of Cusa: Selected Spiritual Writings*, trans. H. Lawrence Bond (1997), esp. I, pp. 87–127.
7. Nicholas of Cusa, *On Learned Ignorance* III, 5, 212, p. 182. For Latin text see *De Docta Ignorantia* III, 5, 212, lines 12–21, ed. and German trans. Hans Gerhard Senger, p. 38.
8. Hilda Graef, *Mary: A History of Doctrine and Devotion* (1985), vol. 1, p. 37.
9. George T. Peck, *The Fool of God: Jacopone da Todi* (1980), p. 134.
10. Peck, *The Fool of God*, pp. 134–5.
11. Bridget of Sweden, *Revelations* 7, 21:6–22, in *Birgitta of Sweden: Life and Selected Revelations*, trans. Albert Ryle Kezel (1990), pp. 203–4.
12. Peck, *The Fool of God*, p. 139.
13. *Birgitta of Sweden: Life and Selected Revelations*, p. 76.
14. Eamon Duffy, *The Stripping of the Altars: Traditional Religion in England 1400–1580* (1992), p. 181.
15. Duffy, *The Stripping of the Altars*, p. 181, Plate 74.
16. Kirsten Hastrup, *Nature and Policy in Iceland 1400–1800: An Anthropological Analysis of History and Mentality* (1990), p. 176.
17. For a few examples of Mary's association with fertility, see Marina Warner, *Alone of All Her Sex: The Myth and the Cult of the Virgin Mary* (1976), pp. 280–1; and F. Marian McNeill, *The Silver Bough: A four volume Study of the National and Local Festivals of Scotland* vol. 1, *Scottish Folklore and Folk-Belief* (1957), p. 68. Almost all accounts of the cults of black Madonnas make reference to fertility and childbirth.
18. McNeill, *The Silver Bough* vol. 1, p. 75.
19. McNeill, *The Silver Bough* vol. 1, p. 175.
20. McNeill, *The Silver Bough* vol. 2, *A Calendar of Scottish National Festivals: Candlemas to Harvest Home* (1959), pp. 22–3.
21. It is not clear that imitation has normally been a strong feature of Marian devotion.
22. Herbert Marcuse, *Eros and Civilisation* (1987[1956]), pp. 68–9.
23. Jerome, *Epistula* 117, quoted in Clarissa W. Atkinson, *The Oldest Vocation: Christian Motherhood in the Middle Ages* (1991), p. 69. An alternative English

translation is given in St Jerome, *Letters and Selected Works*, trans. W. H. Freemantle *et al.* (1979), p. 217.

24. Rupert of Deutz, *In Genesim* III.22, quoted in Barbara Newman, *Sister of Wisdom: St Hildegard's Theology of the Feminine* (1987), p. 117.

25. Arnold of Bonneval, *De operibus sex dierum* (*PL*189,1564BC), trans. from Newman, *Sister of Wisdom*, p. 118.

26. Lotario dei Segni [Pope Innocent III], *De Miseria Condicionis Humane*, ed. Robert E. Lewis (1978), p. 2.

27. [Innocent III] *De Miseria Condicionis Humane*, pp. 102–5, with Latin.

28. [Innocent III], *De Miseria Condicionis Humane*, pp. 104–5, with Latin.

29. Michael O'Carroll, *Theotokos: A Theological Encyclopedia of the Virgin Mary* (1982), pp. 185–6.

30. Peck, *The Fool of God*, pp. 47–9.

31. Peck, *The Fool of God*, pp. 7–8.

32. Peck, *The Fool of God*, p. 49.

33. Newman, *Sister of Wisdom*, pp. 147–8.

34. Newman, *Sister of Wisdom*, p. 178.

35. See, for example, Caroline Walker Bynum, *Fragmentation and Redemption: Essays on Gender and the Human Body in Medieval Religion* (1991), pp. 79–117.

36. St Hildegard's use of this motif is discussed in Newman, *Sister of Wisdom*, p. 118.

37. Bynum, *Fragmentation and Redemption*, p. 97.

38. Richard Hamer, *A Choice of Anglo-Saxon Verse* (1970), pp. 166–7. The historical date of the Crucifixion was believed to have been the same as that of the Annunciation, i.e., 25 March, and it is possible that the poet intends an allusion to this, as well as to the incarnational and redemptive features which are shared by the two events. See Mary Clayton, *The Cult of the Virgin Mary in Anglo-Saxon England* (1990), pp. 206–7.

39. Rupert of Deutz, *Commentary on John's Gospel* 13, in *PL*169,790A-B.

40. R. T. Davies (ed.), *Medieval English Lyrics: A Critical Anthology* (1966), p. 87, lines 37–45.

41. Columba Marmion, *Christ the Life of the Soul* (St Louis: Herder, 1939), p. 377, quoted by James Cardinal Hickey in *Mary at the Foot of the Cross: Teacher and Example of Holiness of Life for Us* (1988), p. 197.

42. Hans Urs von Balthasar, *The Threefold Garland* trans. Erasmo Leiva-Merikakis (1982), p. 102.

43. *Oxford Book of Italian Verse*, ed. St John Lucas (1952), pp. 20–5.

44. Peck, *The Fool of God*, pp. 150–2.

45. Peck, *The Fool of God*, p. 148.

46. Leo Steinberg, 'The Metaphors of Love and Birth in Michelangelo's *Pietàs*' in T. Bowie and C.V. Christenson (eds), *Studies in Erotic Art* (1970), p. 234.

47. Peck, *The Fool of God*, p. 140; John V. Fleming, *An Introduction to the Franciscan Literature of the Middle Ages* (1977), p. 181.
48. Peck, *The Fool of God*, pp. 65–7. Philip Ziegler describes the spread and decline of the Flagellants in the fourteenth century in *The Black Death* (1982), pp. 87–98.
49. William A. Christian, Jr, *Apparitions in Late Medieval and Renaissance Spain* (1981), pp. 220–2.
50. Duffy, *The Stripping of the Altars*, pp. 246–8 and 234–256 *passim*.
51. Duffy, *The Stripping of the Altars*, p. 258.
52. Duffy, *The Stripping of the Altars*, p. 259; Christian, *Apparitions in Late Medieval and Renaissance Spain*, p. 220; Ziegler, *The Black Death*, pp. 276–86.
53. Michael Carroll, *The Cult of the Virgin Mary: Psychological Origins* (1986), pp. 49–76.
54. André Grabar, *Christian Iconography: A Study of its Origins* (1969), pp. 131–2.
55. Duffy, *The Stripping of the Altars*, pp. 238–42.
56. Graef, *Mary: A History of Doctrine and Devotion* vol. 1, p. 122.
57. Graef, *Mary: A History of Doctrine and Devotion* vol. 1, p. 201.
58. Graef, *Mary: A history of Doctrine and Devotion* vol. 1, p. 200.
59. William McLoughlin, 'Our Lady of Sorrows – A devotion within a tradition' in Alberic Stacpoole (ed.), *Mary and the Churches* (1987), p. 115.
60. McLoughlin, 'Our Lady of Sorrows', p. 115; Warner, *Alone of All Her Sex*, pp. 210–11.
61. Graef, *Mary: A History of Doctrine and Devotion* vol. 1, pp. 243–4.
62. Graef, *Mary: A History of Doctrine and Devotion* vol. 1, p. 263.
63. See n. 39.
64. Michael Carroll, *Madonnas that Maim: Popular Catholicism in Italy since the Fifteenth Century* (1992), p. 92. See also Giuliano Procacci, *History of the Italian People*, trans. Anthony Paul (1973), pp. 36–7 and 86–92.
65. Peck, *The Fool of God*, p. 134.
66. Peck, *The Fool of God*, p. 135.

 споспоспо

Conclusion: looking forward

The history of Marian doctrine and devotion is no less fraught with ambiguities than are other aspects of human culture, and there cannot be any proper resolution to a work of this kind. But since a book must have some sort of conclusion, I offer one or two provisional pointers which follow from what has gone above.

Mary in modernity

There has been much Marian devotion which may not unfairly be suspected of having perpetuated an infantile dependence upon an all-powerful mother – an inappropriate dependence which Protestants have implicitly and rightly criticized in their rejection of certain aspects of Catholicism. Yet it is necessary for us to recall our most primitive sense of contentment and of union with our surroundings, and to find in this memory the inspiration to criticize the present, in the search for a possible better future. This sense of contentment and union seems to find its symbolism in the language and imagery relating to motherhood, and this language and imagery is the proverbial baby which many branches of Protestantism threw out with the bath-water of medieval Catholicism. Yet does the cult of the Virgin today include any features which, in a rationalized and commodified world, could supply that memory of infant satisfaction which might inspire revolutionary change, and not just provide temporary solace in the midst of apparently inevitable alienation? There are many reasons for

212

believing that Marian devotion is quite lacking in this kind of potential.

Julia Kristeva has suggested that the appeal of certain aspects of the cult of the Virgin has resided in their evocation of experiences which cannot be articulated in words, and in particular, of the experiences of new motherhood and early infancy. However, she poses the modernist objection to representative imagery: that in a world dominated by commodities, most representations no longer have the power to signify meaning beyond that which can be bought and sold, or which can be manipulated for advertising. She seems to contend that portrayals of Mary's motherhood suffer precisely that fate.[1]

In Chapter 1 I commented on the modern tendency for women's anatomy to be seen predominantly in terms of sexual attraction or medical science, and this again seems to militate against the possibility that Mary's physical maternity might offer that memory of childhood contentment which could provoke action which is orientated towards the future. Against this, one might suggest that to understand the dynamics of Marian devotion partly in terms of the Oedipus complex makes explicit a latent element of sexuality which, following the reasoning of Marcuse, might be accepted and then deliberately sublimated in the interests of creating and striving to realize a vision of future liberation. Moreover, since it has been rare for Marian devotion to be associated directly with any affirmation of the goodness of sexual pleasure, the integration of these diverse elements of human experience might be considered a goal whose attainment would signify that the fissures which characterize domination and repression were being undermined. There nevertheless arises the suspicion that the conscious articulation and acceptance of a sexual aspect to the veneration of Mary will lead only to the discarding of that veneration, rather than to its incorporation in a project of human – including sexual – liberation. Furthermore, Marcuse rightly recognized that sexuality itself can be transformed into an aspect of one-dimensional culture,[2] when it is commonly reduced to a series of superficial pleasures, and used as a device in the widespread promotion of commodity sales. It is not clear how one can guarantee that the rescuing of repressed sexuality will lead to its appropriate sublimation, and not to the despondent barbarism which reduces all human culture to that which is 'merely' – and from that point of view, despicably – sexual.

If it is not sexuality which can provide a route whereby Marian devotion might inspire action for liberation, then it might be suggested instead that the experience of suffering pain could perform such a function. Pain is an experience which is universal, and it may not be as susceptible as pleasure to commercial manipulation. Hence, through reflection on Mary at the Cross, the memory of the mother's pain and the child's distress might provide a point from which to launch a critique of a culture which maintains itself through the infliction of violence. Yet the removal of birthing, dying and illness from the streets and houses of a rationalized society make it hard for the members of that society to set ordinary but intense human suffering in a perspective that both reveals its agony and yet allows one to see beyond it. Furthermore, a culture whose popular entertainment is characterized by the widespread use of 'spatter' (as bloodshed is now called in the film trade) and sado-masochism has evidently developed a high level of resistance to the tragedy of pain and guilt.

Considerations of this kind tend to suggest that those aspects of Marian devotion which might in principle become stimuli to progressive political action are unlikely to be able to generate such an effect under the conditions which obtain in a culture dominated by commodities and rationalization. I hope nonetheless to show that there are perspectives from which the Marian traditions of Christianity appear to provide a more plausible foundation for a radical critique of the social and economic status quo.

Critical moments

At the beginning of *Civilization and its Discontents*, Freud includes a short essay on the subject of religious experience.[3] He says that a friend of his, Romain Rolland, has written quite favourably to Freud in response to the latter's book *The Future of an Illusion*. However, Rolland

> was sorry [Freud] had not properly appreciated the true source of religious sentiments. This, he says, consists in a peculiar feeling, which [seems to be quite common, and] ... which he would like to call a sensation of 'eternity', a feeling as of something 'oceanic' ... One may, he thinks, rightly call oneself religious on the ground of this oceanic feeling alone, even if one rejects every belief and every illusion.[4]

But Freud rejects the idea that this 'oceanic feeling' is the true source of religious sentiments. He suggests that the feeling is an expression of the persistence into adulthood of the infant's experience of continuity with its surroundings, which is the memory that was established prior to the differentiation of the ego from the outside world.

> An infant at the breast does not as yet distinguish his ego from the external world as the source of the sensations flowing in upon him. He gradually learns to do so, in response to various promptings. He must be very strongly impressed by the fact that some sources of excitation, which he will later recognize as his own bodily organs, can provide him with sensations at any moment, whereas other sources evade him from time to time – among them what he desires most of all, his mother's breast – and only reappear as a result of his screaming for help.[5]

In this way, the child begins to learn that it is distinct from its surroundings; but the very earliest experience of union with the world always remains present in some manner in the mind of the adult. This, however, is not the source of 'the religious attitude', even if it subsequently became connected with it. On the contrary, Freud writes:

> The derivation of religious needs from the infant's helplessness and the longing for the father aroused by it seems to me incontrovertible, especially since the feeling is not simply prolonged from childhood days, but is permanently sustained by the fear of the superior power of Fate. I cannot think of any need in childhood as strong as the need for a father's protection. Thus the part played by the oceanic feeling . . . is ousted from a place in the foreground.[6]

Freud's whole approach to Rolland's suggestion is shot through with assumptions drawn from an androcentric analytical base. Apart from his confident assertion about the primacy of the infant's need for paternal protection (and not, say, for maternal nourishment), Freud's understanding of the development of the ego depends upon the notion that the infant experiences itself as primary, and its surroundings as an undifferentiated extension of itself. That is to say, it is not that the infant feels itself to be continuous with the environment in which it is submerged, but rather, that the environment is a continuation of its own self (a view which has been called into question above, in Chapter 5). Actually, Freud lapses into language which suggest that the differentiation of the ego is indeed a process of extracting the self from the prior universe of which it forms a constituent part, and not one of pushing away those features of the world which had once been part of the self, but which subsequently turn out to be 'other' than it. Freud then has to 'correct' himself: 'In this way, then, the ego detaches itself from the external world. Or, to put it more correctly, originally the ego includes everything, later it separates off an external world from itself.'[7] Thus, Freud sees infant development from the standpoint of the male adult who has experienced sharply his own difference from his mother and from the world around him, and who, being anxious to maintain his fragile sense of a masculine self, projects it back into infancy, where it is described as suffering from that *folie de grandeur* which in fact characterizes a later, and very different, stage of emotional development.

My own arguments depend upon the understanding that the infant's sense of continuity with the world is not a characteristic of some inflated sense of self, but that it signifies a mental condition in which all that is comprehended is participation in one's surroundings, with nothing more than the slightest intimation of one's separate identity. It is because we are truly continuous with, and at every point dependent upon, our inanimate environment and its living inhabitants, that the apparently transcendent human self relates to these things so easily as though they were 'mother'. This is also one of the reasons for the motherhood of the Virgin Mary being closely tied to the cultural construction of Nature. There is a true analogy between our participation in the world we call 'environment', and the infant's participation in the union with its mother. Moreover, precisely at this point is found one of the crucial moments in the quest for liberation: for it may well be that the remembrance of this early sense of continuity with one's mother has the implicit ability to call to mind knowledge of one's real continuity with the elements, and with all one's fellow creatures. This perception can become a fundamental criterion by which to assess the workings of domination and the progress of liberation.

The dualism of the dominant 'self' and the subordinate 'other' undermines the knowledge that there is an ultimate unity of nature and interest which underlies the two, and the mastering self tries always to maintain the state of separation. We have seen that Mary has on many occasions been co-opted to the cause of moral dualism and political domination, and there is something of an implicit tendency to do this even on the part of authors who expressly reject such views. Eamon Duffy, for example, acknowledges that the cult of the Virgin has been used in the service of misogynistic attitudes among Christians. He cites the following feminist objection to Marian devotion:

> Woman in her own right, autonomous and with her own sexual identity has, it is claimed, no part in the cult of the Madonna, for Mary herself has value only by her obedience to the Father and her bearing of the Son.[8]

Duffy considers that there is some historical justification for such criticism. However, he is of the opinion that it is not 'a necessary or legitimate development of the cult of the Virgin Mary. [Rather,] the figure of Our Lady is to be understood as *inclusive*, representative of redeemed humanity as a whole, and not merely of womankind.' Thus,

> Mary's receptivity and obedience to the work of God in Christ is not the model for some uniquely *feminine* mode of behaviour, but the pattern for *all* creaturely responsiveness to God, male as well as female.[9]

What Duffy fails to observe is that the relationship between God and Mary is still couched in terms of male initiative and female response, and, moreover, that the terms of this relationship are articulated within an overall cultural context in which female is indeed subordinate to male. Duffy writes: 'in Mary Christianity has exalted a woman to a place second only to Christ himself',[10] as though the words 'only' and 'himself' remove the force of the fact that the woman is secondary to the man!

A fundamental flaw in much Christian teaching about Mary's obedience to God seems to lie in its positing God and the human being as though they were two individuated creatures, of whom one must obey the other's command. This model reproduces elements from the pattern of human domination and seems likely to assist in the legitimation of such a pattern. Yet there are alternative ways of interpreting Mary's relationship with God. Let us look first at the motif of command and obedience.

Is Mary's *fiat* ('Let it be to me according to your word') the response of a slave who accedes to her master's wishes regardless of her own preference? A case can be made for saying that the dominant tradition of interpretation of the Annunciation story gives little ground for such a reading. It seems more in keeping with the general tenor of Mary's cult through the ages (if not in the twentieth century) that Gabriel's news of the Virgin's impending motherhood should be viewed as a message which fulfils Mary's deepest longings. That is to say, she does not have to 'knuckle under' and do as she is told, because it is her own desire which is about to be realized. She is to be the bearer of her own Saviour, who is also the Redeemer of the world. Mary is said to be a figure for Israel, in whom the people's salvation is conceived and for whom it is born; and Christian tradition has maintained that Israel had for generations longed for this salvation – the coming of the Messiah – and that this wish was fulfilled in Jesus. Moreover, biblical scholars have drawn attention to the fact that the Greek word with which Gabriel greets Mary is χαιρε, which is a usual form of greeting, but which has the literal meaning 'Rejoice'. This is also the word used by the Septuagint in prophecies addressed to the 'Daughter of Zion', which look forward to the salvation of the Jewish people. In this way, Mary is cast as a representative of God's people, in whom their deepest hope is about to be realized.[11]

Typology aside, we have seen above that Catholic teaching has invariably held Mary's assent to be an act of free will. None of this detracts from the idea that Mary's acceptance of her vocation was highly courageous. What it does imply is that God's will and Mary's were perfectly conformed to one another.

Now, although this account ostensibly involves no conflict between the Lord and the creature, it may still be unsatisfactory when considered from the standpoint of a critique of domination. It seems to say that the master knows what is best for the subordinate, and that if only the subordinate sees the world clearly, then she will understand that the master's will is in fact what she 'really' wants. Mary thus appears to be the perfect servant, since she has made her master's will her own and carries it out without even being able to know whether or not she has interests which might conflict with the decision of her Lord. Indeed, it is Mary's sinlessness which makes possible her clarity of insight, and since this is itself a gift from God, she appears to be beholden to him as a slave to her owner.

This objection is valid, however, only if we speak of God as though he were a created individual, imposing his will on another creature in an attempt to deny her alterity. And in a world shot through with unjust inequalities, it is indeed hard, and even impossible, to find language which is not loaded with connotations of domination. Yet God is beyond any individuation and therefore beyond the relationships that may follow from individuation, such as domination. Mary's desire coincides with God's will not because she has been coerced into accepting his lordship, but because the life and the will of God are at the foundation of the life and well-being of all God's creatures, and Mary has recognized that. Human relations of domination make us forget the source of our life and well-being and are a symptom of that forgetfulness. But in Mary, the knowledge of the source, sustenance and destiny of her own life ensures that her desire for the conception and birth of Christ is entirely her own.

The Holy Spirit who overshadows Mary does not fertilize her (and this is signified by her remaining a virgin), but 'broods' over her, and thereby brings to fruition the embodiment of divine life which has arisen inside her. For this reason, the comparison which some Jungian writers have made between the Virgin Mary and a virgin forest seems apt.[12] The virgin forest is uncultivated by humanity and abundantly fruitful in itself. The fecundity of God's activity is thus not imposed on Mary, but springs up within and as a part of her, so that her desire, her conception, her gestation and childbearing are radically her own at the same time as being divine. Mary is, as it were, an icon of freedom from domination, who not only inspires in the devotee the hope for a world transformed, but already embodies that transformation in her own life. This sacred integrity may already be suggested by the great Virgin in Majesty figures of twelfth-century Europe, in which Christ arises out of his mother like a sapling out of soil.

Yet there are no images or words adequate to this condition which Christians call glorification. St Robert Bellarmine writes of the bliss which the angels already enjoy in their heavenly homeland, and considers the fact that humanity must sojourn in exile until we too may come to eternal joy. He says:

> Although in this regard we are less than the angels, God's goodness wonderfully consoles us men ... because he has placed a man and a woman from our race, Christ and Mary, ahead of all the angels in the kingdom of heaven ... [13]

Christ and Mary are already in that state of sinless and glorified humanity which in some manner will finally be established on earth, and we cannot know what that condition is like. But we can acquire sufficient sense of it to identify some of the circumstances where it is lacking in the present, and so to move ahead in the constant hope of attaining that which is as yet unknown. For in Christ, the unseen God has been made tangibly present in this world through Mary, and in

Christ and Mary is the promise that this world can be fully restored to a condition worthy of its origin in God.

Notes

1. Julia Kristeva, 'Stabat Mater' in *Histoires d'Amour* (1983), pp. 225–47; and in Toril Moi (ed.), *The Kristeva Reader*, trans. Leon Roudiez (1986), pp. 160–86.
2. Herbert Marcuse, *One Dimensional Man* (1964), pp. 72–4.
3. Sigmund Freud, *Civilization and its Discontents*, trans. Joan Rivière (1963), pp. 1–10.
4. Freud, *Civilization and its Discontents*, p. 1.
5. Freud, *Civilization and its Discontents*, pp. 3–4.
6. Freud, *Civilization and its Discontents*, p. 9.
7. Freud, *Civilization and its Discontents*, p. 5.
8. Eamon Duffy, *What Catholics Believe about Mary* (1989), pp. 20–1.
9. Duffy, *What Catholics Believe about Mary*, p. 21.
10. Duffy, *What Catholics Believe about Mary*, p. 20.
11. This line of scriptural interpretation seems to have begun with the now famous paper by S. Lyonnet, 'χαιρε Κεχαριτωμενη' (in *Biblica* vol. XX (1939), pp. 131–41). It is elaborated by René Laurentin (*Structure et Théologie de Luc I–II* (1957), pp. 152–61), and also by John McHugh (*The Mother of Jesus in the New Testament* (1975), pp. 38–52). Raymond Brown cites Protestant, as well as Catholic, scholars who favour this interpretation, but is himself more sceptical about it (*The Birth of the Messiah: A Commentary on the Infancy Narratives in the Gospels of Matthew and Luke* (1993), pp. 321–4).
12. John Layard, 'The incest taboo and the virgin archetype', *Eranos Jahrbuch* vol. XII (1945), pp. 290–1; Nor Hall, *The Moon and the Virgin: Reflections on the Archetypal Feminine* (1980), p. 11.
13. Robert Bellarmine, *The Mind's Ascent to God* 9:5, in *Spiritual Writings*, trans. John Patrick Donnelly and Roland J.Teske (1989), p. 149.

Appendix: The concept of domination

Weber's concept of domination

Max Weber considered that domination played 'a considerable role' in most kinds of social action, and he even stated: 'Without exception, every sphere of social action is profoundly influenced by structures of dominancy.'[1] Weber defined domination in terms of command and obedience, and wrote: 'No usable concept of domination can be defined in any way other than by reference to power of command.'[2] According to Weber, the level of domination in a social situation is the probability that a particular command will be obeyed by a given group of persons.[3] Weber's definition in itself does not include any reference to the source of the dominant party's power of command, or to the subordinate party's corresponding motivation for obedience. However, he indicates two general sources of domination, when he writes that domination might exist 'by virtue of a constellation of interests (in particular: by virtue of a position of monopoly)', or alternatively, that it might exist 'by virtue of authority, i.e., power to command and duty to obey'.[4] The distinction between these two types of domination is expressed by Frank Parkin in a paraphrase of Weber: 'Whereas no one is expected to obey the capitalist or banker out of a sense of duty, everyone is expected to obey the patriarch or the prince precisely on these grounds.'[5] Obedience to the banker arises out of material necessity: to the patriarch, out of moral or legal obligation. Weber makes it clear that his own concern is almost entirely with domination of the latter kind, that is, domination 'by virtue of authority'. He elucidates this further by explaining that in a relationship of domination

– as he is going to employ the term – the will of the *ruler* influences the conduct of the *ruled* in such a way that, 'to a socially relevant degree', the party which is ruled carries out the ruler's command as though the ruled willed the content of the command for its own sake.[6] Simone de Beauvoir's account of the subordination of women to men implies that, in Weberian terms, the relationship between men and women in the society she describes has been the most extreme example of a relationship of domination, since women have not contested male sovereignty, but have submitted themselves to the point of view of the group which designates them as 'other'.[7]

Weber makes little reference to either the will or the interests of the subordinate party (the 'ruled') in a relationship of domination. However, he does define domination as a special case of *power*,[8] having already defined *power* as the chance of realizing one's will in communal action, against the resistance of others participating in the action.[9] In a situation of domination, therefore, there may be a conflict of wills or interests, but the ruler's command is obeyed by the subordinates regardless of their own preferences. The fact that a situation of domination exists at all nonetheless indicates that some opposition between the parties involved is either presumed to exist or is anticipated as a possibility in the future. So domination is first and foremost a relationship of coercion. Whether or not a relationship of domination exists may be tested by asking the question: what would happen if the subordinate refused to co-operate with the superior's command? If the likelihood is that such non-compliance would be met with the imposition of force (or at least with strong negative sanctions) then it would be plain that the relationship was one of domination, albeit that the imbalance of power is not normally made so explicit.

Domination is typically taken for granted by the participants in the relationship; in many instances, it is part of the fabric of everyday social interaction, and as such, it precedes the entry of any particular participant into the relationship, and similarly continues after the departure of any participant. Weber himself supplies the example of the dominance of a particular language when it is the consequence of political change in a given geographical area[10] – an illustration which indicates well that a relationship of domination is part of the social structure. Domination is a structural relationship of coercion.

The legitimation of domination

A state of domination is maintained by the practical legitimation which it receives from those who have contact with it, and in particular, from those who are subject to it. When a group which is subject to domination ceases to accord legitimacy to the existing structure of command and obedience, then that structure collapses: domination exists in virtue of legitimation. Any enquiry into legitimation must try to establish what count as the real *interests* of the various parties involved in a relationship of domination, since domination is defined specifically in terms of its failure to address the interests of the subordinate party, and legitimation is the process by which people support the status quo even against their own interests.

By what process, then, do subordinates come to legitimate a structure which maintains their own subservience? For the purposes of the present study, this is a question which may be answered on two different levels. The first of these is the interpersonal, or psychological level, at which the question is dealt with in terms of the micro-social relations by which members of a given social group are taught, forced or persuaded to accept subordination to their rulers. Childhood experience or peer pressure, for example, might be cited as partial explanations of some particular group's legitimation of a given authority, or of authority in general. An explanation of this kind is concerned with the actions, and sometimes the thoughts and feelings, of individual actors, rather than with the corporate behaviour of social groups. In contrast to this, the second of the two levels of explanation for legitimation is that of the macro-social, at which an account is given for human behaviour in terms of the functioning of society as a whole.

The Frankfurt School of social theory drew on (and amended) both the large-scale theory of Marxism and the psychoanalytical theory of Freud to account for the means by which members of modern societies are willing to legitimate their own domination, and pointed to the ways in which mass culture tries to disguise or hide the truth about humanity's real interests, and about the injustice and impoverishment of a world shot through with every sort of domination. However, since both Marxism and psychoanalysis are themselves products of a society characterized by economic, political and ideological domination, they may be misconstruing social reality by unwittingly reflecting and thereby helping to legitimate relationships of domination which have not yet been recognized. It follows from this that it would only be under conditions of liberation from domination that any final assessment of interests could be formulated. Hence, the only human interest which can be clearly identified is the general attainment of liberation from domination of any kind. The fact that any existing assumptions about domination are likely to be inadequate means that the criticism of these assumptions must form an essential aspect of the project of liberation. Existing assumptions must be constantly reassessed in the light of new experience.

Domination and rationalization

The Frankfurt School's understanding of rationality was greatly influenced by the work of the Hungarian social theorist Georg Lukács, and in particular, by his essay 'Reification and the Consciousness of the Proletariat'.[11] In this essay, Lukács argued that capitalist society was profoundly affected in all its aspects by commodity relations. This analysis was an elaboration and development of Marx's thinking on the same subject.[12] In a developed capitalist economy, commodity exchange tends to become the universal form of economic life, and as this happens, it obscures the human relationships which in fact are the substance of all economic exchange. In a society in which articles are traded with an immediate view to their use-value, it is clear that the economic relationship is simultaneously a personal one; in a mercantile economy, by contrast, goods are bought and sold without any interest in the human use which they might ultimately serve, and are viewed solely in terms of their value as commodities. The trading of commodities gives the appearance of a series of relationships between objects, without any immediate sign of the human interactions which have generated those commodities and which constitute the activities of exchange. Commodities themselves, and the behaviour of a commodity market, which fundamentally are composed of relationships between *people*, seem to be merely relations between *things*, and for this reason, human relationships are said to be *reified* in commodities. Moreover, Lukács writes, 'Reification requires that a society should learn to satisfy all its needs in terms of commodity exchange.'[13] This means that human relations in general become reified.

The worker sells his or her labour-power as a commodity. Unlike an artisan in some earlier period of history, the worker does not make an article from scratch, having in mind a customer and a use for the finished article, using his own tools, and governing his own time. Rather, the worker sells his or her labour-power to an employer who has determined what objects are to be made, and what small part in their production the worker will perform. The tools with which he or she works are provided by the employer, and the time in which the work is to be carried out is likewise externally established. An aspect of the worker's own person is thereby alienated from him or her, and is sold as a commodity.

The commodification of human persons and relationships is universal not only in the world of paid work, but because so many of the institutions of capitalist society are adapted to the needs of the economy, it comes to affect almost every other aspect of human life. Hence, one bourgeois philosopher can claim that marriage is centrally concerned with the partners' use and 'possession' of one another's sexual organs.[14]

Furthermore, not only human relationships, but also the material world becomes misrepresented through being regarded in terms of commodities. Land, for example, will be seen by the capitalist landlord as a potential yielder of rent, and its inherent qualities - such as fertility - will be overlooked (except in so far as they contribute to its monetary value).[15]

The reification brought about by the dominance of the commodity form in capitalist society is intimately connected to the process of rationalization.[16] Commodities are objects of calculation: their very existence tends to imply measurement and prediction, since it is the estimation of value and profit which eventually renders the production and marketing of commodities a worthwhile activity. Beyond this, the rationalization of production through the division of labour and the costing of labour hours (both of which are aspects of reification) has been essential to the expansion of commodity production.

A rationalized economy also requires, for example, a rationalized legal system. That is to say, it must be possible to calculate what the legal consequences of particular actions will be, without having to risk running up against entirely upredictable factors, such as the exceptional wrath or mercy of some particular judge on some particular occasion.[17] In this way, the social domination of a commodity-based economy – which is itself characterized by the domination of one class over another

– has generated a life-world in which everything becomes ever more machine-like in its relentlessness and insensitivity to both humanity and nature.

At the heart of this process of rationalization is the reduction of dissimilar phenomena to a single common denominator. For the merchant, everything can be converted into money: silk or cinnamon, oil or diamonds – it must all be translated into monetary units before it can be acquired or disposed of. And this applies equally, of course, to the worker's labour power or to ten acres of meadowland.

Adorno and Horkheimer point out that it is the reduction of all things and activities to mathematics which is the ultimate tendency of rationalization. The classification of the world into ever more precise categories for the purposes of increasing control is a practice which culminates in the mathematization of the world, since it is in the symbols and formulae of mathematics that the finest reduction and greatest interchangeability of different phenomena can be achieved. Mathematics is potentially universal in its application to physical phenomena, and hence may be regarded as the lowest of all common denominators.[18]

Lukács also observed, however, that the overall system of capitalist production is not subject to any of this kind of calculation: it is essentially irrational.[19] Although the capitalist producer relies heavily upon the detailed control of the various contributory activities to and within his own business, the market in which he sells the final product is competitive, fundamentally unplanned and ultimately unpredictable. This lack of rational direction characterizes the whole society. It was this thesis which the Frankfurt theorists developed when they argued that instrumental rationality – the principle by which the various parts of society are managed – had become an end in itself. Since no rational goals had been set for the social system as a whole, it had been possible for the instrumental rationality which should have been the means of achieving these goals to be elevated to the status of a supreme good in itself; the concept of reason, on the other hand, had been correspondingly reduced to signify nothing more than instrumental rationality. The irrational pursuit of technical progress had therefore taken on the appearance of being reasonable, even though it was not fulfilling the requirement of human well-being.[20] The critique of domination by instrumental rationality must form an integral part of any project of liberation in contemporary society.

Notes

1. Max Weber, *Economy and Society*, two vols, trans. Guenther Roth *et al.* (1978 [1968]), vol. 2, p. 941.
2. Weber, *Economy and Society* vol. 2, p. 948.
3. Weber, *Economy and Society* vol. 1, p. 53.
4. Weber, *Economy and Society* vol. 2, p. 943.
5. Frank Parkin, *Max Weber* (1982), p. 74.
6. Weber, *Economy and Society* vol. 2, p. 946.
7. Simone de Beauvoir, *Le Deuxième Sexe I: Les Faits et les Mythes* (1949), pp. 17–19.
8. Weber, *Economy and Society* vol. 2, p. 941.
9. Weber, *Economy and Society* vol. 1, p. 53.
10. Weber, *Economy and Society* vol. 2, p. 941.
11. Georg Lukács, *History and Class Consciousness: Studies in Marxist Dialectics*, first edn 1922; trans. Rodney Livingstone, from 1967 edn (1971), pp. 83–222.
12. Lukács, *History and Class Consciousness*, pp. 84 and 83–111 *passim*.
13. Lukács, *History and Class Consciousness*, p. 91. These ideas underlie Marcuse's writing about 'one-dimensional' society.
14. Lukács, *History and Class Consciousness*, p. 100.
15. Lukács, *History and Class Consciousness*, p. 92.
16. Lukács, *History and Class Consciousness*, pp. 88–9.
17. Lukács, *History and Class Consciousness*, pp. 95–7. Note that many of the miracles of the Virgin depend upon a relatively non-rationalized legal procedure: the Virgin intervenes to secure mercy where the rigid application of principles of justice would lead to condemnation. Perhaps the demise of judicial practices of this kind has contributed to the demise not only of these miracle stories, but also of a more general sense of Christian hope.
18. Max Horkheimer and Theodor Adorno, *Dialectic of Enlightenment*, trans. John Cumming (1979), pp. 6–8.
19. Lukács, *History and Class Consciousness*, pp. 99–103.
20. #Jürgen Habermas has pointed out that this diminished concept of reason is very different from the notion of reason as it was employed by the classical philosophers of the eighteenth century. It then had a moral content: action was reasonable if it was right in its practical implications. Now, by contrast, reason signifies only technical control (*Theory and Practice*, trans. John Viertel (1988), pp. 253–5). The theme of domination by technical reason, and the irrationality of that domination, has been taken up by other authors, e.g. Stanley Aronowitz, *Science as Power: Discourse and Ideology in Modern Society* (1988); Brian Easlea, 'Who Needs the Liberation of Nature?', *Science Studies* 4 (1974), pp. 77–92; William Leiss, *The Domination of Nature* (1974).

csesescses

Bibliography

Adams, Carol *The Sexual Politics of Meat*. Cambridge: Polity Press, 1990.

Adorno, Theodor W. *Minima Moralia: Reflections from Damaged Life* (trans. E.F.N. Jephcott). London: NLB, 1974.

Gesammelte Schriften (ed. Gretel Adorno), Band 4. Frankfurt am Main: Suhrkamp Verlag, 1980.

Adorno, Theodor and Max Horkheimer *Dialectic of Enlightenment* (trans. John Cumming). London: Verso Editions, 1979.

Allchin, A. M. *The Joy of All Creation: An Anglican Meditation on the Place of Mary*. London: New City, 1993.

Allen, Prudence *The Concept of Woman: The Aristotelian Revolution, 750 BC–AD 1250*. Grand Rapids, MI. and Cambridge: Eerdmans, 1997.

[Anonymous] *Meditations on the Tarot: A Journey into Christian Hermeticism*. New York: Amity House, 1985.

Anselm, St 'De conceptu virginali et de originali peccato' in *S. Anselmi Opera Omnia* (ed. F.S. Schmitt), vol. 2. Edinburgh: Thomas Nelson, 1946.

The Prayers and Meditations of St Anselm (trans. Benedicta Ward). Harmondsworth: Penguin Books, 1973.

Aronowitz, Stanley *Science as Power: Discourse and Ideology in Modern Society*. Basingstoke: Macmillan Press, 1988.

Atkinson, Clarissa *The Oldest Vocation: Christian Motherhood in the Middle Ages* Ithaca, NY and London: Cornell University Press, 1991.

Balić, Carlo 'The medieval controversy over the Immaculate Conception up to the death of Scotus' in E.D. O'Connor (ed.), *The Dogma of The Immaculate Conception: History and Significance*, pp. 161–212. Notre Dame, IN: University of Notre Dame Press, 1958.

Barrow, John and Frank Tipler *The Anthropic Cosmological Principle*. Oxford: Oxford University Press, 1987.

Barth, Karl *Church Dogmatics* vol. I: *The Doctrine of the Word of God* (trans. G. T. Thomson and Harold Knight). Edinburgh: T & T Clark, 1956.

Bede, St *A History of the English Church and People* (trans. Leo Sherley-Price). Harmondsworth: Penguin Books, 1955.

Bellarmine, St Robert *De Controversiis Christianae Fidei* vol. 2: *De Conciliis, et Ecclesia*. Prague: Wolffgang Wickhart, 1721.

   Spiritual Writings (trans. John Patrick Donnelly and Roland J. Teske, Classics of Western Spirituality Series). New York and Mahwah, NJ: Paulist Press, 1989.

[Benedict St] *The Rule of St Benedict: In Latin and English with Notes* (ed. Timothy Fry *et al.*). Collegeville, MN: The Liturgical Press, 1981.

[Bernard of Clairvaux St] *St Bernard's Sermons on the Blessed Virgin Mary* (trans. A Priest of Mount Melleray). Chulmleigh, Devon: Augustine Publishing Company, 1984.

   The Letters of St Bernard of Clairvaux (trans. Bruno Scott James). Stroud, Glos.: Alan Sutton, 1998 [Burns & Oates, 1953].

Bernard of Clairvaux and Amadeus of Lausanne *Magnificat: Homilies in Praise of the Blessed Virgin Mary* (trans. M.-B. Saïd and Grace Perigo). Kalamazoo, MI: Cistercian Publications, 1979.

Berselli, Costante and Giorgio Gharib (eds) *In Praise of Mary: Hymns from the First Millennium of the Eastern and Western Churches* (trans. Phil Jenkins). Slough: St Paul Publications, 1981.

Bétérous, Paule *Les Collections de Miracles de la Vierge en Gallo et Ibéro-Roman au XIIIe Siècle*, Marian Library Studies, New Series vols. 15–16. Dayton, OH: University of Dayton, 1983–4.

Boss, Sarah Jane 'Mary at the margins: Christology and ecclesiology in modernity'. *The Month*, December 1996, pp. 463–75.

Brandon, S. G. F. *Creation Legends of the Ancient Near East*. London: Hodder & Stoughton, 1963.

[Bridget of Sweden St] *Revelationes Caelestes Seraphicae Matris S. Birgittae Suecae*. Gelder: Sebastian Rauch, 1680.

   The Revelations of St Bridget, Princess of Sweden (selection, trans. from Durandus edn 1606, reprinted Cologne 1628). London: Thomas Richardson and Son, 1873.

   Birgitta of Sweden: Life and Selected Revelations (trans. Albert Ryle Kezel, Classics of Western Spirituality Series). New York and Mahwah, NJ: Paulist Press, 1990.

British Methodist/Roman Catholic Committee *Mary, Mother of the Lord: Sign of Grace, Faith and Holiness*. London and Peterborough: CTS Publications and Methodist Publishing House, 1995.

Brock, Sebastian 'Mary in Syriac tradition' in Alberic Stacpoole (ed.) *Mary's Place in Christian Dialogue* pp. 182–91. Slough: St Paul Publications, 1982.

Brodrick, James *The Life and Work of Blessed Robert Francis Cardinal Bellarmine, SJ*, two vols. London: Burns, Oates & Washbourne, 1928.

Saint Peter Canisius, SJ London, Geoffrey Chapman, 1963 [Sheed & Ward, 1938].

Brown, Raymond *The Birth of the Messiah: A Commentary on the Infancy Narratives in Matthew and Luke*. London: Geoffrey Chapman, 1993.

Brownmiller, Susan *Femininity*. London: Paladin Books, 1986.

Bynum, Caroline Walker 'Jesus as mother and abbot as mother: some themes in twelfth-century Cistercian writing', in *Jesus as Mother: Studies in the Spirituality of the High Middle Ages*. Berkeley, Los Angeles and London: University of California Press, 1982, pp. 110–69.

Fragmentation and Redemption: Essays on Gender and the Human Body in Medieval Religion. New York: Zone Books, 1991.

Cadden, Joan *Meanings of Sex Difference in the Middle Ages: Medicine, Science, and Culture*. Cambridge, New York and Victoria: Cambridge University Press, 1993.

Canisius, St Peter *De Maria Virgine Incomparabili, et De Genitrice Sacrosancta*. Ingolstadt: David Sartorius, 1677; and in J.-J. Bourassé (ed.) *Summa Aurea de Laudibus BVM* vol. 8, cols. 613–1450. Paris: Migne, 1862.

Carroll, Michael *The Cult of the Virgin Mary: Psychological Origins*. Princeton, NJ: Princeton University Press, 1986.

Madonnas that Maim: Popular Catholicism in Italy since the Fifteenth Century. Baltimore, MD and London: Johns Hopkins University Press, 1992.

Carter, Brandon 'Large number coincidences and the anthropic principle in cosmology' in M. S. Longair (ed.) *Confrontation of Cosmological Theories with Observational Data*. Dordrecht and Boston, MA: D. Reidel, 1974.

Cassagnes-Brouquet, Sophie *Vierges Noires: Regard et Fascination*. Rodez: Editions du Rouergue, 1990.

Catta, Etienne 'Sedes Sapientiae' in H. du Manoir (ed.) *Maria: Etudes sur la Sainte Vierge* tom. VI, pp. 689–866. Paris: Beauchesne, 1961.

Chenu, M.-D. *Nature, Man and Society in the Twelfth Century: Essays on New Theological Perspectives in the Latin West* (trans. Jerome Taylor and Lester K. Little). Chicago and London: University of Chicago Press, 1968.

Chodorow, Nancy *The Reproduction of Mothering: Psychoanalysis and the Sociology of Gender*. Berkeley, Los Angeles and London: University of California Press, 1978.

Christian, William A. Jr, *Apparitions in Late Medieval and Renaissance Spain*. Princeton, NJ: Princeton University Press, 1981.

Clark, Alice *Working Life of Women in the Seventeenth Century*. London: George Routledge & Sons, 1919.

Clayton, Mary *The Cult of the Virgin Mary in Anglo-Saxon England*. Cambridge: Cambridge University Press, 1990.

Coyle, Kathleen *Mary in the Christian Tradition from a Contemporary Perspective*. Leominster: Gracewing, 1996.

Crew, Phyllis Mack *Calvinist Preaching and Iconoclasm in the Netherlands: 1544–1569*. Cambridge: Cambridge University Press, 1978.

Dahlberg, Andrea 'Transcendence of bodily suffering: an anthropological study of English Catholics at Lourdes'. PhD thesis, London School of Economic and Political Science, 1987.

    'The body as a principle of holism: three pilgrimages to Lourdes' in John Eade and Michael J. Sallnow (eds) *Contesting the Sacred: The Anthropology of Christian Pilgrimage*, pp. 30–50. London and New York: Routledge, 1991.

Daley, Brian E. (ed. and trans.) *On the Dormition of Mary: Early Patristic Homilies*. Crestwood, NY: St Vladimir's Seminary Press, 1998.

Daly, Mary *The Church and the Second Sex*. London: Geoffrey Chapman, 1968.

    Gyn/Ecology: The Metaethics of Radical Feminism Boston, MA: Beacon Press, 1978.

    Pure Lust: Elemental Feminist Philosophy. London: The Women's Press, 1984.

Davies, R.T. (ed.) *Medieval English Lyrics: A Critical Anthology*. London: Faber & Faber, 1966.

D'Avray, David *The Preaching of the Friars: Sermons Diffused from Paris before 1300*. Oxford: Clarendon Press, 1985.

Deason, Gary B. 'Reformation theology and the mechanistic conception of nature', in David C. Lindberg and Ronald H. Numbers (eds) *God and Nature: Historical Essays on the Encounter between Christianity and Science*, pp. 167–91. Berkeley, Los Angeles and London: University of California Press, 1986.

de Beauvoir, Simone *Le Deuxième Sexe* 1: *Les Faits et les Mythes*. Paris: Gallimard, 1949.

de Bruyn, Lucy *Woman and the Devil in Sixteenth-Century Literature*. Tisbury, Wilts.: The Compton Press, 1979.

de Suduiraut, Sophie Guillot *La Vierge à l'Enfant d'Issenheim: Un chef d'oeuvre bâlois de la fin du Moyen Age*. Paris: Réunion des Musées Nationaux, 1998.

Dines, Jennifer 'Mary and the archetypes'. *The Month*, August/September 1987, pp. 288–94.

Dirvin, Joseph I. *Saint Catherine Labouré of the Miraculous Medal*. Rockford, IL: Tan Books, 1984 [1958].

Duffy, Eamon 'Mater Dolorosa, Mater Misericordiae'. *New Blackfriars* 69:816 (May 1988), pp. 210–27.

    What Catholics Believe about Mary. London: CTS Publications, 1989.

    The Stripping of the Altars: Traditional Religion in England 1400–1580. New Haven, CT and London: Yale University Press, 1992.

du Manoir, Hubert (ed.) *Maria: Etudes sur la Sainte Vierge*, eight vols. Paris: Beauchesne, 1949–71.

[Eadmer of Canterbury] *Eadmeri Monachi Cantuariensis Tractatus de Conceptione Sanctae Mariae* (ed. H. Thurston and P. Slater). Freiburg-im-Breisgau: Herder, 1904.

Easlea, Brian 'Who needs the liberation of nature?' *Science Studies* 4 (1974), pp. 77–92.

Fathering the Unthinkable: Masculinity, Scientists and the Nuclear Arms Race. London: Pluto Press, 1983.

Elder, E. Rozanne (ed.) *From Cloister to Classroom: Monastic and Scholastic Approaches to Truth.* Kalamazoo, MI: Cistercian Publications, 1986.

Elliott, J. K. (ed.) *The Apocryphal New Testament.* Oxford: Clarendon Press, 1993.

[Emmerich Anne] *The Life of the Blessed Virgin Mary from the Visions of Anne Emmerich* (trans. M. Palairet). Rockford, IL: Tan Books, 1970 [Burns & Oates, 1954].

Erasmus of Rotterdam 'A pilgrimage for religion's sake' (from *Colloquies*, 1526; trans. Craig R. Thompson) in D. Englander *et al.* (eds) *Culture and Belief in Europe 1450–1600: An Anthology of Sources.* Oxford: Basil Blackwell, 1990.

Fildes, Valerie *Breasts, Bottles and Babies.* Edinburgh: Edinburgh University Press, 1986.

Fleming, John V. *An Introduction to the Franciscan Literature of the Middle Ages.* Chicago: Franciscan Herald Press, 1977.

Forsyth, Ilene *The Throne of Wisdom: Wood Sculptures of the Madonna in Romanesque France.* Princeton, NJ: Princeton University Press, 1972.

Freedberg, David *The Power of Images: Studies in the History and Theory of Response.* Chicago and London: University of Chicago Press, 1989.

Freud, Sigmund *Totem and Taboo* (trans. James Strachey). London: Routledge & Kegan Paul, 1950 [German edn 1913].

Civilization and its Discontents (trans. Joan Rivière). London: Hogarth Press, 1963 [German edn 1930].

The Complete Introductory Lectures on Psychoanalysis (trans. James Strachey). London: George Allen & Unwin, 1971.

Moses and Monotheism (trans. James Strachey). London: Hogarth Press, 1974 [German edn 1939].

The Interpretation of Dreams (trans. James Strachey). Harmondsworth: Penguin Books, 1976 [German edn 1930].

Gebara, Ivone and Maria Clara Bingemer *Mary, Mother of God, Mother of the Poor* (trans. Phillip Berryman). Tunbridge Wells: Burns & Oates, 1989.

Gilson, Etienne *History of Christian Philosophy in the Middle Ages.* London: Sheed & Ward, 1980.

Gimpel, Jean *The Medieval Machine: The Industrial Revolution of the Middle Ages.* London: Victor Gollancz, 1977.

The Cathedral Builders (trans. Teresa Waugh). Salisbury, Wilts.: Michael Russell, 1983.

Gold, Penny Schine *The Lady and the Virgin: Image, Attitude and Experience in Twelfth-Century France*. Chicago: University of Chicago Press, 1985.

Gousset, Cardinal *La Croyance Générale et Constante de l'Eglise Touchant l'Immaculée Conception de la Bienheureuse Vierge Marie*. Paris: Jacques Lecoffre, 1855.

Grabar, André *Christian Iconography: A Study of its Origins*. London: Routledge & Kegan Paul, 1969.

Graef, Hilda *Mary: A history of Doctrine and Devotion* (two vols bound in one). London: Sheed & Ward, 1985.

Graham, Elaine *Making the Difference: Gender, Personhood and Theology*. London: Mowbray, 1995.

Griffin, Susan *Pornography and Silence*. London: Women's Press, 1981.

Habermas, Jürgen *Theory and Practice* (trans. John Viertel). Cambridge: Polity Press, 1988.

Hall, Nor *The Moon and the Virgin*. London: Women's Press, 1980.

Hamer, Richard *A Choice of Anglo-Saxon Verse*. London: Faber & Faber, 1970.

Hannaford, Robert 'Women and the human paradigm: an exploration of gender discrimination'. *New Blackfriars* 70:827 (May 1989), pp. 226–33.

Harris, Errol E. 'Science and nature', in George F. McLean and Hugo Meynell (eds) *Person and Nature* (Studies in Metaphysics, vol. 1), pp. 25ff. Lanham, NY and London: The International Society for Metaphysics, 1988.

Haskins, Susan *Mary Magdalen*. London: HarperCollins, 1993.

Hastrup, Kirsten *Nature and Policy in Iceland 1400–1800: An Anthropological Analysis of History and Mentality*. Oxford: Clarendon Press, 1990.

Haynes, Robert 'The "purpose" of chance in light of the physical basis of evolution', in John M. Robson (ed.) *Origin and Evolution of the Universe: Evidence for Design?*, pp. 1–31. Kingston and Montreal: McGill-Queen's University Press, 1987.

Hegel, G. W. F. *Phenomenology of Spirit* (trans. A.V. Miller). Oxford: Oxford University Press, 1977.

Heiser, Lothar *Maria in der Christus-Verkündigung des orthodoxen Kirchenjahres*. Trier: Paulinus-Verlag, 1981.

Held, David *Introduction to Critical Theory: Horkheimer to Habermas*. London: Hutchinson, 1980.

Herbert, Albert Joseph *The Tears of Mary and Fatima: Why?* Paulina, LA: Albert J. Herbert, 1992.

Herolt, Johannes *Miracles of the Blessed Virgin Mary* (trans. C. C. Swinton Bland; intro. Eileen Power). London: George Routledge, 1928.

Hickey, James, Cardinal *Mary at the Foot of the Cross: Teacher and Example of Holiness of Life for us*. San Francisco: Ignatius Press, 1988.

Hildegard of Bingen *Scivias* (trans. Columba Hart and Jane Bishop, Classics of Western Spirituality Series). New York and Mahwah, NJ: Paulist Press, 1990.

Hirn, Yrjö *The Sacred Shrine: A Study of the Poetry and Art of the Catholic Church*. London: Faber & Faber, 1958.

Homer *Odyssey*, from *Homeri Opera* (ed. T.W. Allen), vols III and IV. Oxford: Oxford University Press, 1917.

    The Odyssey (trans. E.V. Rieu). Harmondsworth: Penguin Books, 1946 and subsequent reprints.

Hopkins, Gerard Manley *Poems and Prose* (ed. W. H. Gardner). Harmondsworth: Penguin Books, 1953.

Horkheimer, Max and Theodor W. Adorno *Dialektik der Auflärung: Philosophische Fragmente*. Frankfurt am Main: Fischer Verlag, 1988 [1944]. English translation *Dialectic of Enlightenment* (trans. John Cumming). London: Verso, 1979.

Houselander, Caryll *The Reed of God*. London: Sheed & Ward, 1944.

Hunt, Lynn (ed.) *The Invention of Pornography: Obscenity and the Origins of Modernity, 1500–1800*. New York: Zone Books,1996.

[Innocent III, Pope] Lotario dei Segni *De Miseria Condicionis Humane* (ed. Robert E. Lewis). Athens, GA: University of Georgia Press, 1978.

Iogna-Prat, D., E. Palazzo and D. Russo (eds) *Marie: Le Culte de la Vierge dans la Société Médiévale*. Paris: Beauchesne, 1996.

Irenaeus of Lyons *Proof of the Apostolic Preaching* (trans. Joseph P. Smith, Ancient Christian Writers Series, 16). London: Longmans, Green & Co., 1952.

Jacobus de Voragine *The Golden Legend: Readings on the Saints* (trans. William Granger Ryan), two vols. Princeton, NJ.: Princeton University Press, 1993.

James, John *Chartres: The Masons who Built a Legend*. London: Routledge & Kegan Paul, 1982.

Jay, Martin *Adorno*. London: Fontana, 1984.

Jelly, Frederick M. *Madonna: Mary in the Catholic Tradition*. Huntington, IN: Our Sunday Visitor, 1986.

Jerome, St *Letters and Selected Works* (trans. W. H. Freemantle, with G. Lewis and W. G. Martley, Nicene and Post-Nicene Fathers, vol. VI). Grand Rapids, MI: Eerdmans, 1979.

[John Duns Scotus] Ioannis Scoti *Theologiae Marianae Elementa* (ed. P. Carolus Balić). Sibenik (Yugoslavia): Typographia Kačić, 1933.

[John Damascene] Jean Damascène *Homélies sur la Nativité et la Dormition* (ed. and French trans. Pierre Voulet). Paris: Les Editions du Cerf, 1961.

[John of Segovia] Ioannis de Segovia *Allegationes et Avisamenta pro Immaculata Conceptione Beatissime Virginis* (for the Council of Basel, 1436). Brussels: Culture et Civilization, 1965 [facsimile edn of that by Balthasar Vivien, Brussels, 1664].

Johnston, Francis *Fatima: The Great Sign*. Chulmleigh, Devon: Augustine Publishing Company, 1980.

Jordanova, Ludmilla J. 'Natural facts: a historical perspective on science and sexuality', in Carol P. MacCormack and Marilyn Strathern (eds) *Nature, Culture and Gender*, pp. 42–69. Cambridge: Cambridge University Press, 1980.

Sexual Visions: Images of Gender in Science and Medicine between the Eighteenth and Twentieth Centuries. Hemel Hempstead: Harvester Wheatsheaf, 1989.

Jugie, Martin *La Mort et l'Assomption de la Sainte Vierge: Etude Historico-doctrinale*. Vatican City: Biblioteca Apostolica Vaticana, 1944.

Kappeler, Susanne *The Pornography of Representation*. Cambridge: Polity Press, 1986.

Kealey, Edward J. *Harvesting the Air: Windmill Pioneers in Twelfth-Century England*. Woodbridge, Suffolk: Boydell, 1989.

Keller, Evelyn Fox *Reflections on Gender and Science*. New Haven, CT and London: Yale University Press, 1985.

Secrets of Life, Secrets of Death: Essays on Language, Gender and Science. New York and London: Routledge, 1992.

Kelly, J. N. D. *Early Christian Doctrines*. London: A. and C. Black, 1977.

Koehler, Th. 'Maternité spirituelle, maternité mystique' in Hubert du Manoir (ed.) *Maria* tom. VI, pp. 551–638. Paris: Beauchesne, 1961.

Kristeva, Julia 'Stabat Mater', in *Histoires d'Amour*, pp. 225–47. Paris: Denoël, 1983.

'Stabat Mater' (trans. Leon Roudiez), in Toril Moi (ed.) *The Kristeva Reader*, pp. 160–86. Oxford: Basil Blackwell, 1986.

Laqueur, Thomas *Making Sex: Body and Gender from the Greeks to Freud*. Cambridge, MA. and London: Harvard University Press, 1990.

Laurentin, René *Marie, l'Eglise et le Sacerdoce: 1. Essai sur le Développement d'une Idée Religieuse*. Paris: Nouvelles Editions Latines, 1952.

Structure et Théologie de Luc I-II. Paris: Gabalda, 1957.

Court Traité sur la Vierge Marie. Paris: P. Lethielleux, 1968.

Bernadette of Lourdes (trans. John Drury). London: Darton, Longman & Todd, 1979.

The Life of Catherine Labouré, 1806–1876 (trans. Paul Inwood). London and Sydney: Collins, 1983.

Layard, John 'The incest taboo and the virgin archetype'. *Eranos Jahrbuch* vol. XII (1945), pp. 253–307.

Le Goff, Jacques *The Birth of Purgatory* (trans. Arthur Goldhammer). London: Scolar Press, 1984.

le Marchant, Jean *Miracles de Notre-Dame de Chartres* (ed. Pierre Kunstmann). Chartres: Société Archéologique d'Eure-et-Loir, and Ottawa: Editions de l'Université d'Ottawa, 1973.

Leiss, William *The Domination of Nature*. Boston: Beacon Press, 1974.

Liguori, Alphonsus de' *The Glories of Mary* two vols (trans. Anon.). London: St Peter's Press, 1937.

Little, Lester K. *Religious Poverty and the Profit Economy in Medieval Europe*. London: Paul Elek, 1978.

Lloyd, G. L. *The Man of Reason: 'Male' and 'Female' in Western Philosophy*. London: Methuen, 1984.

Loarte, Gaspar *Instructions and Advertisements, how to Meditate upon the Misteries of the Rosarie of the most holy Virgin Mary* [in English]. Rouen: Cardin Hamillon, 1613.

Lossky, Vladimir *The Mystical Theology of the Eastern Church* (trans. Fellowship of St Alban and St Sergius). Cambridge and London: James Clarke, 1957.

Lukács, Georg *History and Class Consciousness: Studies in Marxist Dialectics* (first ed. 1922; trans. Rodney Livingstone from 1967 edn). London: Merlin Press, 1971.

Luther, Martin 'The Magnificat translated and explained' [1520–21] (trans. A. T. W. Steinhauser), in *Works of Martin Luther* vol. III, pp. 117–200. Grand Rapids, MI: Baker Book House, 1982 [1930].

Lyonnet, S. 'Χαιρε Κεχαριτωμενη'. *Biblica* vol. XX (1939), pp. 131–41.

Mackenney, Richard *Tradesmen and Traders: The World of the Guilds in Venice and Europe, c.1250–c.1650*. London and Sydney: Croom Helm, 1987.

MacLean, Ian *The Renaissance Notion of Woman: A study in the Fortunes of Scholasticism and Medical Science in European Intellectual Life*. Cambridge: Cambridge University Press, 1983.

Maeckelberghe, Els ' "Mary": maternal friend or virgin mother?' (trans. David Smith), in A. Carr and E. S. Fiorenza (eds) *Motherhood: Experience, Institution, Theology*, I *Concilium* 206 (6/1989)]. Edinburgh: T & T Clark, 1989.

Maitland, Sara *A Map of the New Country: Women and Christianity*. London: Routledge & Kegan Paul, 1983.

Mâle, Emile *The Gothic Image: Religious Art of France in the Thirteenth Century* (trans. Dora Hussey). New York: Harper & Row, 1972.

Marcuse, Herbert *One-Dimensional Man*. London: Routledge & Kegan Paul, 1986 [1964].

Eros and Civilisation. London: Routledge & Kegan Paul, 1987 [1956].

Marlowe, Christopher *Doctor Faustus*, in *The Complete Plays* (ed. J. B. Steane), pp. 259–339. Harmondsworth: Penguin Books, 1969.

Mary of Agreda *Mystical City of God* (trans. Γ. Marison [i.e., G. J. Blatter]), four vols. Catholic Information Service of New Mexico (distributed by Corcoran: Wheeling, West Virginia), 1914.

McHugh, John *The Mother of Jesus in the New Testament*. London: Darton, Longman & Todd, 1975.

McLoughlin, William 'Our Lady of Sorrows – A devotion within a tradition', in Alberic Stacpoole (ed.) *Mary and the Churches*, pp. 114–21. Dublin: The Columba Press, 1987.

236

McNeill, F. Marian *The Silver Bough: A four volume Study of the National and Local Festivals of Scotland* vol. 1: *Scottish Folklore and Folk-Belief.* Glasgow: William MacLellan, 1957.

  The Silver Bough vol. 2: *A Calendar of Scottish and National Festivals: Candlemas to Harvest Home.* Glasgow: William MacLellan, 1959.

Merchant, Carolyn *The Death of Nature.* London: Wildwood House, 1982.

Meyers, Ruth A. 'The Wisdom of God and the Word of God: Alcuin's mass "of wisdom"', in Martin Dudley (ed.) *Like a Two-Edged Sword: The Word of God in Liturgy and History*, pp. 39–59. Norwich: The Canterbury Press, 1995.

Miegge, Giovanni *The Virgin Mary: The Roman Catholic Marian Doctrine* (trans. Waldo Smith). London: Lutterworth Press, 1955.

Miles, Margaret 'The Virgin's one bare breast: female nudity and religious meaning in Tuscan early Renaissance culture', in Susan Rubin Suleiman (ed.) *The Female Body in Western Culture*, pp. 193–208. Cambridge, MA: Harvard University Press, 1986.

Mills, Patricia Jagentowicz *Woman, Nature and Psyche.* New Haven, CT and London: Yale University Press, 1987.

Mitchell, Timothy *Passional Culture: Emotion, Religion, and Society in Southern Spain.* Philadelphia: University of Pennsylvania Press, 1990.

Moore, R. I. *The Origins of a Persecuting Society: Power and Deviance in Western Europe, 950–1250.* Oxford: Basil Blackwell, 1987.

More, Thomas *Utopia* (trans. Paul Turner). Harmondsworth: Penguin, 1965.

Moscucci, Ornella *The Science of Woman: Gynaecology and Gender in England, 1800–1929.* Cambridge: Cambridge University Press, 1990.

Moylan, Tom 'Bloch against Bloch: The theological reception of *Das Prinzip Hoffnung* and the liberation of the utopian function', in J. O. Daniel and T. Moylan (eds) *Not Yet: Reconsidering Ernst Bloch*, pp. 96–121. London: Verso, 1997.

Murray, Robert *Symbols of Church and Kingdom: A Study in Early Syriac Tradition.* Cambridge: Cambridge University Press, 1977.

Newman, Barbara *Sister of Wisdom: St Hildegard's Theology of the Feminine.* Aldershot: Scolar Press, 1987.

[Nicholas of Cusa] *Nicolai de Cusa De Docta Ignorantia* Buch III (Latin, with German trans., ed. Hans Gerhard Senger; *Schriften des Nikolaus von Kues*, Heft 15c). Hamburg: Verlag von Felix Meiner, 1977.

  The Vision of God (trans. Emma Gurney Salter). London: Dent, and New York: Dutton, 1978 [1960].

  On God as Not-Other: A translation and an appraisal of De Li Non Aliud (with Latin text; ed. and trans. Jasper Hopkins). Minneapolis: University of Minnesota Press, 1979.

Nicholas of Cusa: Selected Spiritual Writings (trans. H. Lawrence Bond, Classics of Western Spirituality Series). Mahwah, NJ: Paulist Press, 1997.

Nigel of Canterbury *Miracles of the Virgin, in Verse: Miracula Sancte Dei Genitricis Marie, Versificie* (ed. Jan Ziolkowski from BL Ms Cotton Vespasian D.xix). Toronto: Pontifical Institute of Medieval Studies, 1986.

O'Carroll, Michael *Theotokos: A Theological Encyclopedia of the Blessed Virgin Mary*. Dublin: Dominican Publications, 1982.

O'Connor, Edward Dennis (ed.) *The Dogma of the Immaculate Conception: History and Significance*. Notre Dame, IN: University of Notre Dame Press, 1958.

O'Donnell, Christopher *At Worship with Mary: A Pastoral and Theological Study*. Wilmington, DE: Michael Glazier, 1988.

Olier, Jean-Jacques *Vie Intérieure de la Très-Sainte Vierge* (collected from Olier's writings), two vols. Rome: Salviucci, 1866.

O'Malley, John W. *The First Jesuits* Cambridge, MA and London: Harvard University Press, 1994.

Oxford Book of Carols (ed. Percy Dearmer, Ralph Vaughan Williams and Martin Shaw). Oxford: Oxford University Press, 1964 [1928].

Oxford Book of English Verse, 1250–1918 (ed. Arthur Quiller-Couch). Oxford: Clarendon Press, 1939.

Oxford Book of Italian Verse (ed. St John Lucas). Oxford: Oxford University Press, 1952.

Paredes, Joseph *Mary and the Kingdom of God: A Synthesis of Mariology* (trans. Joseph Davies and Josefina Martinez). Slough: St Paul Publications, 1991.

Parkin, Frank *Max Weber*. Chichester: Ellis Horwood, and London and New York: Tavistock, 1982.

Peck, George T. *The Fool of God: Jacopone da Todi*. University, AL: University of Alabama Press, 1980.

Pelikan, Jaroslav *The Christian Tradition: A History of the Development of Doctrine 1. The Emergence of the Catholic Tradition (100–600)*. Chicago and London: The University of Chicago Press, 1971.

Perdue, Peter C. 'Technological Determinism in Agrarian Societies', in Merritt Roe Smith and Leo Marx (eds) *Does Technology Drive History? The Dilemma of Technological Determinism*, pp. 169–200. Cambridge, MA and London: The MIT Press, 1994.

Perry, Nicholas and Loreto Echeverría *Under the Heel of Mary*. London: Routledge, 1988.

[Pius IX] *Apostolic Constitution of Pius IX Defining the Dogma of the Immaculate Conception* (reprinted from *Our Lady*, Papal Teachings Series). Boston, MA: St Paul Books & Media, n.d.

Pliny (the Elder) *Natural History* (Latin text with trans. by H. Rackham, Loeb Classical Library), vol. I. London: William Heinemann, 1938.

Pope, Barbara Corrado 'Immaculate and powerful: the Marian revival in the nineteenth century', in Clarissa Atkinson *et al. Immaculate and Powerful: The Female in Sacred Image and Social Reality*, pp. 173–200. Crucible, 1985.

Preater, Jason ' "Not wood but flesh": confraternity statues in post-Tridentine Andalusia', *Maria: A Journal of Marian Studies*, forthcoming.

Preston, James J. (ed.) *Mother Worship: Themes and Variations* Chapel Hill, NC: University of North Carolina Press, 1982.

Procacci, Giuliano *History of the Italian People* (trans. Anthony Paul). London: Pelican Books, 1973.

Rahner, Karl 'Le principe fondamentale de la théologie Mariale'. *Recherches de Science Religieuse* 42 (1954), pp. 481–522.

'The Immaculate Conception', in *Theological Investigations* vol. 1 (trans. Cornelius Ernst), pp. 201–13. London: Darton, Longman and Todd, 1961.

'Virginitas in partu', in *Theological Investigations* vol. 4 (trans. Kevin Smyth), pp. 134–62. London: Darton, Longman & Todd, 1966.

Mary Mother of the Lord (trans. W. J. O'Hara). Wheathampstead: Anthony Clarke, 1974 [1963].

'Human aspects of the birth of Christ', in *Theological Investigations* vol. 13 (trans. David Bourke), pp. 189–94. London: Darton, Longman & Todd, 1975.

Rahner, K., C. Ernst and K. Smyth (eds) *Sacramentum Mundi: An Encyclopedia of Theology*, six vols. London: Burns & Oates, 1968–1970.

Ranke-Heinemann, Ute *Eunuchs for the Kingdom of Heaven: The Catholic Church and Sexuality*. Harmondsworth: Penguin Books, 1990.

Ratzinger, Joseph, Cardinal *Daughter Zion: Meditations on the Church's Marian Belief* (trans. John H. McDermott). San Francisco: Ignatius Press, 1983.

'On the position of Mariology and Marian spirituality within the totality of faith and theology' (trans. Graham Harrison), in Helmut Moll (ed.) *The Church and Women: A Compendium*. San Francisco: Ignatius Press, 1988.

Reich, Wilhelm *The Mass Psychology of Fascism* (trans. Vincent R. Carfagno). London: Souvenir Press (Educational and Academic), 1972.

Richert, Hans-Georg (ed.) *Marienlegenden aus dem Alten Passional*. Tübingen: Max Niemeyer Verlag, 1965.

Rickert, Margaret *The Reconstructed Carmelite Missal: An English Manuscript of the Late XIV Century in the British Museum (Additional 29704-05)*. London: Faber & Faber, 1952.

Roberts, C. H. (ed.) *Catalogue of Greek and Latin Papyri in the John Rylands Library, Manchester* vol. III: *Theological and Literary Texts (nos. 457–551)*. Manchester: The University Press, 1938.

Roschini, Gabriel M. *Mariologia*, four vols. Rome: Angelus Belardetti, 1948.

'Royauté de Marie', in Hubert du Manoir (ed.) *Maria* tom. I, pp. 601–18. Paris: Beauchesne, 1949.

Rubin, Miri *Corpus Christi: The Eucharist in Late Medieval Culture* Cambridge: Cambridge University Press, 1991.

Ruether, Rosemary Radford *Sexism and God-Talk: Towards a Feminist Theology*. London: SCM Press, 1983.

Russo, Daniel 'Les représentations mariales dans l'art d'Occident: essai sur la formation d'une tradition iconographique', in D. Iogna-Prat *et al.* (eds) *Marie: Le Culte de la Vierge dans la Société médiéval*, pp. 173–291. Paris: Beauchesne, 1996.

Sanday, Peggy Reeves *Female Power and Male Dominance: On the Origins of Sexual Inequality*. Cambridge: Cambridge University Press, 1981.

Saward, John *The Mysteries of March: Hans Urs von Balthasar on the Incarnation and Easter*. London: Collins, 1990.

Scheeben, Matthias *Mariology*, two vols (trans. T. L. M. J. Geukers). St Louis and London: Herder Book Co., 1946/7.

Schiebinger, Londa 'Skeletons in the closet: the first illustrations of the female skeleton in eighteenth-century anatomy', in C. Gallagher and T. Laqueur (eds) *The Making of the Modern Body: Sexuality and Society in the Nineteenth Century*, pp. 42–82. Berkeley, CA: University of California Press, 1987.

Schillebeeckx, E. *Mary, Mother of the Redemption*. London: Sheed & Ward, 1964.

Schluchter, Wolfgang *Rationalism, Religion and Domination: A Weberian Perspective* (trans. Neil Solomon). Berkeley and Los Angeles: University of California Press, 1989.

Sebastian, Wenceslaus 'The controversy over the Immaculate Conception from after Duns Scotus to the end of the eighteenth century', in E. D. O'Connor (ed.) *The Dogma of the Immaculate Conception: History and Significance*, pp. 213–70. Notre Dame, IN: University of Notre Dame Press, 1958.

Semmelroth, Otto *Mary: Archetype of the Church* (trans. Maria von Eroes and John Devlin). Dublin: Gill & Son, 1964.

Sichtermann, Barbara *Femininity: The Politics of the Personal* (trans. John Whitlam). Oxford: Polity Press, 1986.

Siebert, Rudolf J. *The Critical Theory of Religion: The Frankfurt School*. Berlin, New York and Amsterdam: Mouton, 1985.

Southern, R. W. 'The English origins of the "Miracles of the Virgin"'. *Medieval and Renaissance Studies* 4 (1958), pp. 176–216.

Stauffer, Ethelbert *New Testament Theology* (trans. John Marsh). London: SCM Press, 1955.

Steinberg, Leo 'The metaphors of love and birth in Michelangelo's *Pietàs*,' in T. Bowie and C. V. Christenson (eds) *Studies in Erotic Art*. New York and London: Basic Books, 1970.

   The Sexuality of Christ in Renaissance Art and Modern Oblivion London: Faber, 1983.

Stirnimann, Heinrich *Marjam: Marienrede an einer Wende*. Freiburg: Universitätsverlag, 1989.

Stoller, Robert *Sex and Gender* vol. 1: *The Development of Masculinity and Femininity*. London: H. Karnac, 1984 [1974].

Presentations of Gender New Haven, CT and London: Yale University Press, 1985.

Perversion: The Erotic Form of Hatred. London: II. Karnac, 1986 [1975].

Stratton, Suzanne L. *The Immaculate Conception in Spanish Art*. Cambridge, New York and Melbourne: Cambridge University Press, 1994.

Suárez, Francisco *De Mysteriis Vitae Christi: Commentarii et Disputationes in Tertiam Partem D. Thomae* in *Opera Omnia* (ed. Charles Berton) vol. XIX. Paris: Vivès, 1860.

Tar, Zoltán *The Frankfurt School: The Critical Theories of Max Horkheimer and Theodor W. Adorno*. New York: Schocken Books, 1985.

Tawney, R. H. *Religion and the Rise of Capitalism*. Harmondsworth: Penguin Books, 1975.

Theweleit, Klaus *Male Fantasies* vol. 1 (trans. Stephen Conway, Erica Carter and Chris Turner). Cambridge: Polity Press, 1987.

Thomas Aquinas, St *Summa Theologiae* (trans. Order of Preachers) vol. 4. London: Blackfriars with Eyre and Spottiswoode, 1963.
Vol. 8, 1963.
Vol. 13, 1963.
Vol. 32, 1963.
Vol. 39, 1964.

Thomas, Keith *Religion and the Decline of Magic: Studies in Popular Beliefs in Sixteenth- and Seventeenth-Century England*. Harmondsworth: Penguin Books, 1978.

Man and the Natural World: Changing Attitudes in England 1500–1800 Harmondsworth: Penguin Books, 1984.

Turner, Victor and Edith Turner *Image and Pilgrimage in Christian Culture: Anthropological Perspectives*. Oxford: Basil Blackwell, 1978.

Vloberg, Maurice 'Les types iconographiques de la Mère de Dieu dans l'art Byzantin', in Hubert du Manoir (ed.) *Maria* tom. II, pp. 483–540. Paris: Beauchesne, 1952.

'The iconography of the Immaculate Conception', in E. D. O'Connor (ed.) *The Dogma of the Immaculate Conception: History and Significance*, pp. 463–512. Notre Dame, IN: University of Notre Dame Press, 1958.

von Balthasar, Hans Urs *The Threefold Garland* (trans. Erasmo Leiva-Merikakis). San Francisco: Ignatius Press, 1982.

von Eschenbach, Wolfram *Parzival* (trans. A. T. Hatto). Harmondsworth: Penguin Books, 1980.

von Speyr, Adrienne *Handmaid of the Lord* (trans. E. A. Nelson). San Francisco: Ignatius Press, 1985.

Warner, Marina *Alone of All Her Sex: The Myth and the Cult of the Virgin Mary*. London: Quartet Books, 1978.

Watts, Alan *Myth and Ritual in Christianity*. London and New York: Thames & Hudson, 1954.

Weber, Max *Ancient Judaism* (trans. H. H. Gerth and D. Martindale). New York: Free Press, 1952.

From Max Weber: Essays in Sociology (trans. H. H. Gerth and C. Wright Mills). London: Routledge & Kegan Paul, 1970.

Economy and Society (trans. Guenther Roth, Claus Wittich *et al.* [1968] from German edn, 1964), two vols. Berkeley, CA: University of California Press, 1978.

The Protestant Ethic and the Spirit of Capitalism (trans. Talcott Parsons from German edn 1920–22). London: Unwin Paperbacks, 1985.

'Science as a vocation' (trans. Michael John, from German edn, 1922), in Peter Lassman *et al. Max Weber's 'Science as a Vocation'*, pp. 3–31. London: Unwin Hyman, 1989.

Webster, James Carson *The Labors of the Months in Antique and Medieval Art: To the End of the Twelfth Century* (Northwestern University Studies in the Humanities, number 4). New York: AMS Press, 1970.

Weinreich-Haste, Helen 'Brother Sun, Sister Moon: does rationality overcome a dualistic world view?' in Jan Harding (ed.) *Perspectives on Gender and Science*. London, New York and Philadelphia: The Falmer Press, 1986.

White, Lynn Jr, *Medieval Technology and Social Change*. Oxford: Clarendon Press, 1962.

Medieval Religion and Technology: Collected Essays. Berkeley, Los Angeles and London: University of California Press, 1978.

Whiting, Robert *The Blind Devotion of the People: Popular Religion and the English Reformation*. Cambridge: Cambridge University Press, 1989.

Wiggershaus, Rolf *The Frankfurt School* (trans. Michael Robertson). Cambridge: Polity Press, 1994.

Wilkins, Eithne *The Rose-Garden Game: The Symbolic Background to the European Prayer-Beads*. London: Victor Gollancz, 1969.

Winston-Allen, Anne *Stories of the Rose: The Making of the Rosary in the Middle Ages*. University Park, PA: Pennsylvania State University Press, 1997.

Wolter, Allan B. and Blane O'Neill *John Duns Scotus: Mary's Architect*. Quincy, IL: Franciscan Press, 1993.

[Wynkyn de Worde] *The Myracles of Oure Lady* (ed. from Wynkyn de Worde's edition, by Peter Whiteford). Heidelberg: Carl Winter-Universitätsverlag, 1990.

Yalom, Marilyn *The History of the Breast*. London: HarperCollins, 1997.

Zeitlin, Irving *Ancient Judaism*. Cambridge: Polity Press, 1984.

Ziegler, Philip *The Black Death.* Harmondsworth: Penguin Books, 1982.

Zimdars-Swartz, Sandra *Encountering Mary: Visions of Mary from La Salette to Medjugorje*. Princeton, NJ: Princeton University Press, 1991.

Index

243